Felt, Fiber, and Stone

Creative Jewelry Designs & Techniques

Suzanne O'Brien

Dedication

I dedicate this book to my mother Oma, who has been a loving and creative inspiration to me from day one. And I give special thanks to my daughter, Darla, for her understanding and patience with me while I worked away for hours on the computer (sometimes neglecting my motherly duties and offering fewer home-made meals and less TLC than usual).

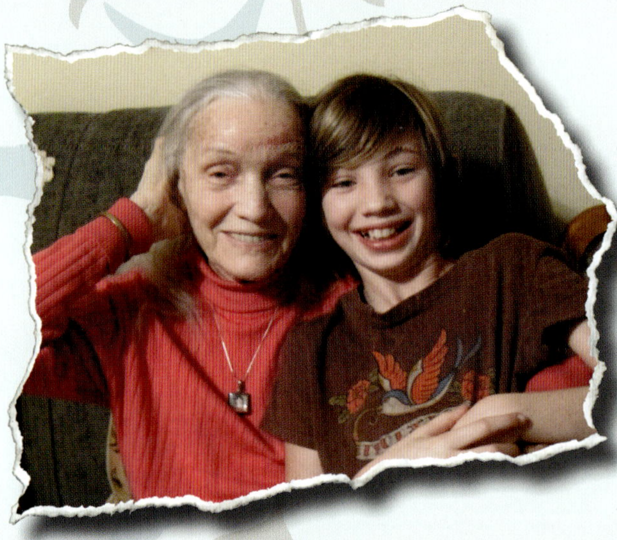

Library of Congress Control Number: 2010939971

Designed by Caroline Siecke-Pape
Type set in Village Idiot BB / Myriad Pro

ISBN: 978-0-7643-3668-3
Printed in China

Schiffer Books are available at special discounts for bulk purchases for sales promotions or premiums. Special editions, including personalized covers, corporate imprints, and excerpts can be created in large quantities for special needs. For more information contact the publisher:

Published by Schiffer Publishing Ltd.
4880 Lower Valley Road
Atglen, PA 19310
Phone: (610) 593-1777; Fax: (610) 593-2002
E-mail: Info@schifferbooks.com

For the largest selection of fine reference books on this and related subjects, please visit our web site at
www.schifferbooks.com
We are always looking for people to write books on new and related subjects. If you have an idea for a book please contact us at the above address.

This book may be purchased from the publisher.
Include $5.00 for shipping.
Please try your bookstore first.
You may write for a free catalog.

In Europe, Schiffer books are distributed by
Bushwood Books
6 Marksbury Ave.
Kew Gardens
Surrey TW9 4JF England
Phone: 44 (0) 20 8392 8585; Fax: 44 (0) 20 8392 9876
E-mail: info@bushwoodbooks.co.uk
Website: www.bushwoodbooks.co.uk

Contents

Introduction

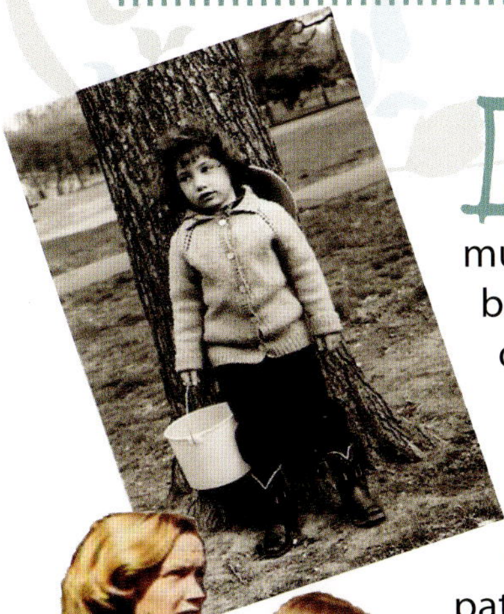

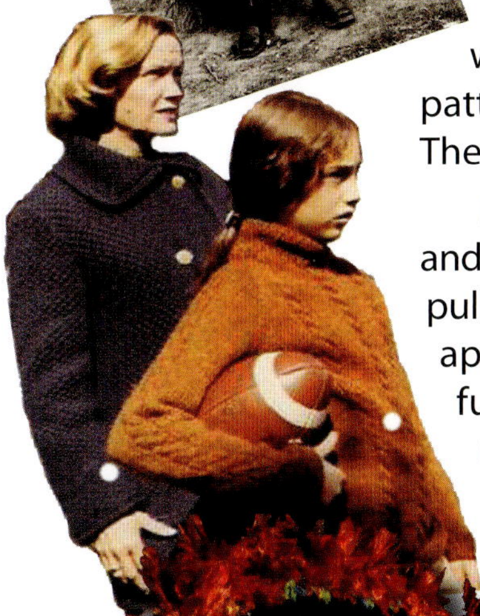

I was raised in a small apartment on the Upper West Side of Manhattan in the late 1950s. Born to a musician father and a fresh-off-the-boat Dutch mother (who could knit or crochet absolutely anything!), I spent many happy childhood hours listening to my father practice his bassoon while watching my mother whip out afghans using traditional patterns with very nontraditional colors. The results were exquisite.

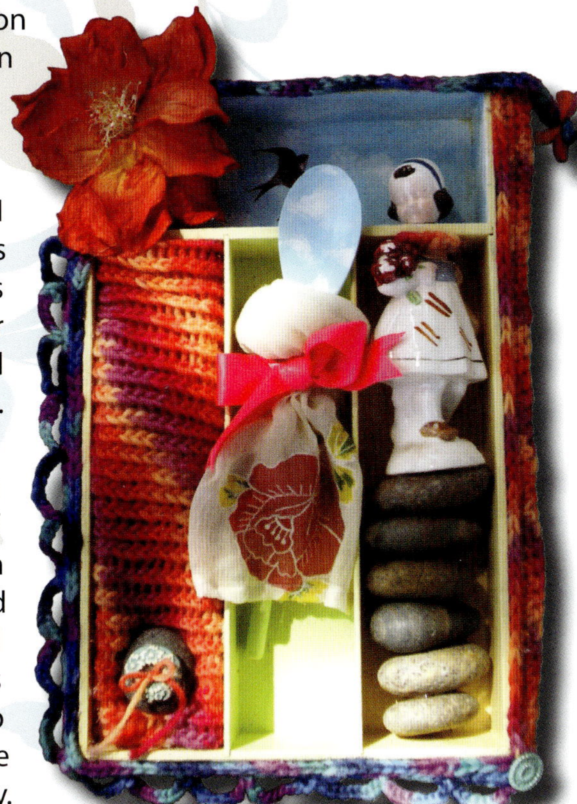

My niche through college was drawing and fine art. After college, I found myself pulled in a different direction and began applying my talents to decorative and functional items. I started with visual merchandising for Bloomingdale's and Ralph Lauren, then moved on to product development for a large home textile company in New York City.

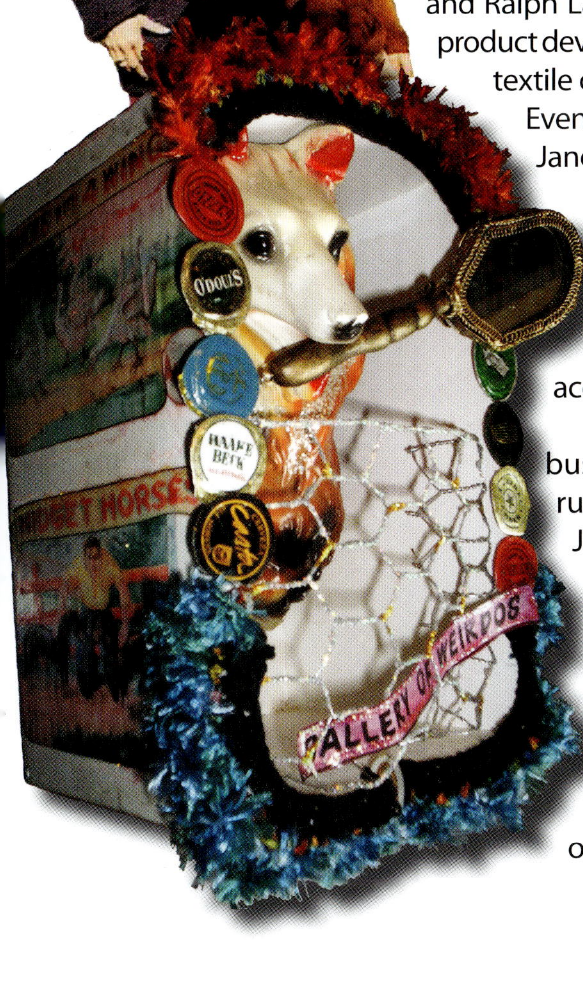

Eventually I opened a store, Plain Jane Kids, with my two best friends. We designed and made all of our own products by hand. Our style had a fresh retro flair that fit in well with homes like yours and mine! (We also designed many celebrity nurseries!) My speciality was fancifully decoupaged furniture and wooden accessories.

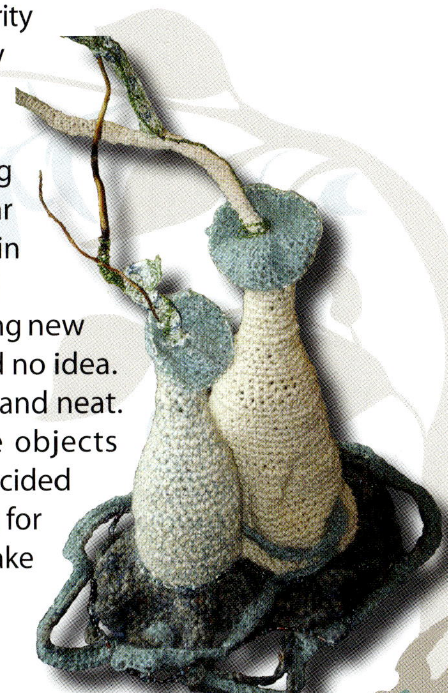

Plain Jane Kids developed into a thriving business, but after a wonderful fifteen-year run, unforseen circumstances caused Plain Jane Kids to close its doors.

It was time to move on to an exciting new project! But what would that be? I had no idea. But I did know I wanted to work small and neat. (No more schlepping around large objects while covered in paint!) One night I decided to crochet a simple bucket-style bag for my eight-year-old daughter, Darla, to take on sleepovers.

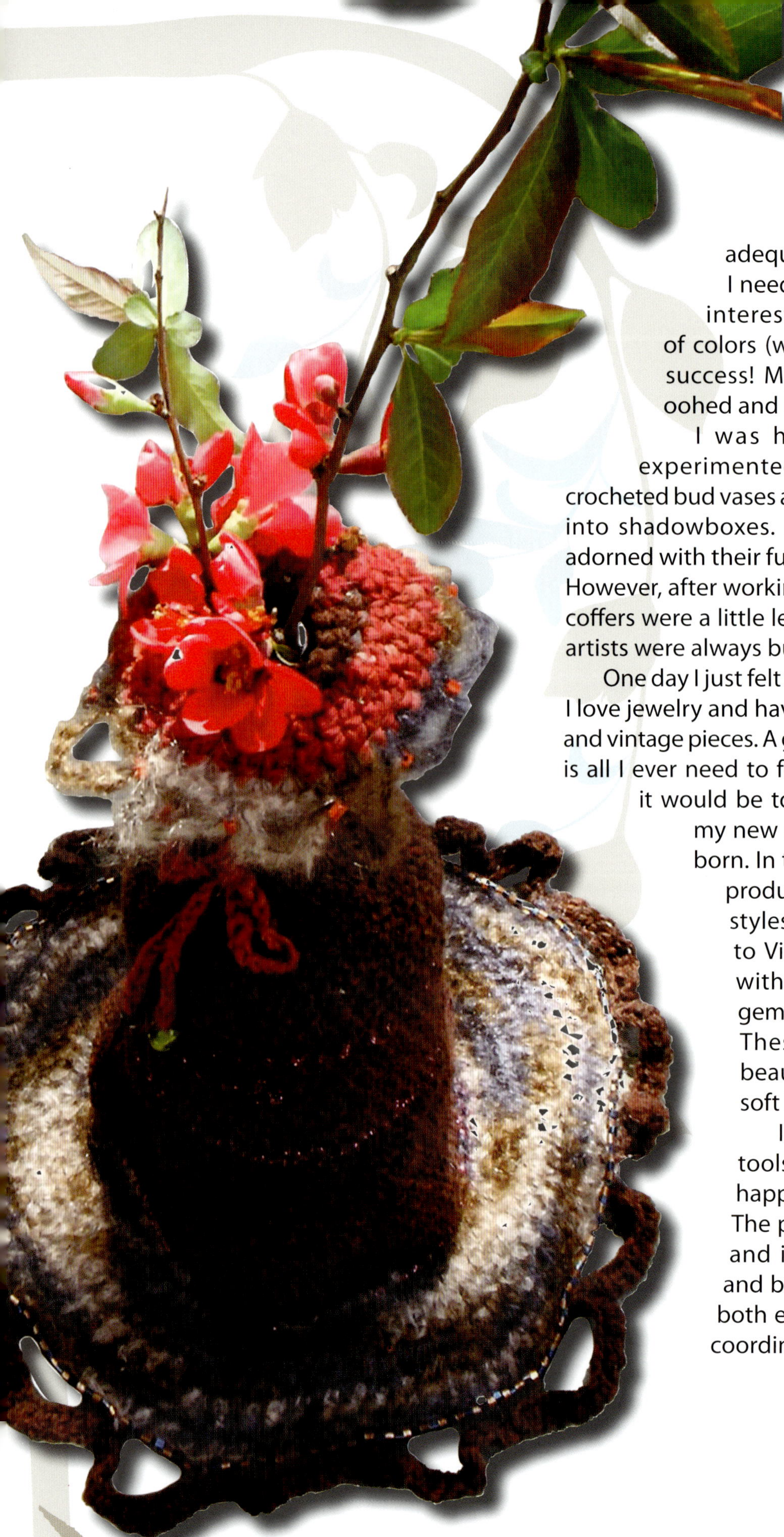

Let me tell you, even after all those years in the presence of my mother's genius, my crocheting skills were still, at best, basic. However, I found that they were more than adequate for making the sculptural shape I needed for my bag. What made the bag interesting and exciting was the choice of colors (wild!) and textures (woolly!) It was a success! My daughter loved it and everyone oohed and aahed when they saw it.

I was hooked (bad pun alert!). I first experimented transforming wine bottles into crocheted bud vases and lamps, and turning found objects into shadowboxes. I loved my whimsical little pieces adorned with their funky beads and bits of broken plates. However, after working a few craft fairs, I noticed that my coffers were a little less than full! By contrast, the jewelry artists were always busy.

One day I just felt as if a light bulb went off in my head. I love jewelry and have always collected Native American and vintage pieces. A great pair of jeans and a cool necklace is all I ever need to feel dressed up. I thought, what fun it would be to make my own jewelry. That night my new company, Oh Susanna Designs, was born. In the three years since, I have lovingly produced hundreds of pieces inspired by styles that range from Native American to Victorian. I especially enjoy working with organic elements such as natural gemstones, pearls, shells, wood and glass. These materials possess such innate beauty that they need only be given a soft bed of fiber in which to dwell.

I hope that this book gives you the tools and inspiration needed for many happy hours of making your own jewelry. The process is very zen-like and relaxing, and in the end you will have a unique and beautiful conversation piece that will both express your own personal style and coordinate perfectly with your wardrobe!

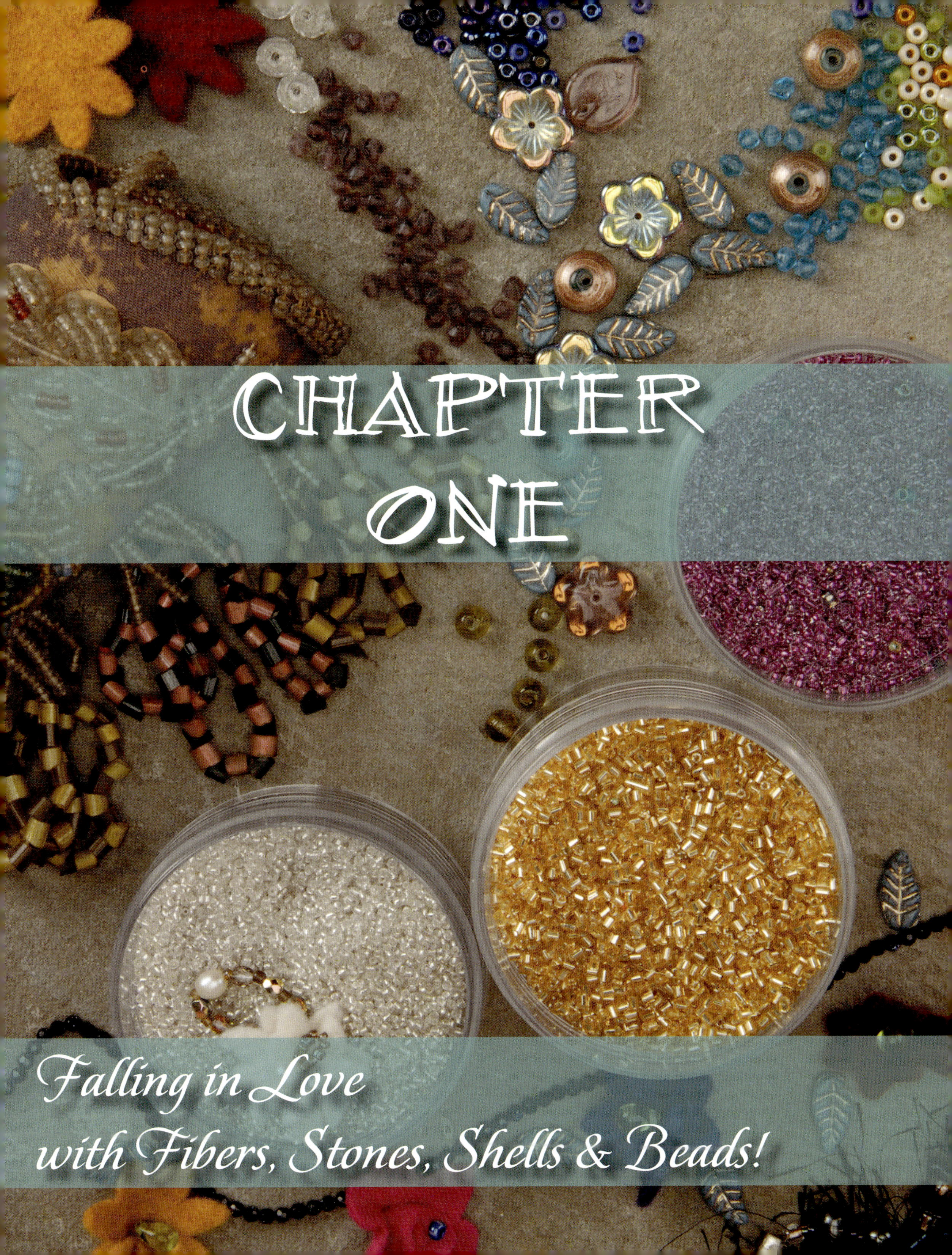

CHAPTER ONE

Falling in Love with Fibers, Stones, Shells & Beads!

It's not difficult to fall in love with the materials that I use. Each has an intrinsic beauty all its own. (Mother nature is a way cool designer!) Making unique and personal jewelry is all about how you (the artist!) choose to marry the materials together.

Let's get started by briefly categorizing and describing our materials, beginning with fibers.

Tell all your creative pals to give you their leftovers. You can inherit fantastic scraps this way (plus it's a recycling thing!).

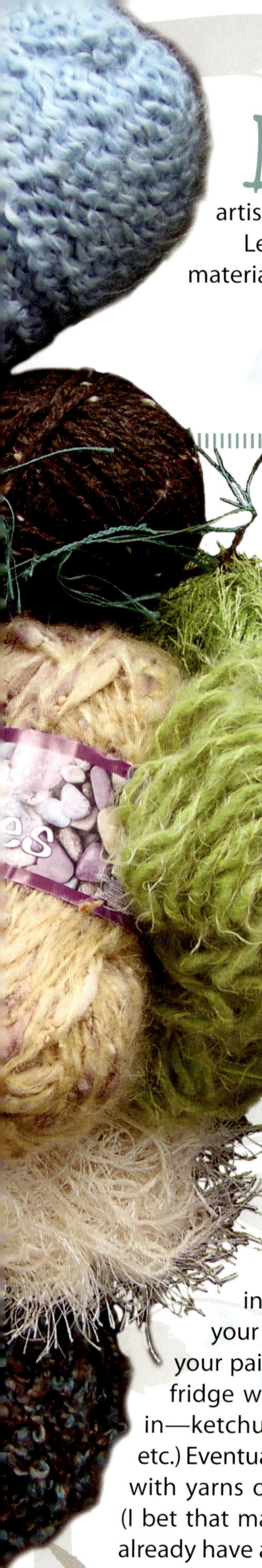

FIBERS

Fibers can be soft, fuzzy, fluffy, lumpy, bumpy, coarse, thick, or thin. They can be sleek, shiny, or sparkly, and made of natural materials or synthetic ones (for those with allergies). They can come from sheep, lamas, alpacas, goats, bunnies, and even your pet dog! These days we are lucky because so many amazing small companies are raising and shearing their own animals and spinning and dying their fibers into a luscious rainbow of colors. You will be dazzled by the range of colors available at any quality yarn shop! In fact, when getting started, the choices can be quite overwhelming.

A good place to start is the remnant bins and close-out sections. These often have great buys because traditional knitters and crocheters generally need materials in larger quantities. One great aspect of my technique is that you don't need multiple balls or skeins of yarn to make my jewelry. Bits and pieces go a long way! (You never know when that last yard of burgundy mohair will be exactly the right color for a snappy pair of earrings to go with your new dress!) Think of your initial shopping adventures as stocking your paint box. (You know, like stocking your fridge with the basics when you first move in—ketchup, mustard, Worcestershire sauce, etc.) Eventually you will have baskets brimming with yarns of all colors, textures, and types. (I bet that many of you crafty gals out there already have a fine stash of supplies!)

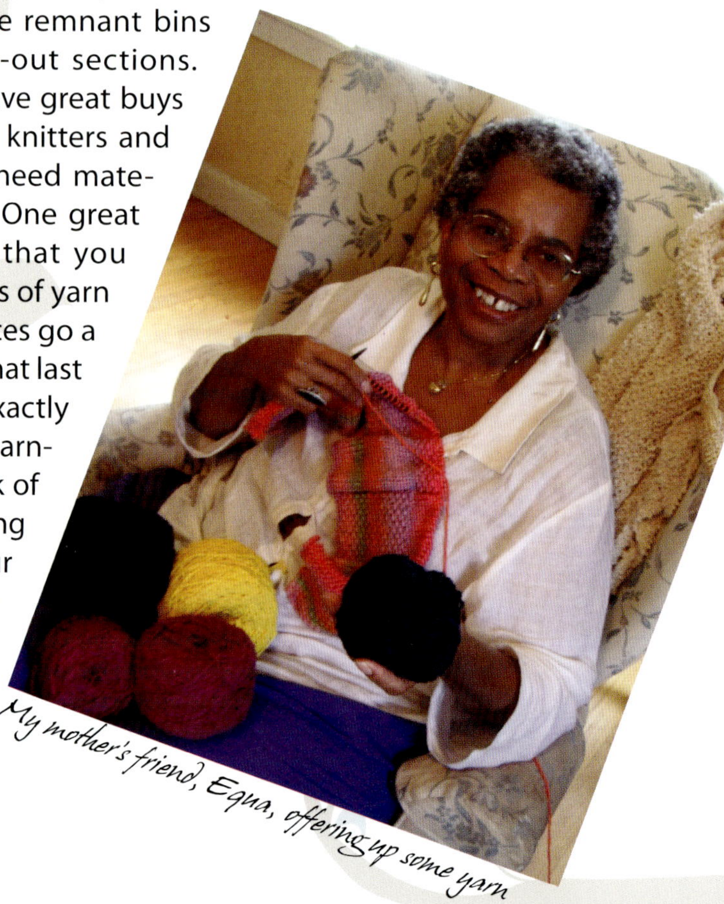

My mother's friend, Equa, offering up some yarn

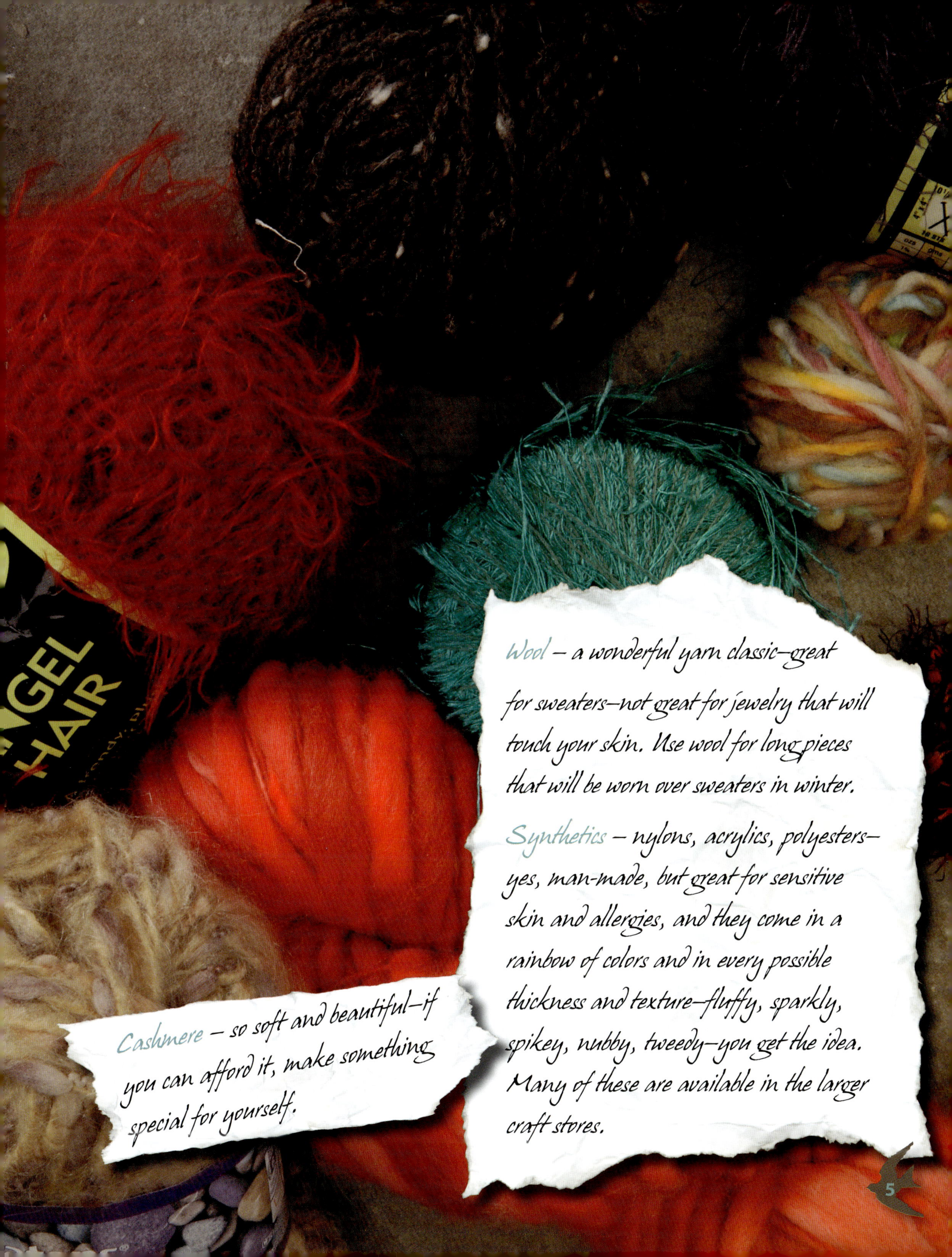

Wool – a wonderful yarn classic—great for sweaters—not great for jewelry that will touch your skin. Use wool for long pieces that will be worn over sweaters in winter.

Synthetics – nylons, acrylics, polyesters—yes, man-made, but great for sensitive skin and allergies, and they come in a rainbow of colors and in every possible thickness and texture—fluffy, sparkly, spikey, nubby, tweedy—you get the idea. Many of these are available in the larger craft stores.

Cashmere – so soft and beautiful—if you can afford it, make something special for yourself.

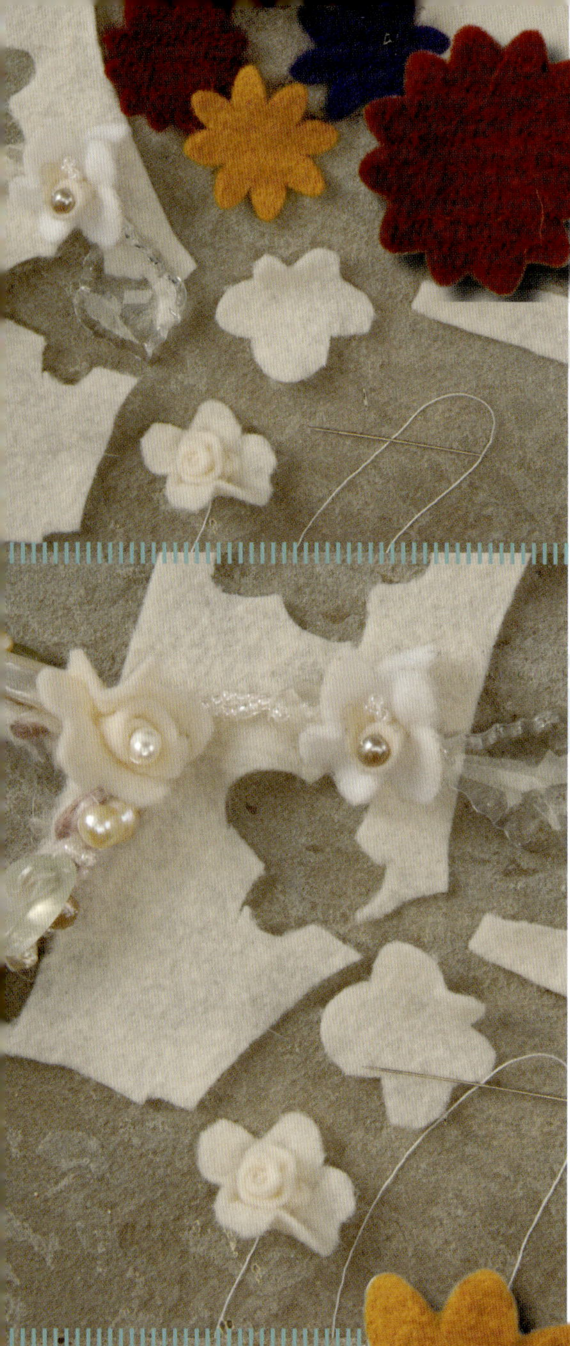

FELT

For me, felt will always evoke fond memories of grade school. It seemed that every classroom had cheery felt graphics on the walls. We used it to make puppets, bags, signs, and hats. You name it, you could make it out of felt. Felt was the supply of choice, the king of craft supplies. Then, for a period of years, there was a backlash against felt and it was no longer "cool" to use. Considered childish and corny, no real artist would consider it for any "serious" project. Well guess what? Felt is back in vogue! Now artists are making felt from scratch and using it for amazing pieces.

When I first started making fiber jewelry, I worked with my neighbor and dear friend Suzy Arnowitz. Suzy taught me how to make the sweet little felt flowers you see throughout my work. And Suzy should know her stuff; her family is in the felt business! Her grandfather was a felt king in the 1940s. In fact, he owned a felt importing and manufacturing business right here in upstate New York that is still in the family today!

In the good old days, most fine felt was imported from Europe, where it was made of pure wool. It was an indispensable fiber prized for its warmth and durability, whether it was used for an exquisite doll or a soldier's blanket.

Over the last 50 years the materials used for felt have been broadened. You can now find felt made out of wool blends and completely synthetic fibers. Felt made from pure wool is quite expensive and harder to find in a range of colors. By contrast, you will find a broad range of colors in synthetic fibers at your local sewing or craft store. The synthetic felts are not as beautiful as the "real deal" wools, but will work just fine for the small flowers used in my work. All you will need to get started is a quarter or a half yard. (That will be enough for entire garden of felt flowers! A little bit goes a long way.)

Here is a list of colors I recommend to get started:

- Burgundy
- Mustard yellow
- Cream/ off-white
- Bright pink
- Brown
- White
- Light pink/ rose
- Purple

I like to tea-stain my whites and light colors to make them more organic in appearance. For this, a wool or wool blend is recommended because 100% synthetics do not take the dyes well.

Instructions: In a large pot of boiling water steep 10 or more bags of black type tea. While the tea water is still warm (be careful not to burn yourself!), submerge your fabric for a half-an-hour to an hour. Remove the fabric from the tea water, rinse it, and dry it in a hot dryer. The end result will be a subtle, irregular staining. Remember, you don't have to use black tea. Experiment! Cut your fabrics into 12"x12" squares and spend a morning trying different teas, stains, and juices (beet juice!). After just one morning you'll have a great group of swatches to choose from for hours of fun!

ORGANIC BEADS

While many prefer the refined look of cut gemstones, I love, love, love organic beads! That is, beads in a mostly natural state, tweaked only gently to bring out their natural beauty. Give me a chunk of turquoise with its rough outer surface smoothed to a waxy, undulating perfection, or a jagged and irregular piece of quartz with its sharp, faceted sides polished to a bright shine that, to my eyes, is as beautiful as any diamond, at a fraction of the cost. The stones I find myself most drawn to are turquoise, amethyst, coral, garnet, gaspeite, kyanite, fluorite, jade, apatite, pearls and quartz of all colors and types. (All great for your "paint box"!) These materials come in a range of sizes, shapes and finishes, including shiny or waxy, and rough or smooth. Some even have cracks or inclusions of different colors run-

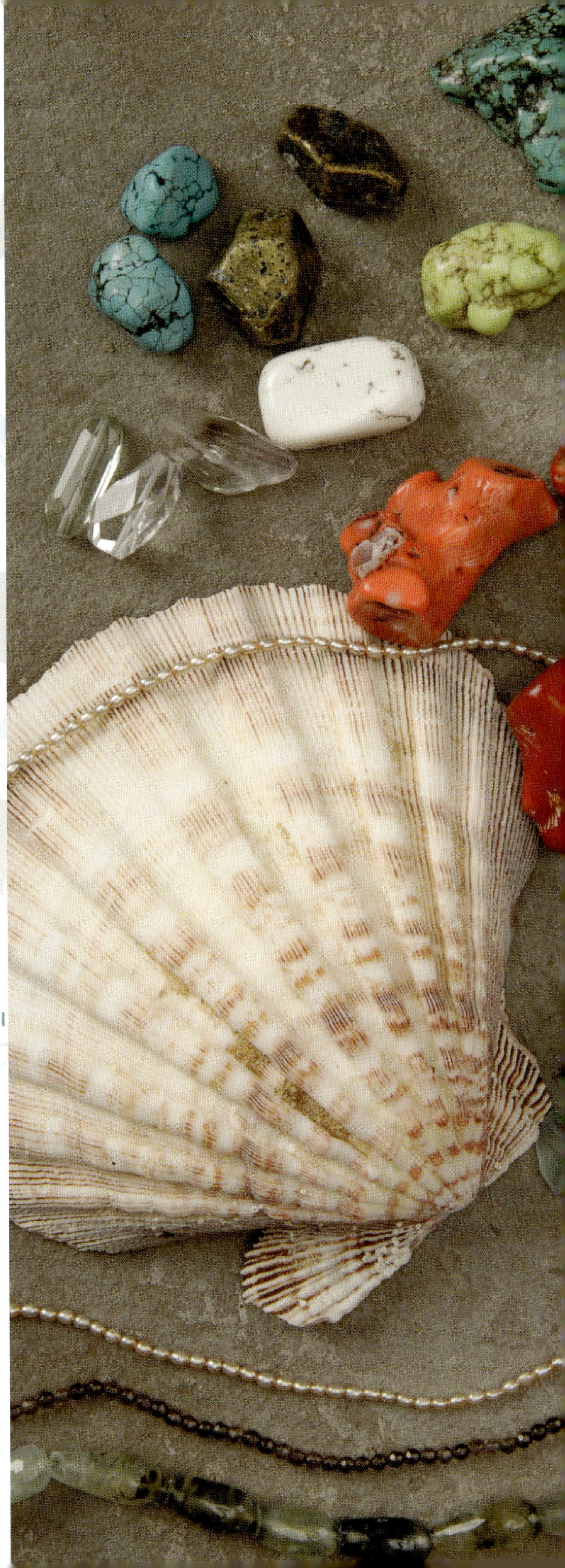

ning through them. Organic beads are perfectly suited for fluffy, soft fibers, and their unique qualities help to shape and influence my work.

I also use an assortment of glass seed beads in sizes ranging from the tiniest to the largest. These colorful little glass beads are the chorus line of my jewelry show, the supporting actresses to the stars, the wind beneath the wings of the larger gemstones and shells, the…(you get the idea). Inexpensive and small, they are indispensable. They add color, shine and texture to any work. I can't live without them.

You may also want to collect some special, fancier, focal elements, such as large metal charms, chandelier crystals (vintage or new), carved stones and shells (many beautiful pieces are imported with carved flowers, dragons, etc.). You might also try mexican milagros, large chunks of gemstones or coral, and whole shells. All make perfect focal points for the simple projects at the beginning of this book.

Just like the scraps of yarn you collect from your friends, you should collect and save broken necklaces. I use small zip-lock bags to keep like-style beads together. You can also use nice glass jars or any other suitable containers to stash your broken treasures. Also, don't be too picky! You never know when that oddball abandoned bit will be perfect for your new masterpiece! (Recycle! Recycle! Recycle!) Yard sales are a great resource for you thrifty folks who enjoy the hunt. Keep your mind open when looking over yard sale jewelry. Aunt Gertie's necklace might be gaudy, but between those awful fake pearls are marvelous tiny glass beads. You get the idea—look beyond the obvious.

Where to buy: I purchase my beads and stones from anywhere and everywhere. For those with little time for the hunt, a nice selection of stones and beads (as well as tools, wire, fibers, etc.) can be found at "one-stop"shops such a Michael's Crafts or A.C. Moore. (Check the resource appendix for more.) Also, you can go online to places like Fire Mountain Gems (a fave of mine) and others. When possible, I chose my stones in person so that I can pick out the exact strands I want. You can't do that online (although the folks at Fire Mountain Gems are very helpful, and they have a fantastic selection and range of materials).

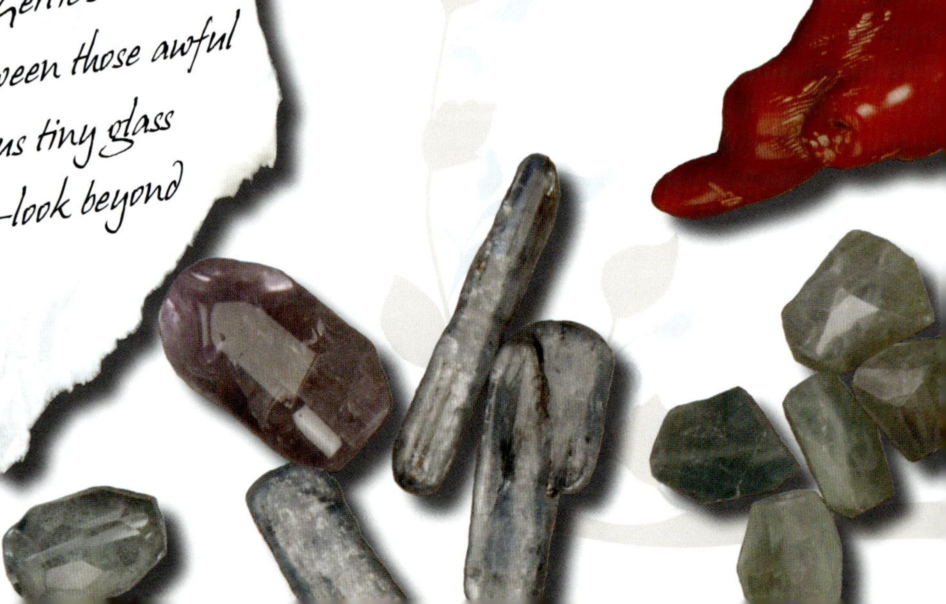

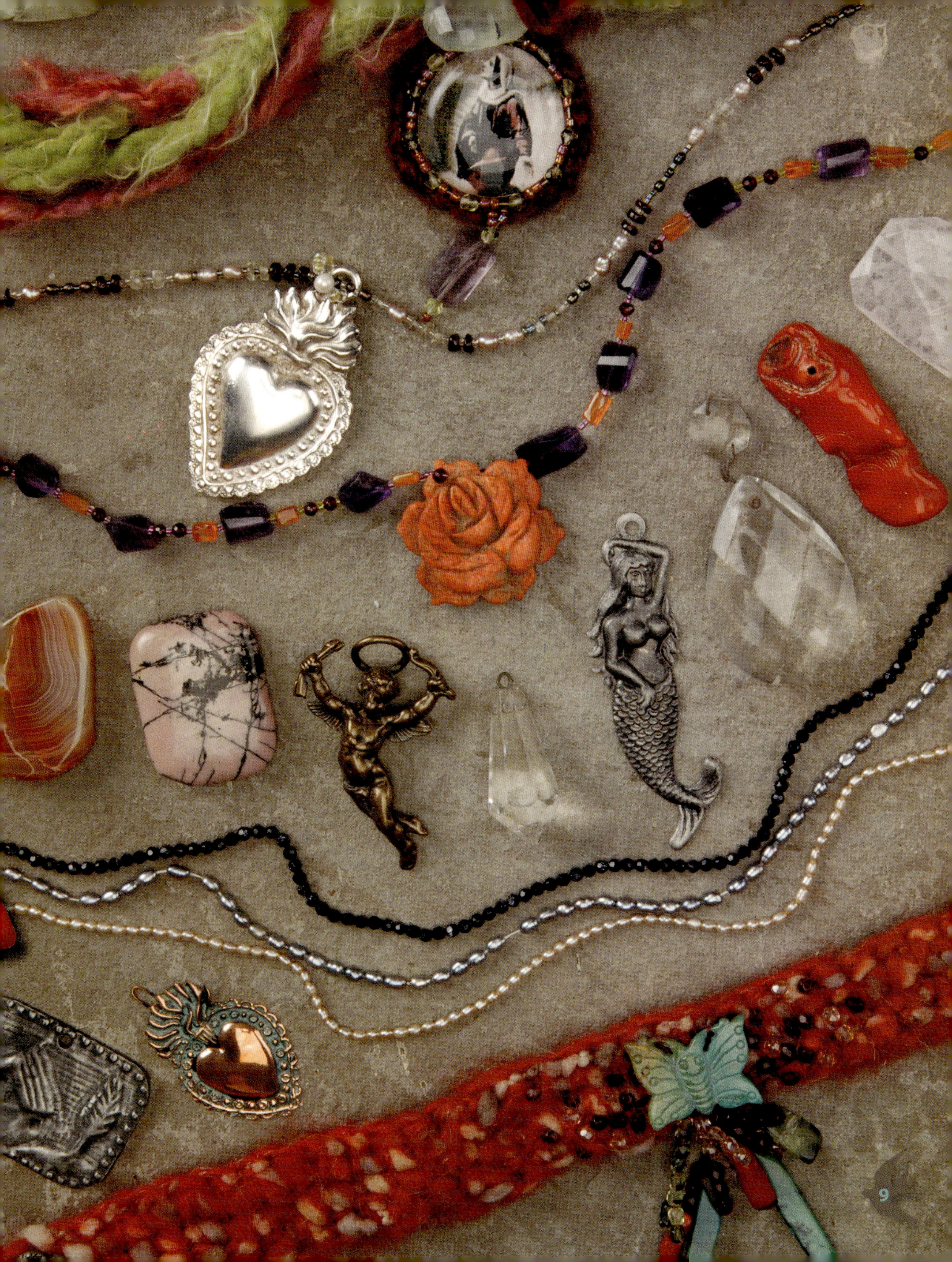

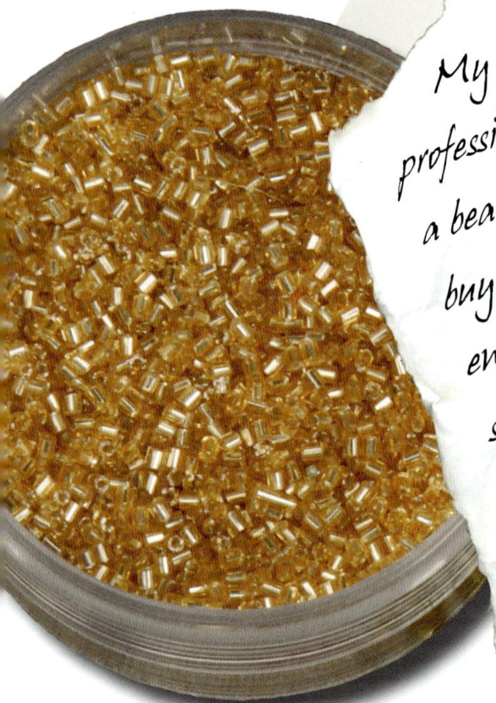

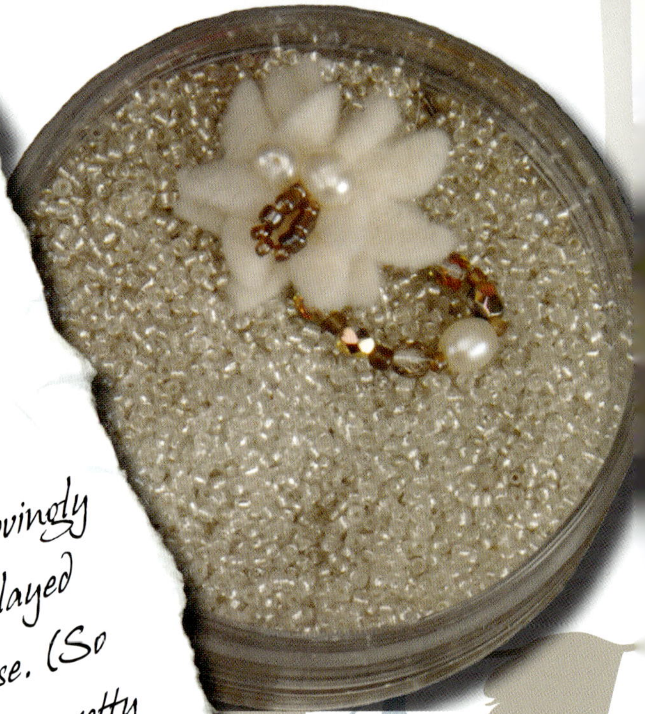

My pal Lizzy (a librarian by profession and weekend artist) is a bead hoarder. She is addicted to buying colorful seed beads. She has enough to wrap around the world several times! In her home, every color and size is separated and lovingly stored in neat glass bottles displayed in collections all over the house. (So remember folks, beads make a pretty display!)

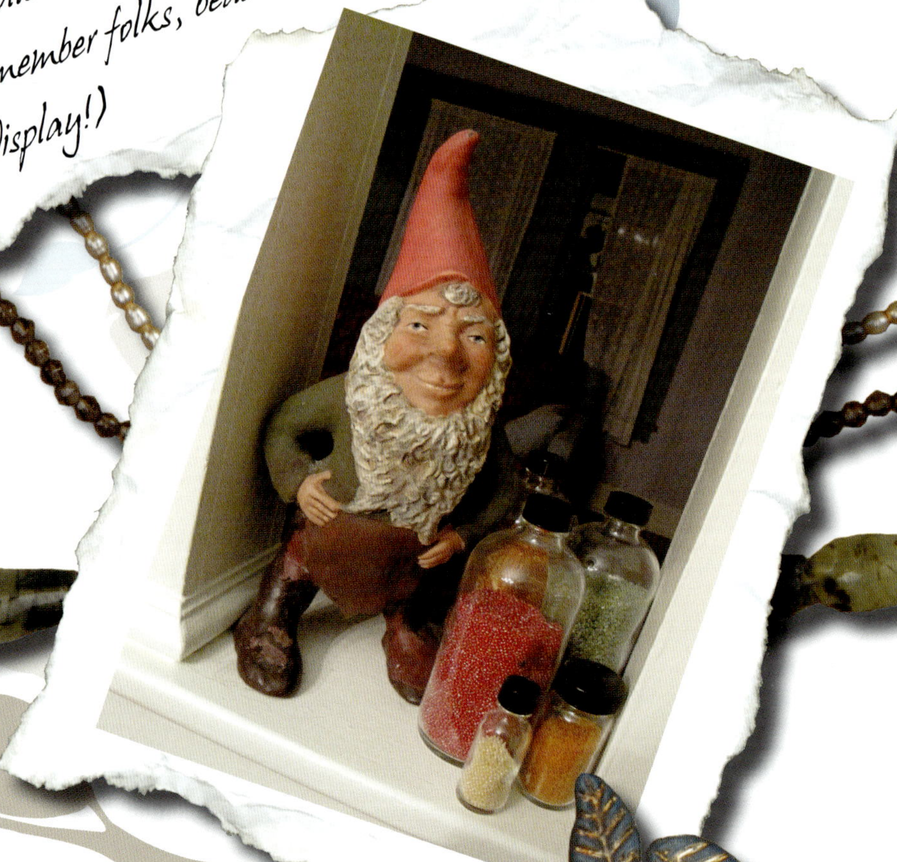

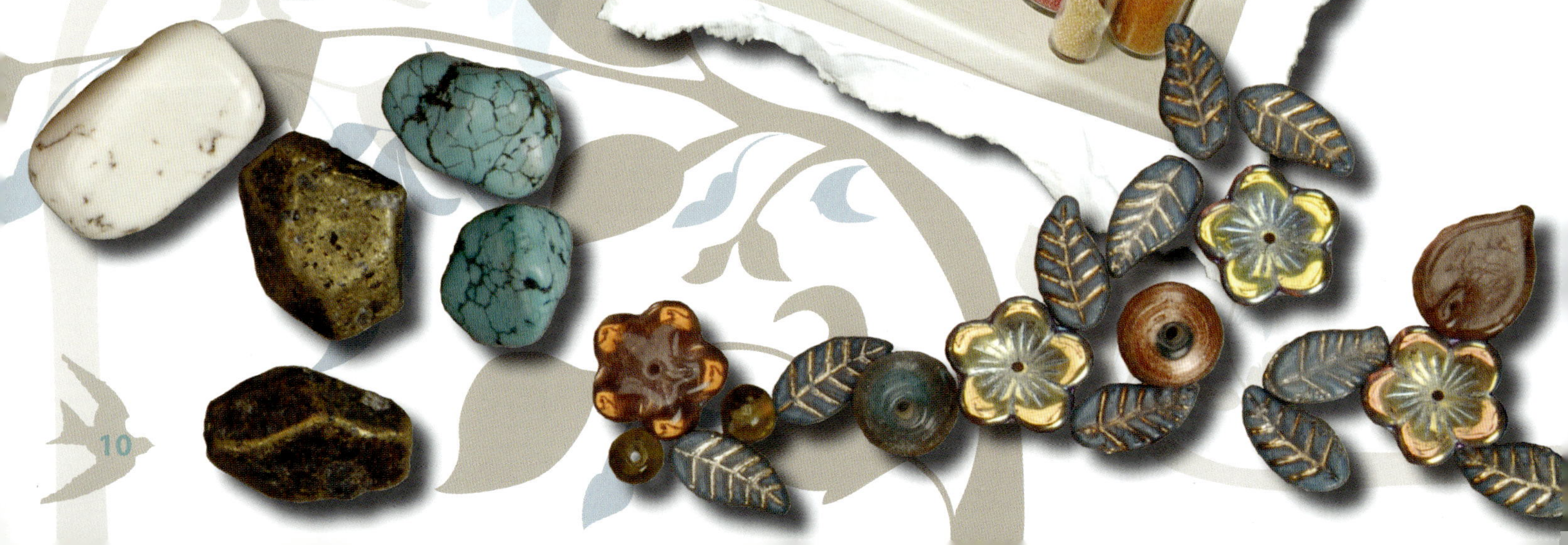

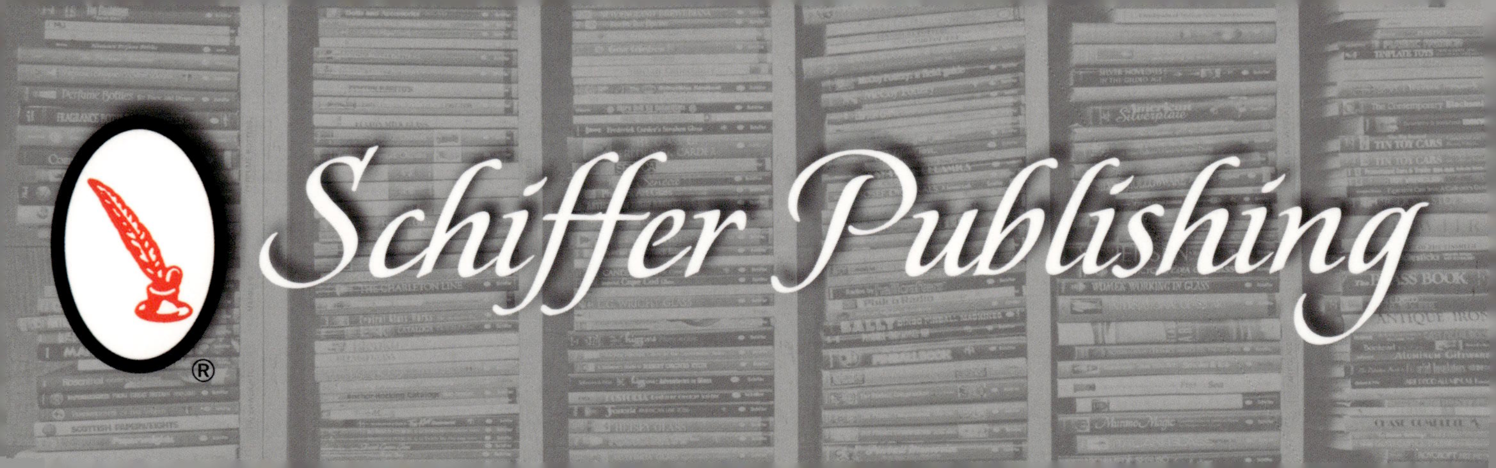
Schiffer Publishing

Ready to Write a Book?

We're always seeking authors for a wide variety of topics. This is your opportunity to shine! See our website to view an extensive list of our titles. If this idea appeals to you, we'd love to hear from you. Review our book submission guidelines at our website by clicking on the "Submit a Book Proposal" link. Then email your proposal and ideas to **info@schifferbooks.com** or write to the attention of **Acquisitions** at the address below. You can also call 610-593-1777 to make an appointment to speak with an editor.

Schiffer Publishing
has books covering a wide variety of interests including:

Antiques, Collectibles, & The Arts
Advertising • Automobilia • Black Collectibles • Breweriana • Ceramics • Clocks • Corkscrews • Decoys • Dolls • Fine Art • Folk Art • Furniture • Graphic Art • Holidays • Hunting • Jewelry • Kitchen • Lighting • Leatherwork • Metalware • Native American Crafts • Nautical • Pinball • Quilts • Rugs • Sports • Teddy Bears • Telephones • Textiles • Toys • Video Games • Vintage Fashion • Watches • Writing Instruments and more.

Design, Lifestyle, & D-I-Y
Architecture • Astrology • Counter Culture • Culinary Arts • Erotica • Interior Design • Kitchens and Baths • Landscaping • Numerology • Paranormal • Pin-Ups • Pop Art • Tarot • Tattooing • Textile Design • UFOs • Witchcraft • Basketry • Beads & Jewelry Making • Carving • Furniture Making • Gourds • Home & Garden • Metalwork • Modeling • Pyrography • Sculpture • Textiles • Weaving • Wood Turning • Tools and more.

Military, Aviation, & Automotive History
WWI & WWII Armor/Aviation: German • U.S. • British • Russian • the Jet Age • Unit Biographies and Autobiographies • Edged Weapons • Firearms • Uniforms and more.

Maritime
Seamanship • Navigation • Ship Management • Towing • Transportation • Boats & Boat Building • Medical • Legal and more.

Regional
History • Children's Books • Architecture • Photography • Landscaping • Paranormal • Souvenir • Guidebooks • Cooking and more.

To learn more, go to **www.schifferbooks.com**
Call 610-593-1777, 8:30a.m.-5:30 p.m. EST
or write to 4880 Lower Valley Road
Atglen, PA 19310 USA
and ask for a free catalog(s).

In the UK and Europe contact
Bushwood Books at 44 (0) 20 8392-8585
info@bushwoodbooks.co.uk

Bookmark printed in China

G-1

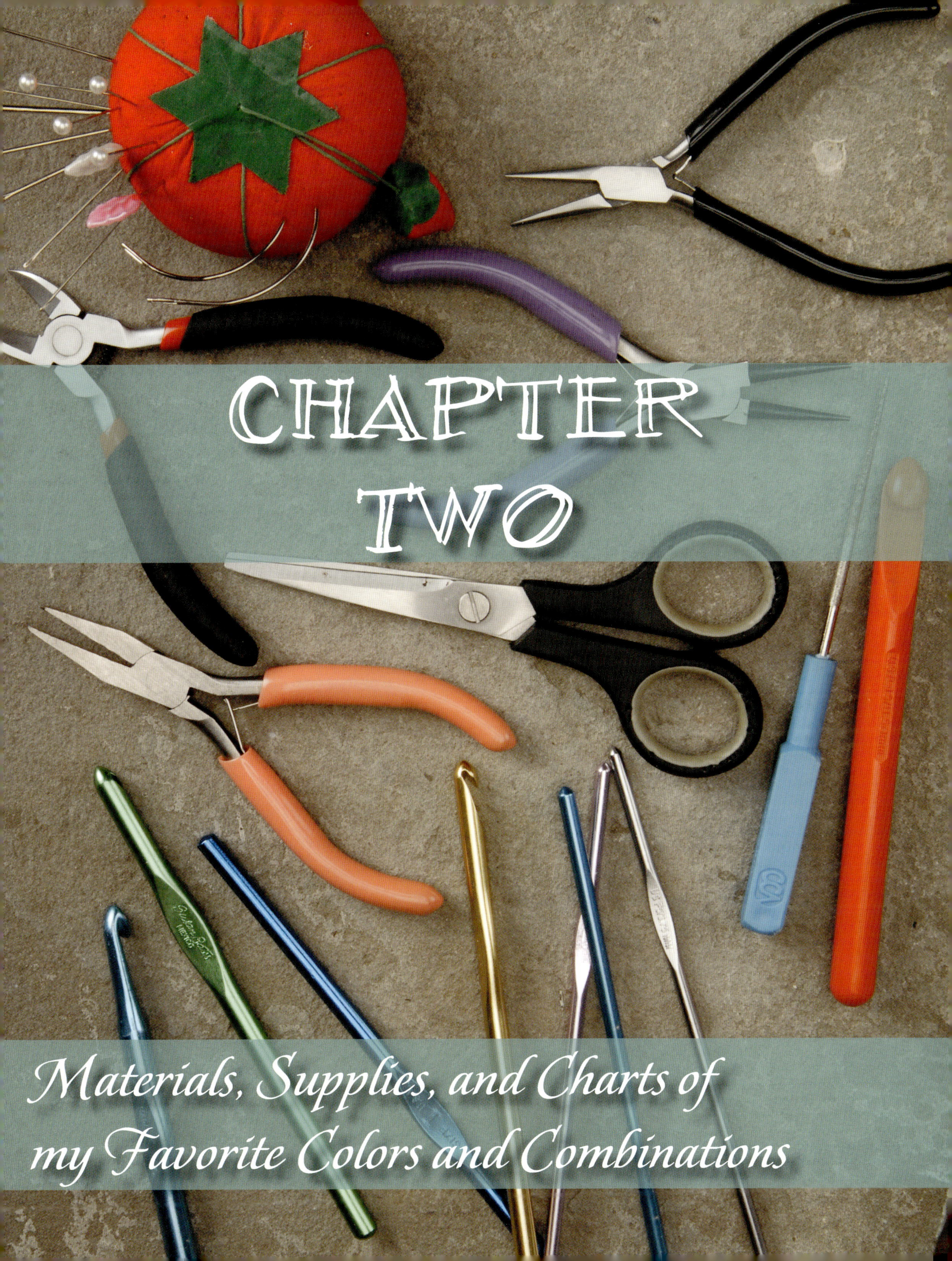

CHAPTER TWO

Materials, Supplies, and Charts of my Favorite Colors and Combinations

Many of you will already have at least some of the supplies you'll need. (Beaders will need the crocheting supplies, and crocheters will need the beading supplies!) Below is a list of suggested supplies and tools broken down by category.

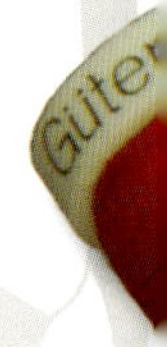

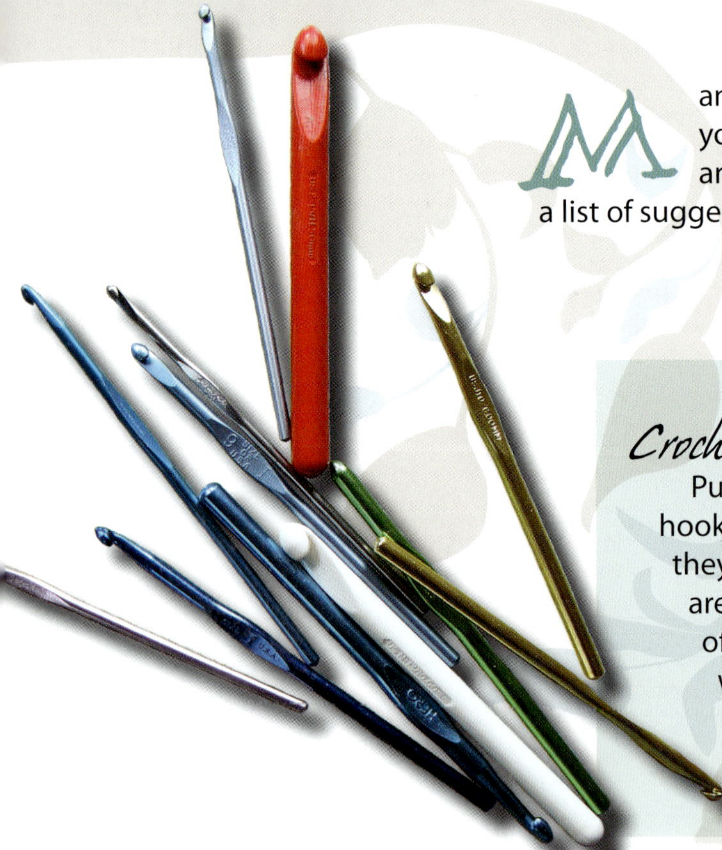

Crochet Hooks:

Purchase a variety of crochet hooks. I like the way the metal hooks feel. However, if you already have and like plastic hooks, they will do fine. The sizes I use most are US 8/H to 10/K. These are larger size hooks that can accommodate multiple strands of yarn. Purchasing an inexpensive set of crochet needles will provide you with a wide range of sizes to accommodate any weight of fiber.

Sewing Needles:

Purchase a few very fine needles for beading and finishing work. The needles may be called English beading needles or milliner's needles. Keep in mind that you need sewing-type needles (not twisted wire beading-type needles) because you will need to sew through fibers of yarn to attach your beads. Also purchase some strong needles with larger holes. (The Dritz company makes a nice seven needle repair assortment.)

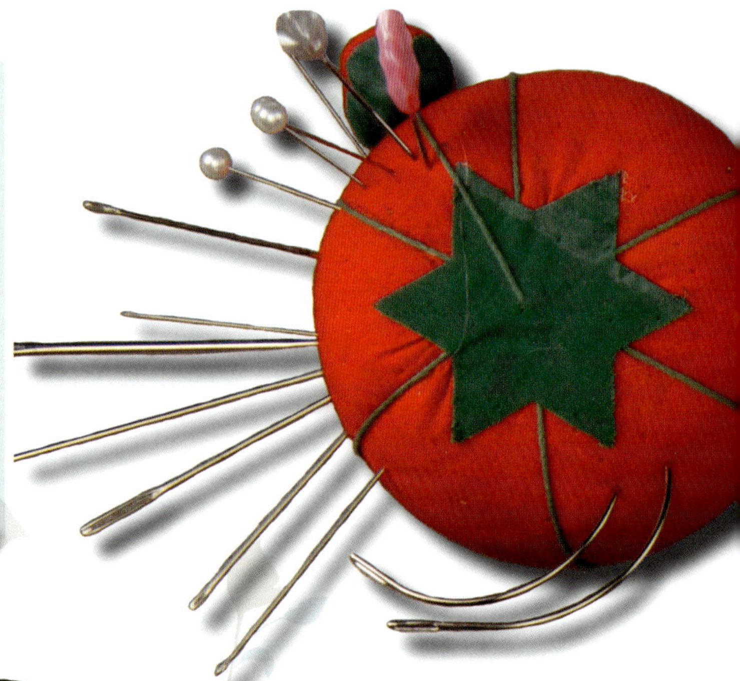

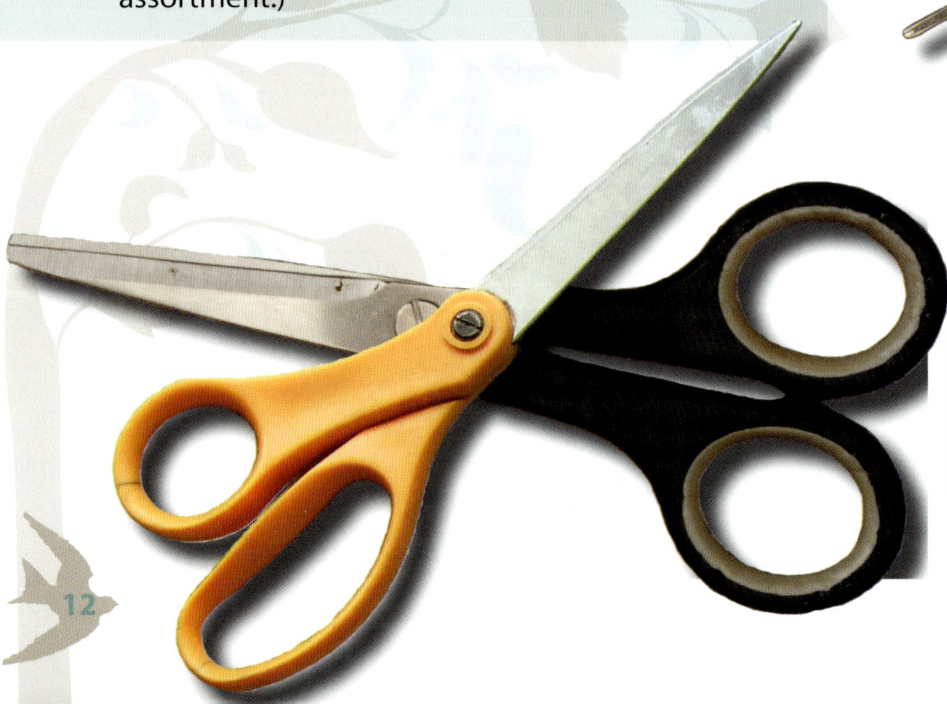

Scissors:

Nothing is more lovely than a nice pair of sharp scissors.

Thread:

Purchase an assortment of strong threads. I like upholstery thread for the heavier jobs and fine nylon beading thread for the more delicate jobs. (GUTERMANN makes a good quality upholstery thread and NYMO makes a good beading thread. Both are available at most shops.) Remember to buy an assortment of colors so that you can match your work. I suggest buying the following basic colors—white or natural, black, teal or turquoise, and sage or grey.

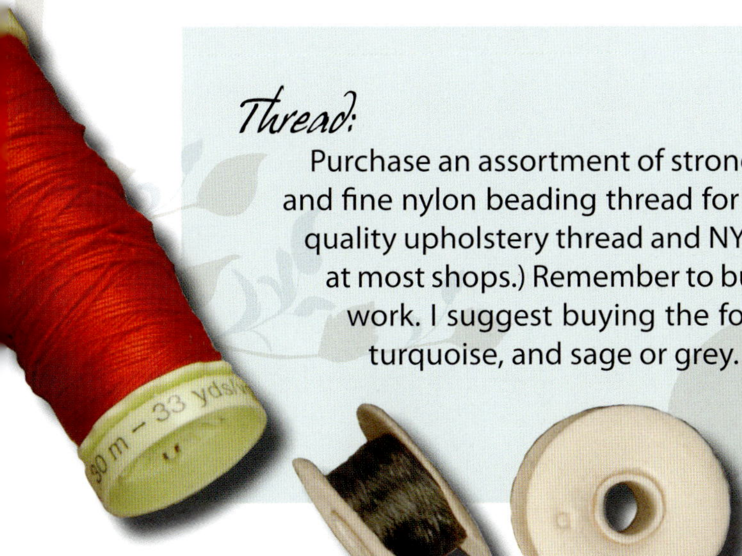

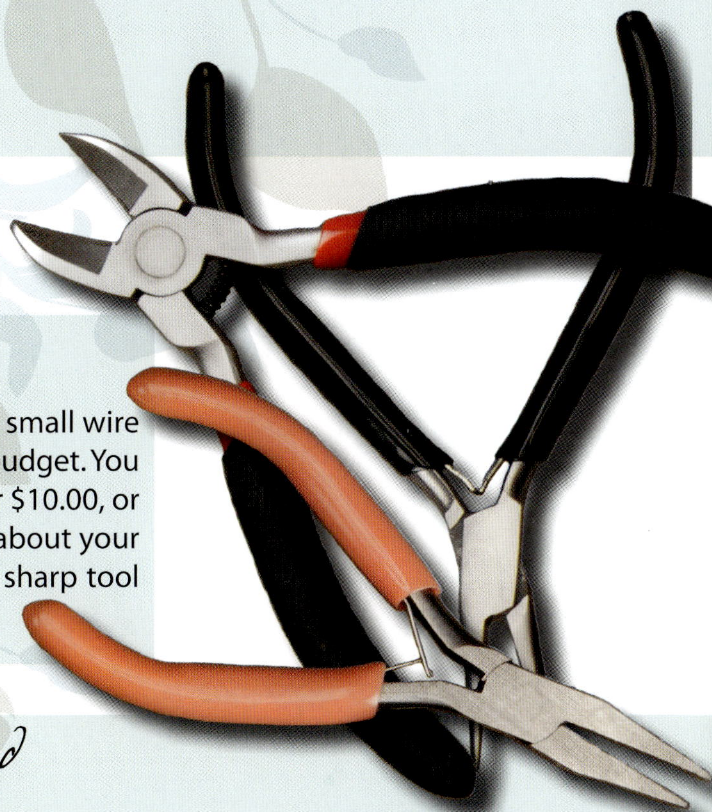

Beading Tools:

You will need jewelry-making needle-nose pliers and small wire cutters. These tools are available at a price to satisfy every budget. You can buy a tool package at the larger craft stores for under $10.00, or you can spend $30.00 or more apiece. If you get serious about your crafting you will use these tools a lot and, believe me, a sharp tool is a pleasure!

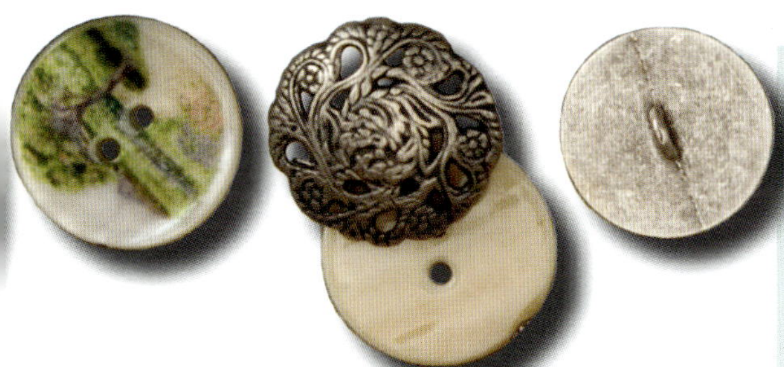

Findings and Closures:

Purchase a variety of buttons for closures. (I use 3/4" to 1" buttons). Simple mother-of-pearl buttons are always beautiful and easy to find.

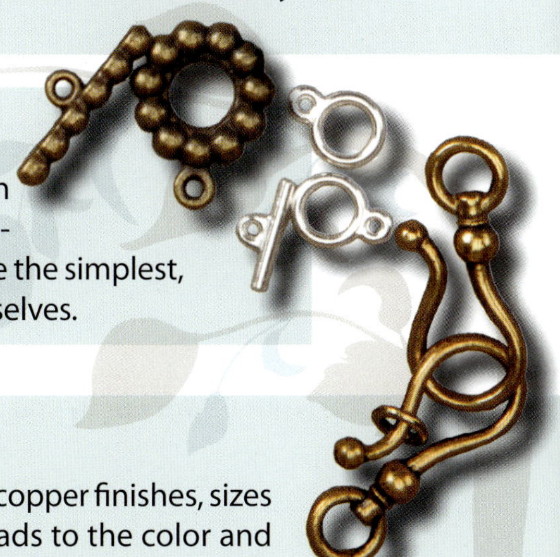

Toggles and Clasps:

I like to use a medium to large size toggle in a plain silver finish or an antique bronze/brass finish. There are tons of choices in this category. Because I won't spend the big bucks for sterling silver components, I choose the simplest, most plain toggles so that they won't draw too much attention to themselves.

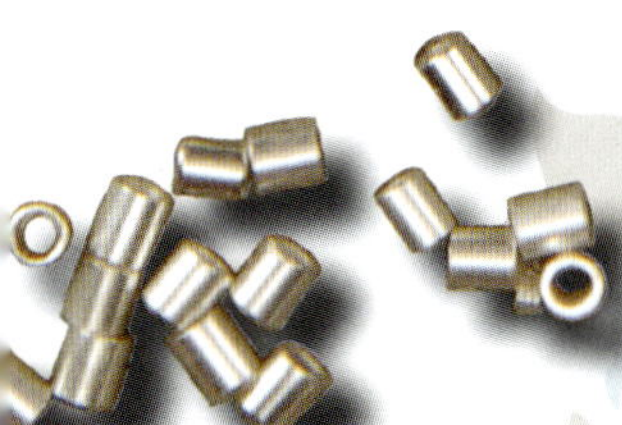

Crimp Beads and Wire:

I mostly use crimp beads in silver, antique brass or copper finishes, sizes #0 or #1. However, you should match your crimp beads to the color and size of your toggles, clasps and buttons. I use nylon-coated bead-stringing wire, size XXS or .010.

MY FAVORITE COLORS TO USE

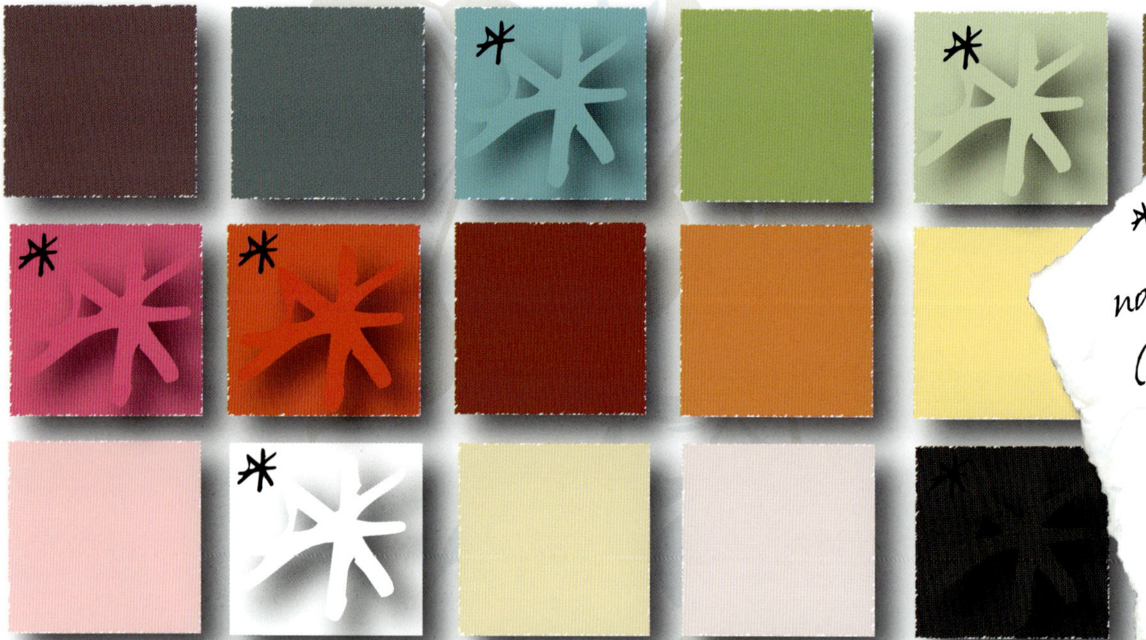

* must-haves in novelty / eyelash yarn (this is the hairy, fun stuff) all other yarns should be soft & fluffy with some texture.

MY FAVORITE COLOR COMBOS

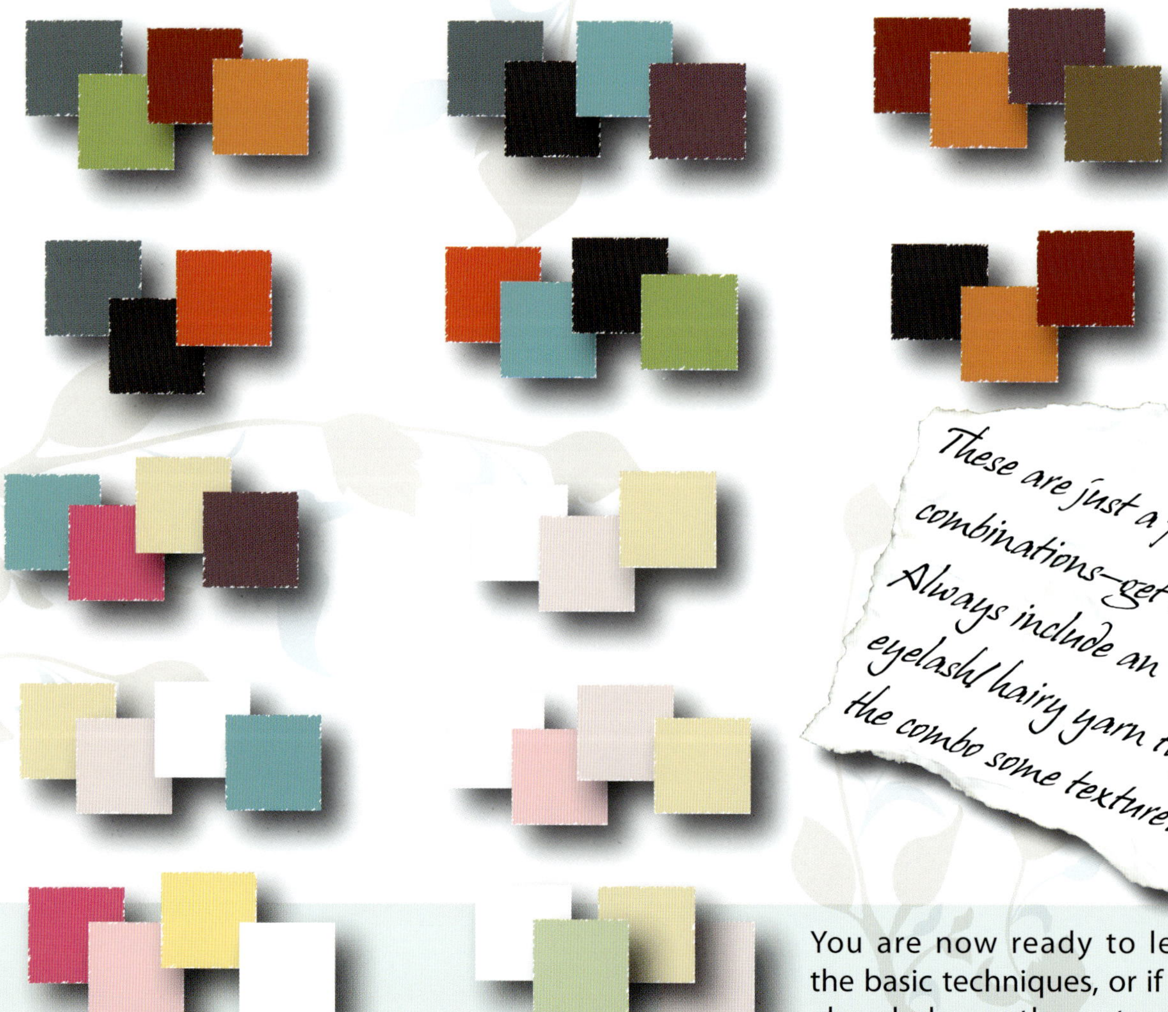

These are just a few color combinations—get creative!! Always include an eyelash/hairy yarn to give the combo some texture.

You are now ready to learn the basic techniques, or if you already know them, to start your first project!

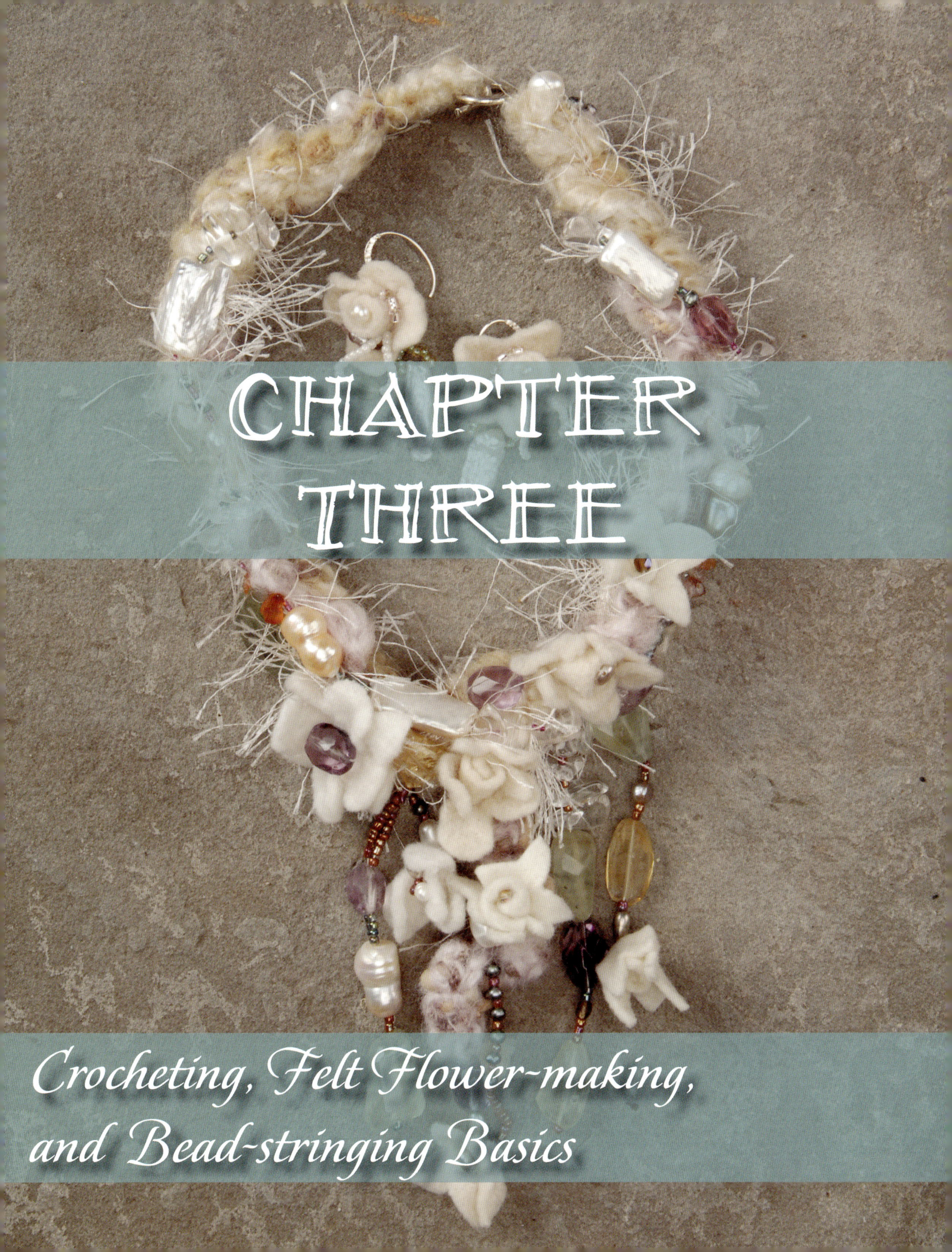

CHAPTER THREE

Crocheting, Felt Flower-making, and Bead-stringing Basics

Unlike my mother (the knitting and crocheting wizard!), I cannot follow a pattern. Sadly, her genetic pattern-following abilities were not passed down. All that counting and structure causes my poor little brain to freeze! Yes, I'm hopeless. So, I have developed a system of easy skills that, used together, compensate for my shortcomings. Better yet, the skills are the same whether the project is simplicity itself or extremely elaborate.

In this chapter you'll learn the basic skills I use for my designs. My hope is that once you have mastered these skills and used them to make some of the projects in this book, the simplicity of the process will inspire you to design and create your own fabulous, one-of-a-kind masterpieces. If you come from a beading background and never thought that you could crochet, don't panic! It's easy! (At least the way I do it!)

BASIC CROCHET STITCHES

It's best to learn crocheting basics using a medium size hook and one strand of medium to heavy fiber. Don't use an eyelash yarn or anything too fuzzy. You want to be able to see your work clearly. Relax, have a glass of wine (or two!) or a nice, warm pot of tea!

The Chain Stitch or Foundation Stitch:

This is the first step to any crochet project. First, take a ball of yarn. Start by making a open loop at one end of your fiber. **A}** Put your hook into the loop and pull the loop snug but not tight around the shaft of your hook. **B}** Use the end of the hook to catch your fiber, and then the pull your hook out of the loop. **C}** Repeat this process until your "links" reach the desired length.

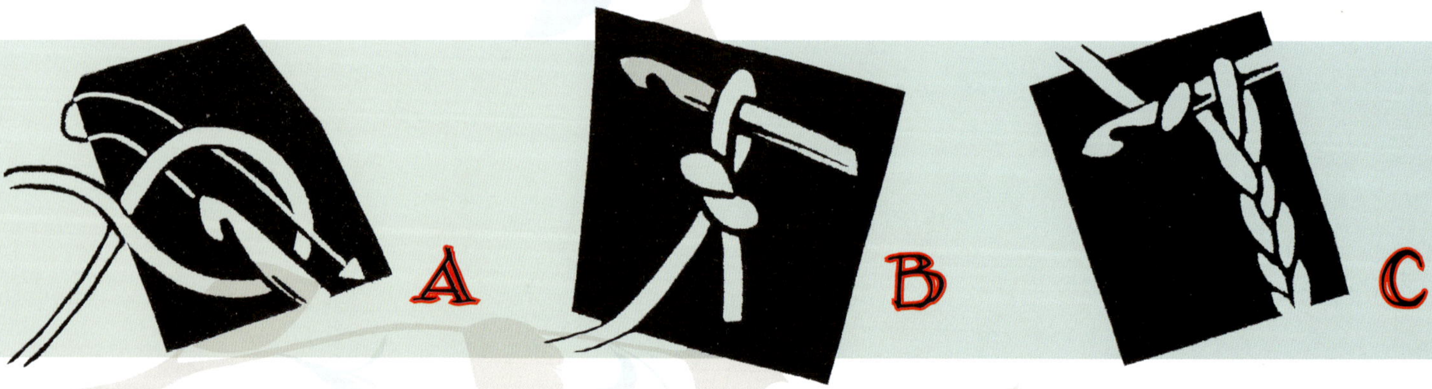

The Single Crochet Stitch:

This is the stitch I use the most. It makes a simple, flat surface (but it's anything but plain when you use funky yarns!). **A&B}** Insert your hook into the second chain (after turning around) and pull it through to create a loop. **C}** Now you have two loops on your hook.

D&E} Wind another loop onto your hook and draw/pull it through the two loops. This will leave you with one loop on your hook. That's it! It's that simple! Now simply repeat. Make sure that when you finish the first row (the one added to the foundation chain) you are putting your hook under and through both yarn pieces of the previous row.

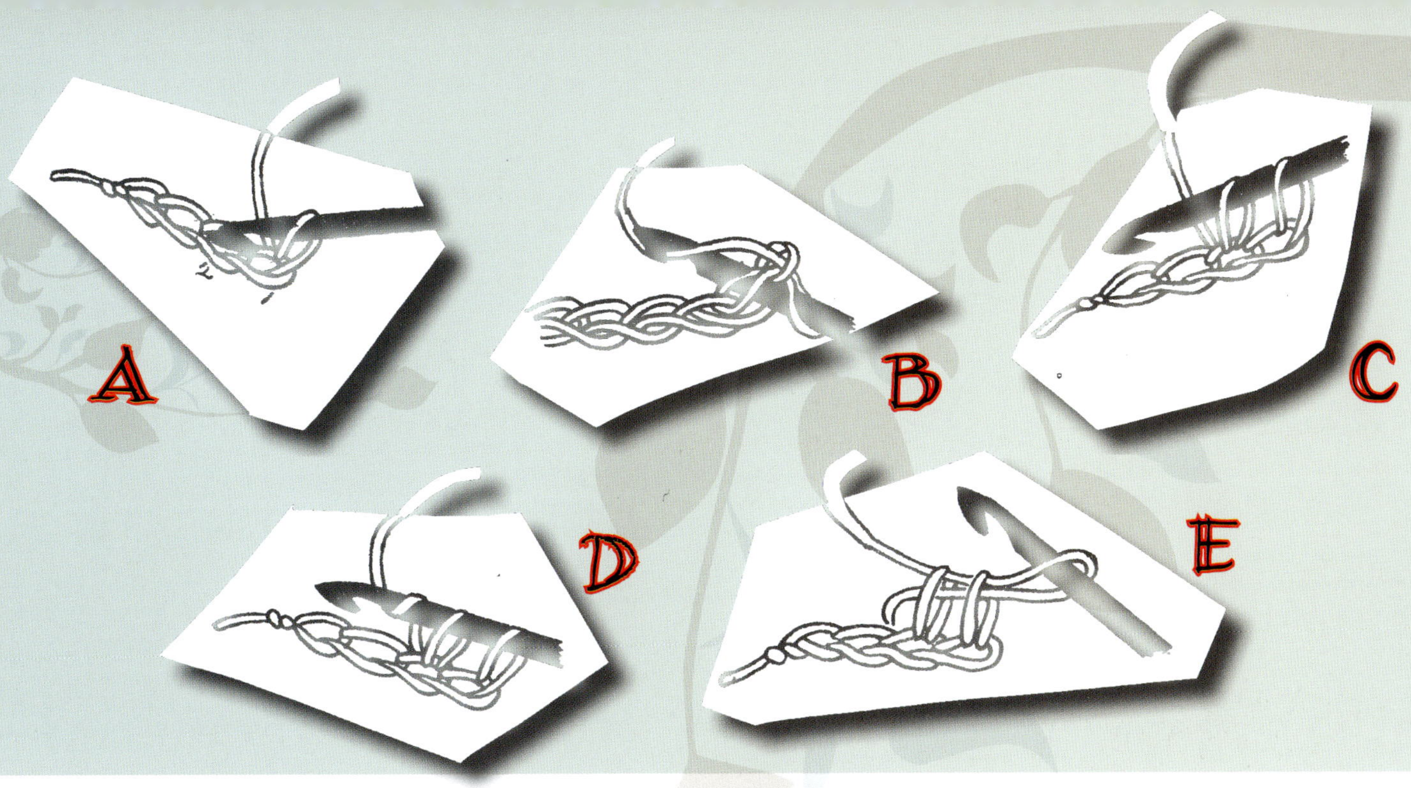

Turning Around:

To make a new row, always add one plain chain stitch before you insert your hook into your first single crochet stitch of the next row. If you do not add this chain stitch, you will decrease the width of your work with every row and end up with a crooked edge. (Although, as I will explain later, this can be used to a produce a desired effect.)

The Slip Stitch:

This is a stitch that is used to add outline color or to join two pieces together, as when you want to make a circle by joining together a foundation chain. To make a slip stitch, put your hook through both pieces of the previous row and wind them around the hook. Then pull the hook all the way back through (even the existing loop). When done, there should be only one loop on the hook.

That's it! Practice the chain stitch until it comes easily. Then make a foundation chain twenty links long. Then turn around and do the single crochet stitch till the end. Then turn around and repeat for a bunch of rows. You will be able to see if you are working with a consistent tension on your yarn. If you use too little tension, the work will appear to have holes. If you use too much tension, the work will be hard to put your hook through! Also, if you are decreasing or increasing the number of stitches (remember that extra chain stitch when turning around!) the work will have an uneven edge. Practice, practice, practice. I'm sure that in no time at all you'll find crocheting as relaxing as I do!

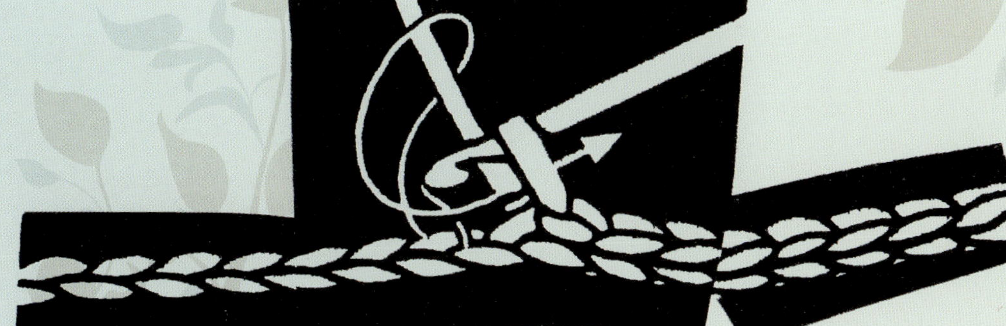

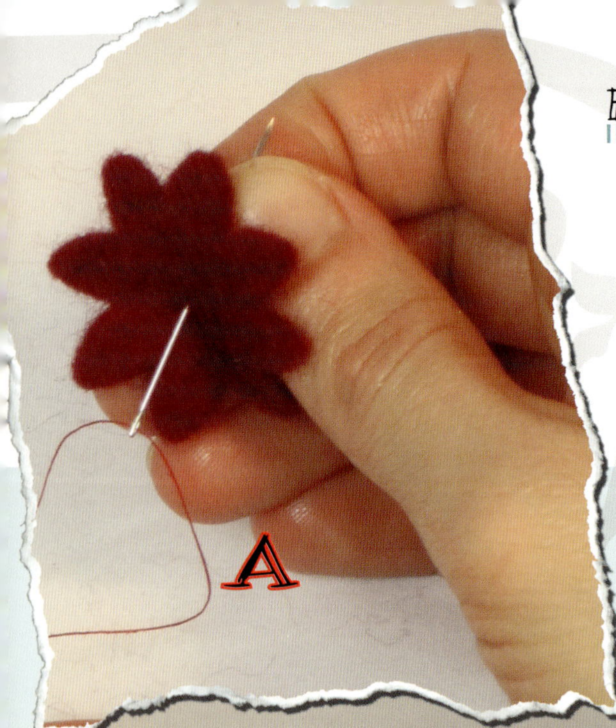

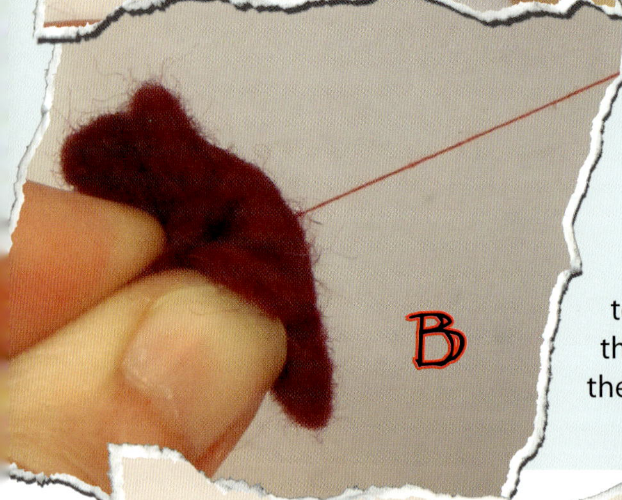

FELT FLOWER-MAKING

To make these sweet little felt flowers you will need felt, a sharp pair of scissors, and a fine needle with strong thread.

The Daisy Flower:

First, using the provided pattern as a guide, cut your "daisy" flower out of felt. Don't be overly concerned with being too exact. A slight variation between the flowers will just give them more individuality and character.

Second, take about 12 inches of strong thread, knot one end and put a needle on the other (i.e. as if for single strand sewing).

Third, pierce the needle through the center of your flower and pull the needle and thread until the knot is against the felt {A.

Using the fingers of one hand, pinch the petals of the flower together on the side of the flower with the knotted end of the thread. (The needle and thread will be on the "unpinched" side of the flower.) {B

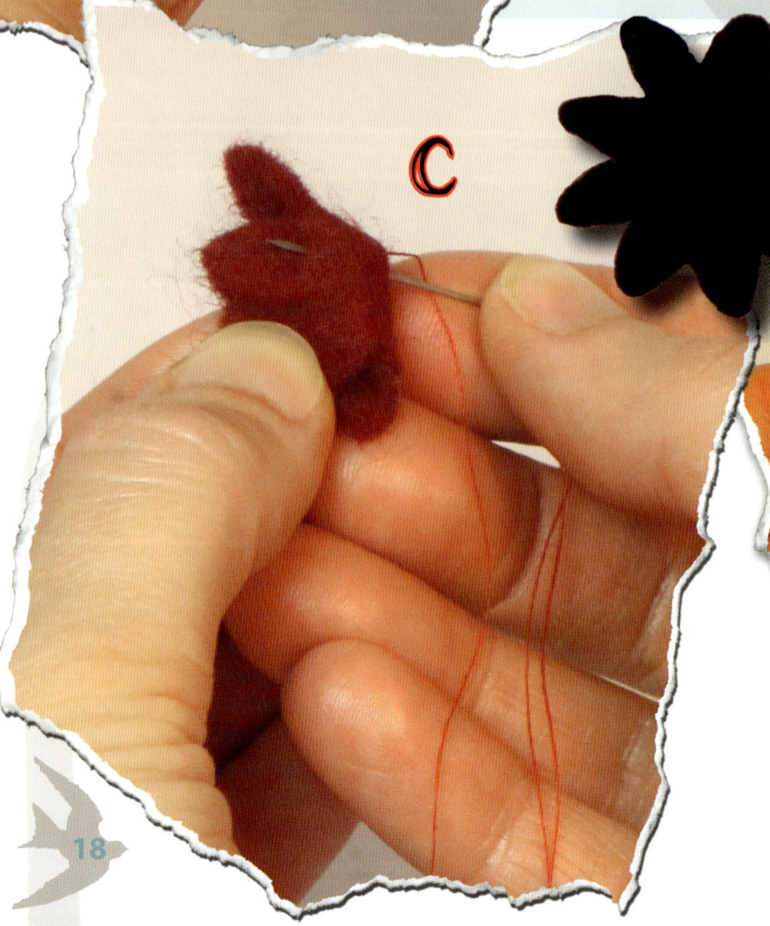

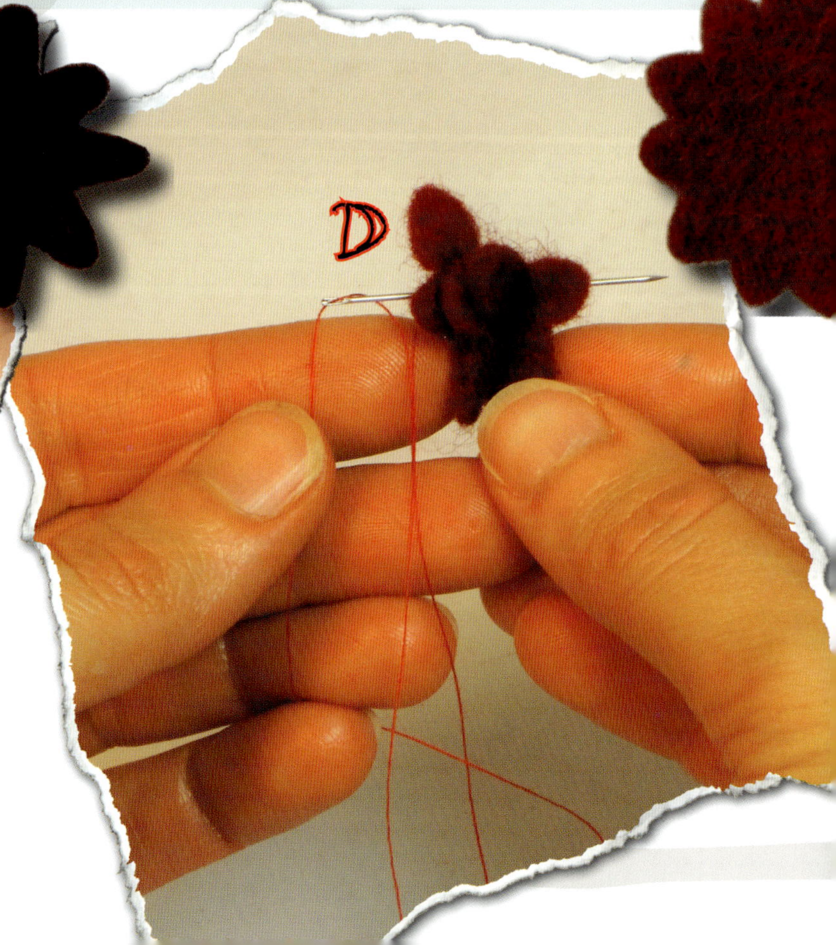

The very simple daisy flower pattern to cut from felt

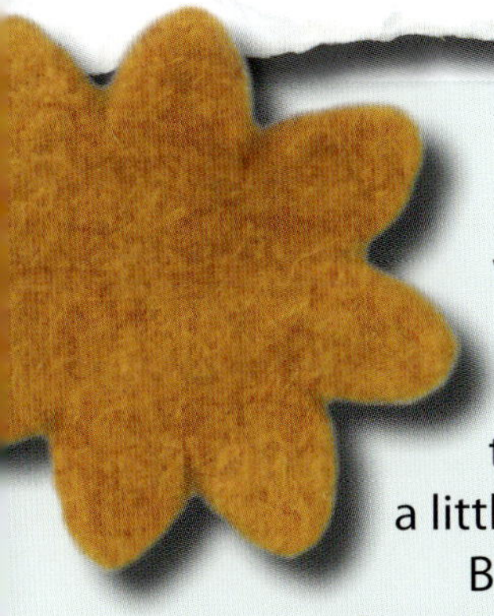

To make the first stitch, pierce the needle back into the center of the flower, near where the thread exits (for an "invisible" stitch) and then out through a petal, a little less than half-way up the petal. {C

Use three or four more tiny stitches to sew opposing petals to one another, also a little less than half-way up the petal. {D, E & F Be careful not to pull the thread too tight on the stitches or the flower will not "open" up when finished. Also, remember that perfection is not required! In fact, I prefer imperfection, as it will make the flower appear more "natural." To finish the flower, pierce the needle back through the back of the center/base of the flower, make several knots in the felt, and cut the excess thread. {G

Voila! A "daisy" flower!

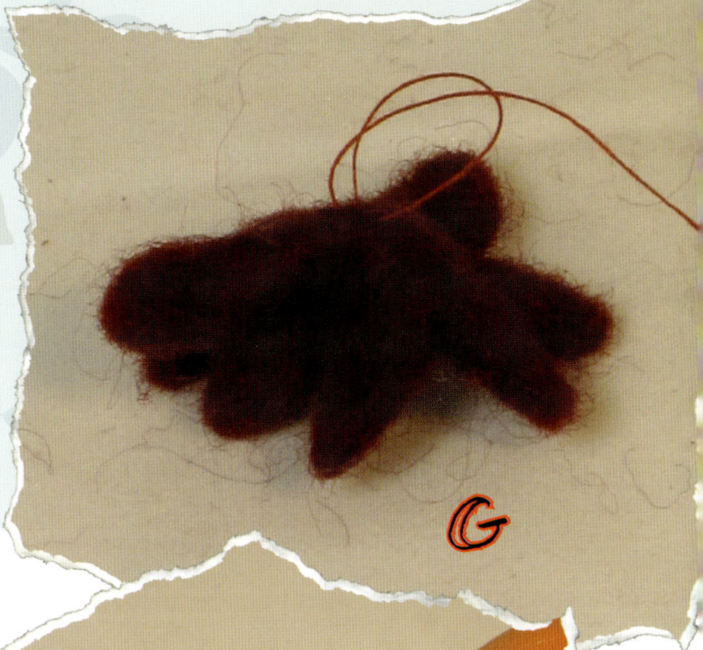

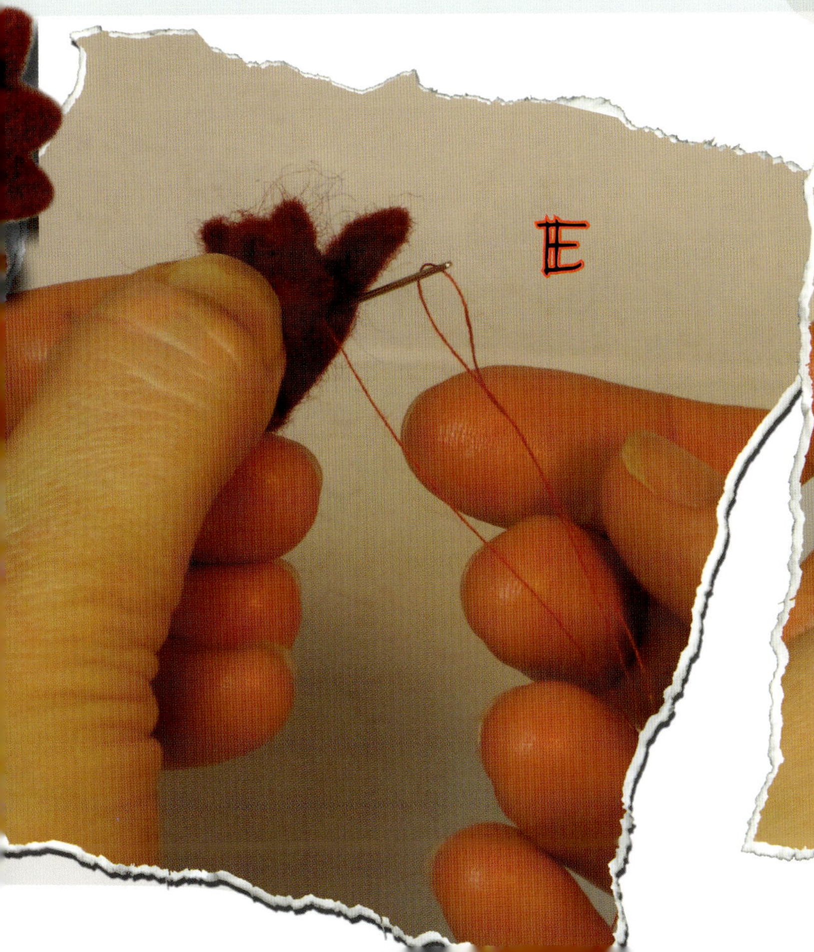

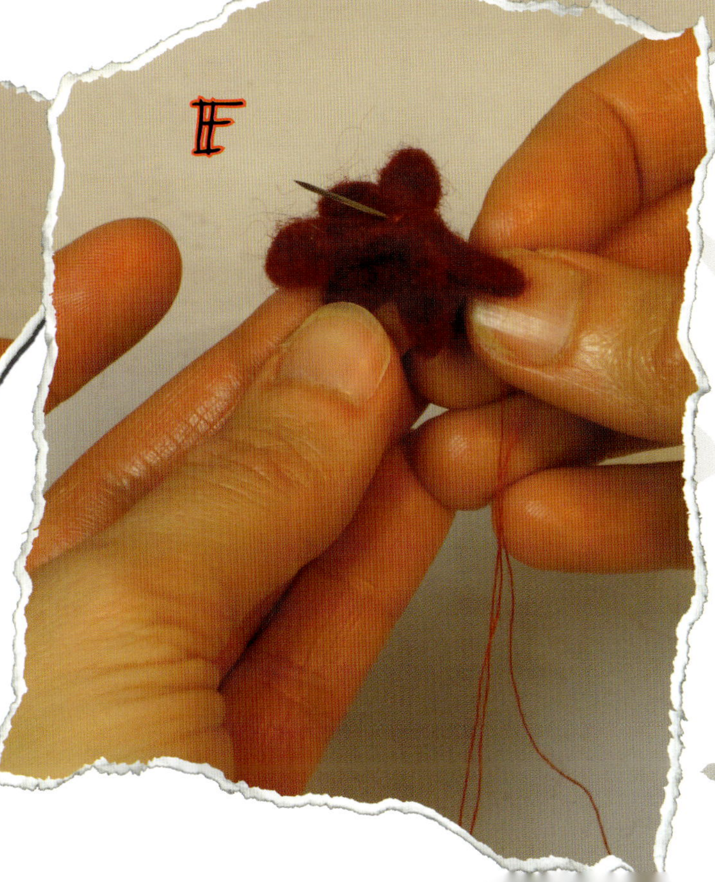

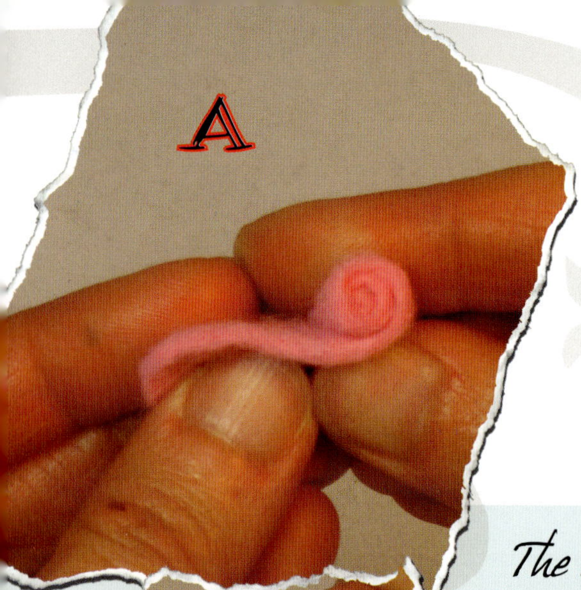

Note: These "rose" flowers are definitely the hardest of the basic skills to master. It's a lot of scrunching and finessing of the felt, and your fingers will feel clumsy at first.

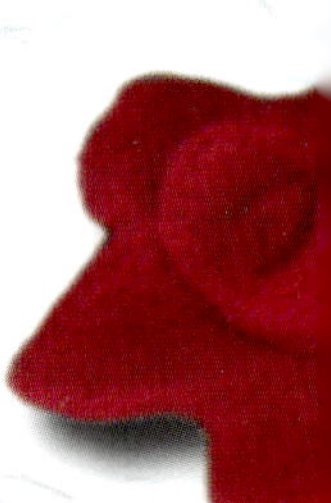

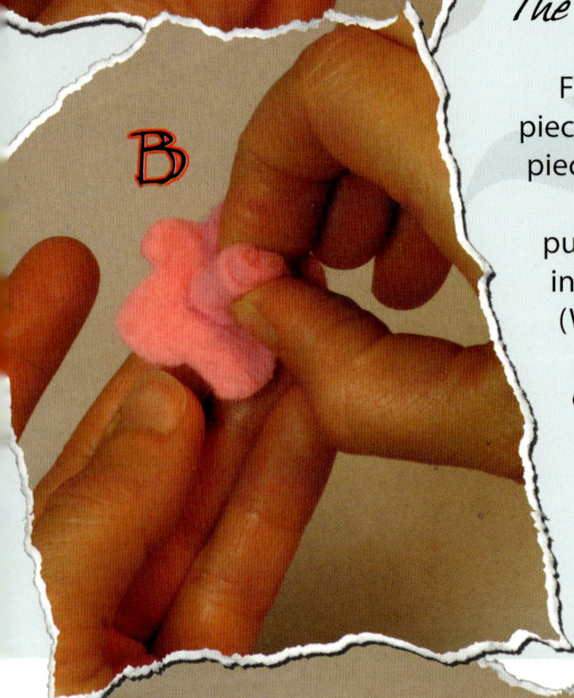

The Rose Flower:

First, using the provided pattern as a guide, cut your two "rose" flower pieces out of felt, i.e. the center (pennant-like) piece and the outer petal piece.

Second, take about 12 inches of strong thread, knot one end and put a needle on the other (i.e. as if for single strand sewing). Third, starting with the narrower end, roll the center piece into a "jelly-roll" shape. (When done the wider end will be on the outside.) **{A**

Fourth, place one end of the rolled center piece into the middle of the outer petal piece and, using the fingers of one hand, pinch the center piece into the middle of the outer petal piece and hold it pinched from the "back" of the flower. **{B & C**

Using your other hand, take the threaded needle and pierce it into the middle of the center piece of the flower (from the front) and out through the back of the outer petal piece. **{D & E**

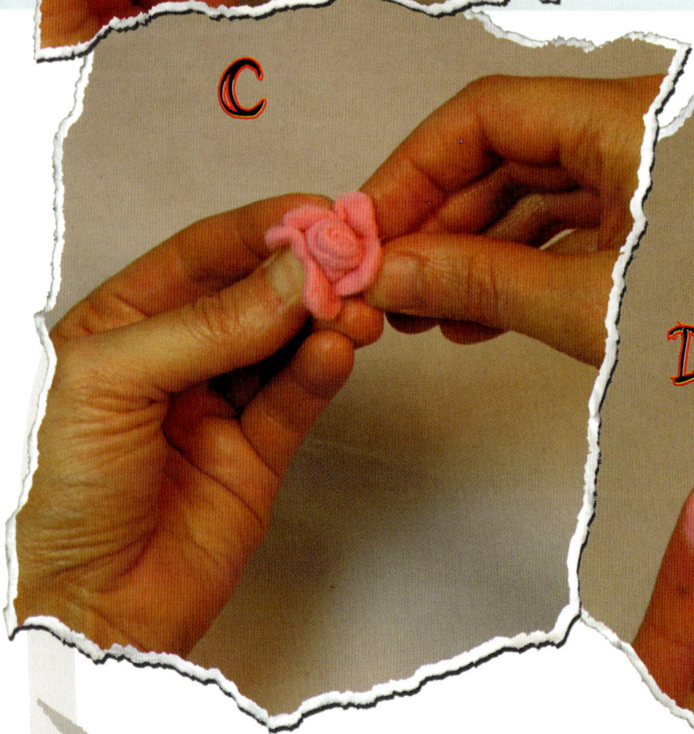

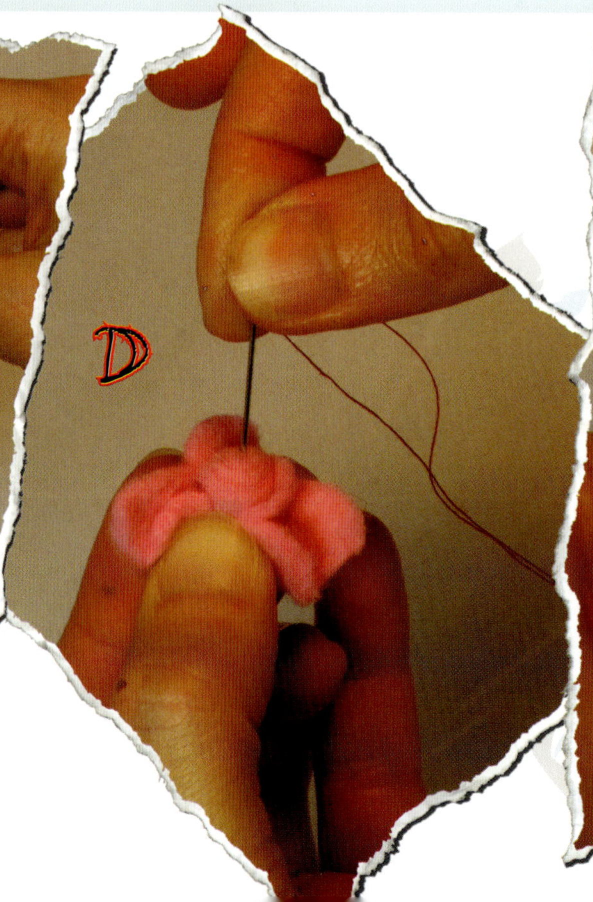

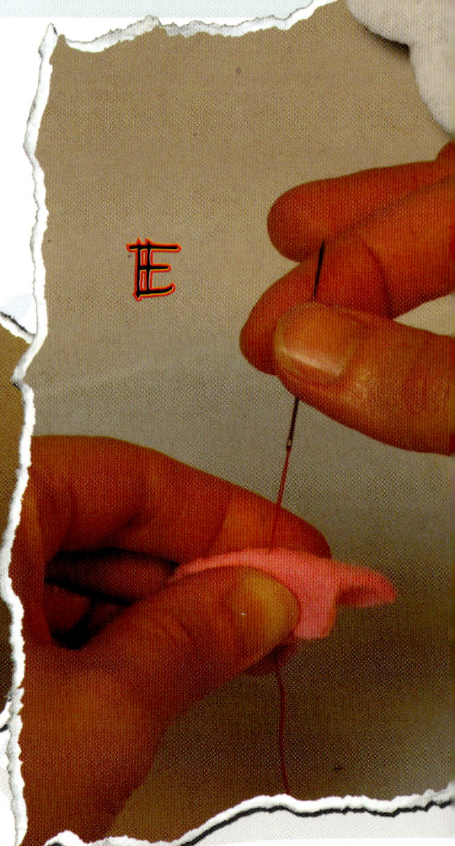

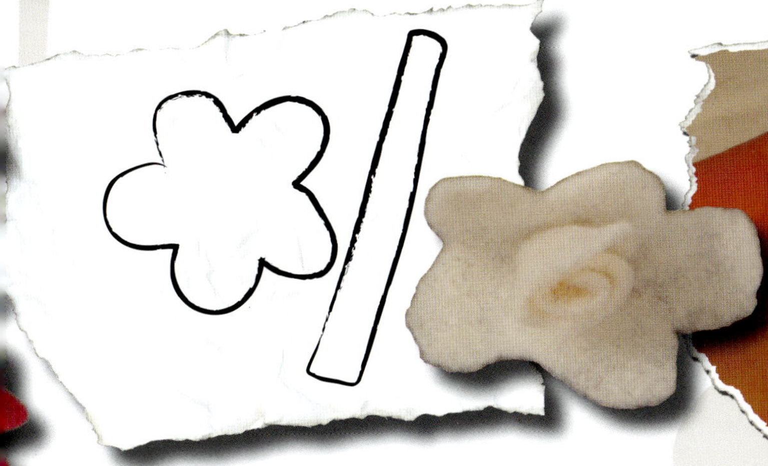

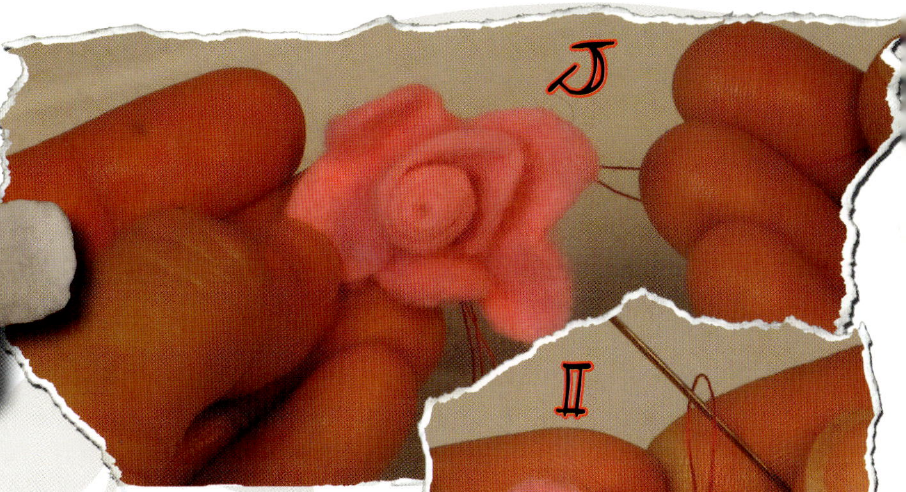

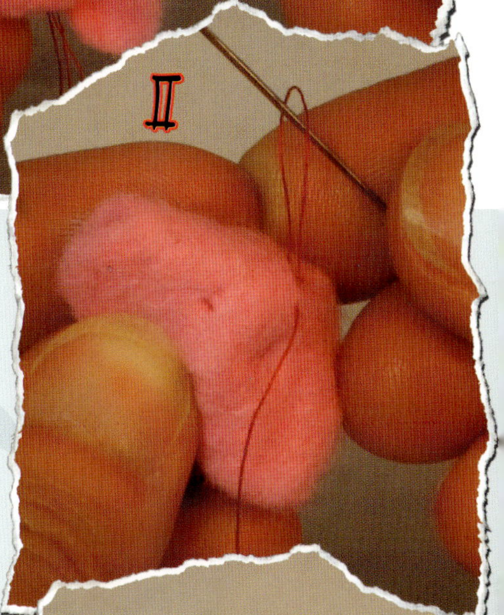

Fifth, complete the "rose" flower as you did the "daisy" flower, i.e. for the first stitch, pierce the needle back into the center of the flower near where the thread exits, then through the center piece and out through a petal, again, a little less than half-way up the petal. {F

Use three or four more tiny stitches to sew opposing petals to one another, also a little less than half-way up the petal. Be sure to catch the center piece of the flower with every stitch! {G & H Also, again, be careful not to pull the thread too tight or the flower will not "open" up when finished. Remember that perfection is not required! Finally, finish off the "rose" by piercing the needle back through the center/base of the flower, making several knots in the felt, and cutting the excess thread. {I & J

Voila! A rose! If you like, you can also shape your rose after it is complete by trimming the petals with a sharp pair of scissors.

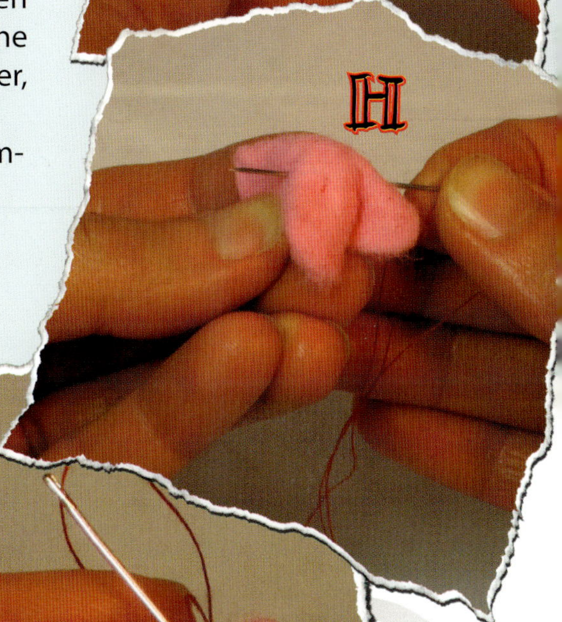

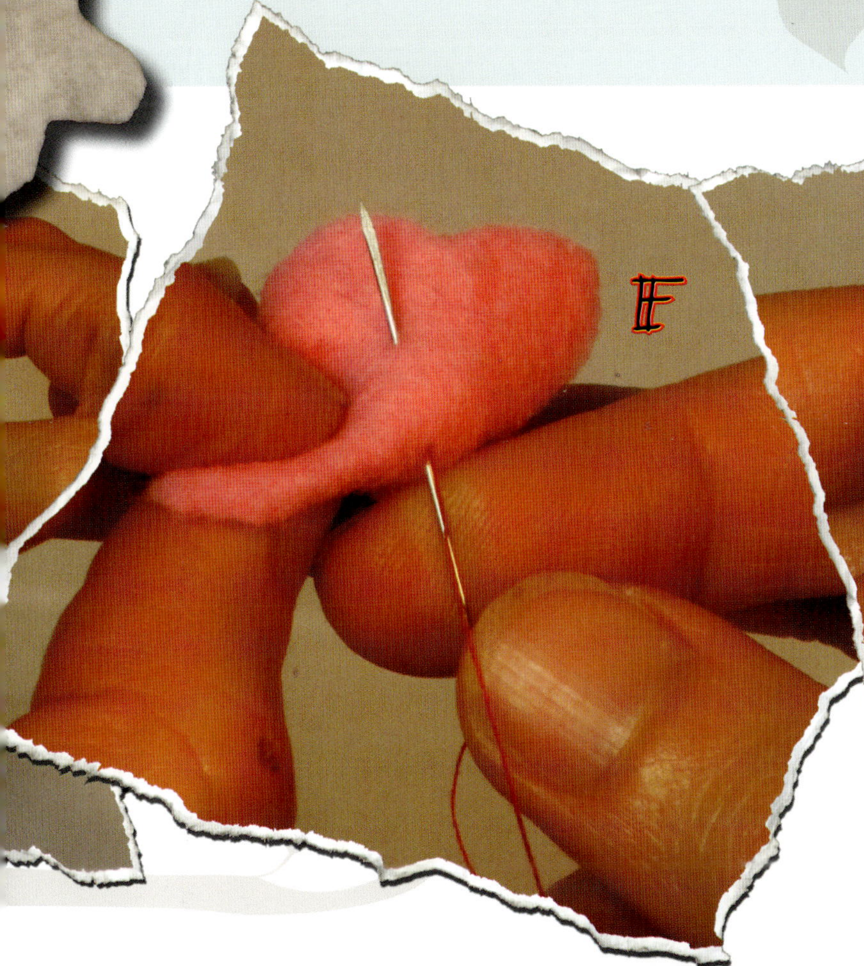

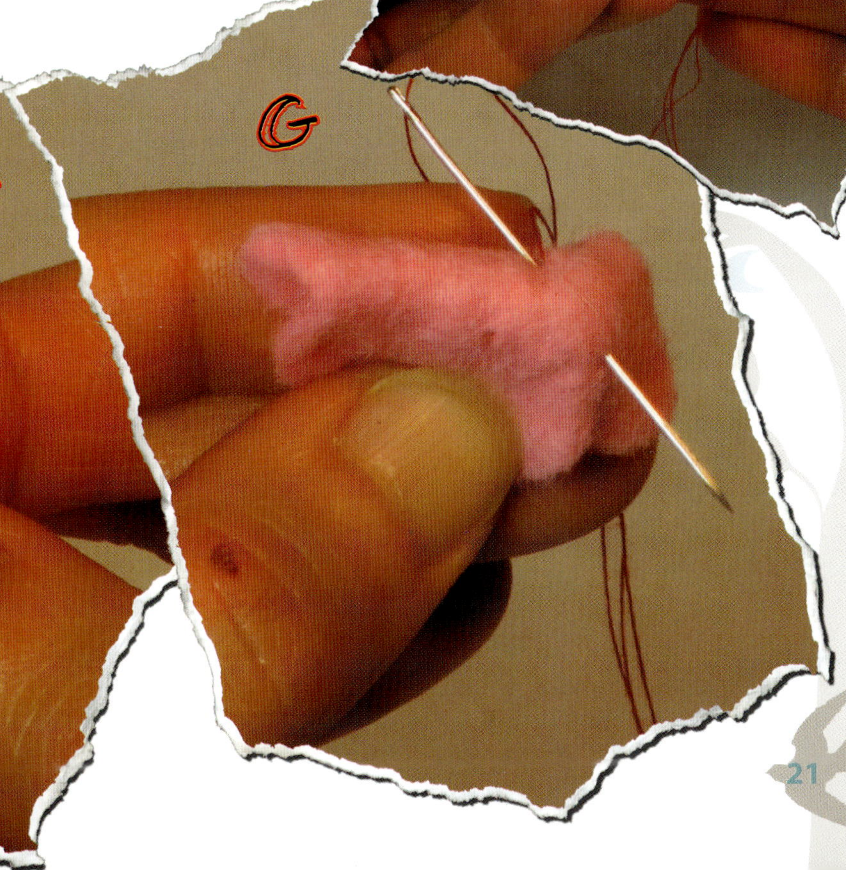

BASIC BEADING

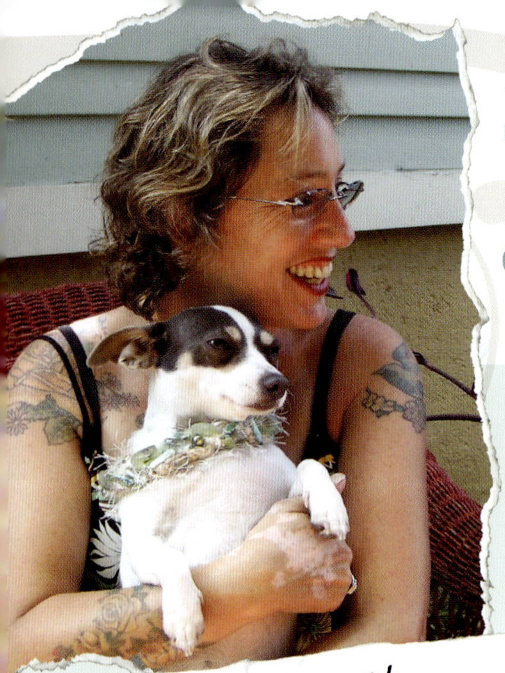

Me and my dog, Olive, wearing one of her necklaces.

Once again, my beading technique is basic. (The dazzle comes from the bead choice!)

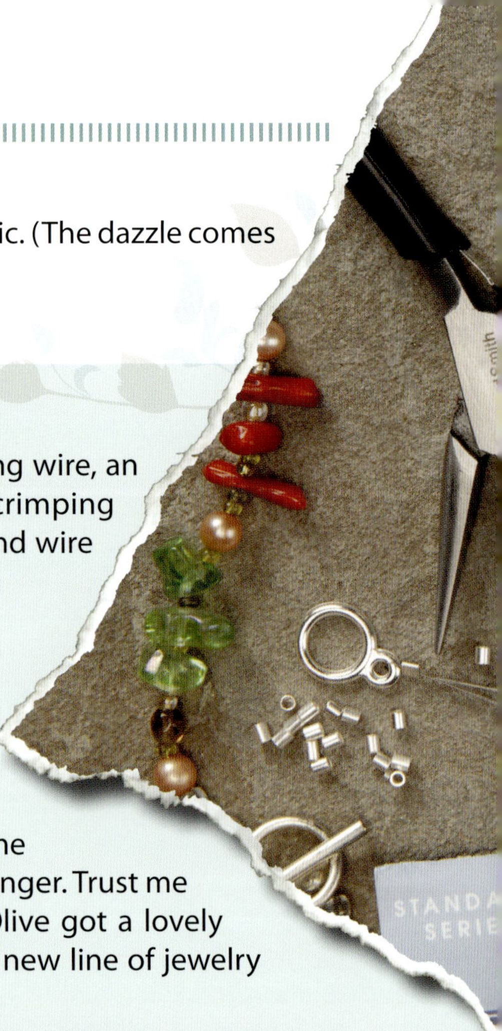

Tools and Supplies:

For basic beading you will need beading wire, an assortment of beads, a toggle or clasp, crimping beads, and a pair of needle-nosed pliers and wire cutters.

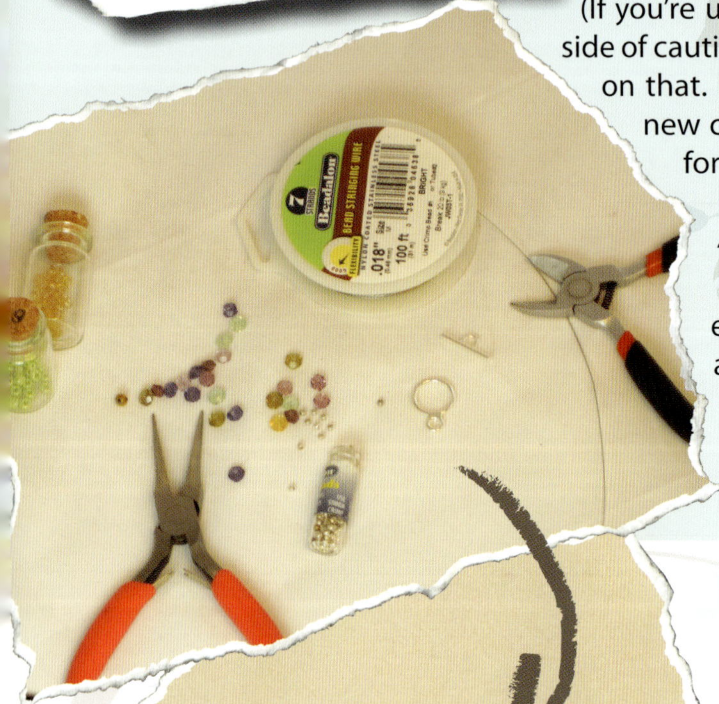

Cut Your Wire:

First, decide how long you want your necklace or bracelet to be. Then, using wire cutters, cut your wire to a length approximately 4 inches longer. (If you're unsure, it's better to err on the side of caution and cut the wire a little longer. Trust me on that. Long story short, my dog Olive got a lovely new collar and I got an idea for a new line of jewelry for pets!)

Attach One End of Your Toggle or Closure:

First, choose your toggle. Make it a habit to always start either with the "bar" end or the "O" end. This way you won't accidentally use the same part for both ends. (This is especially true if you buy your parts in bulk.) Again, trust me on that. (Long story short, another new collar for Olive!)

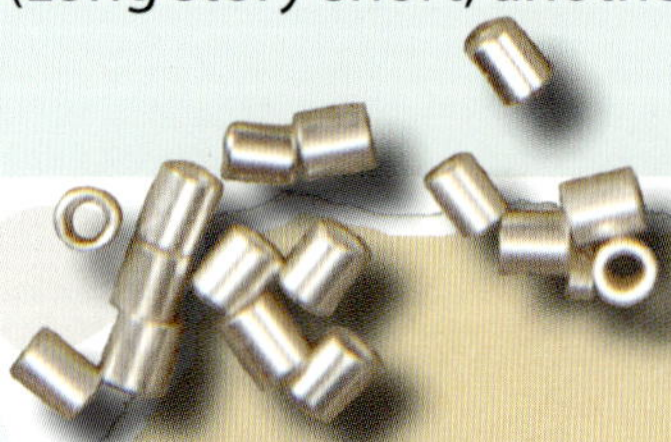

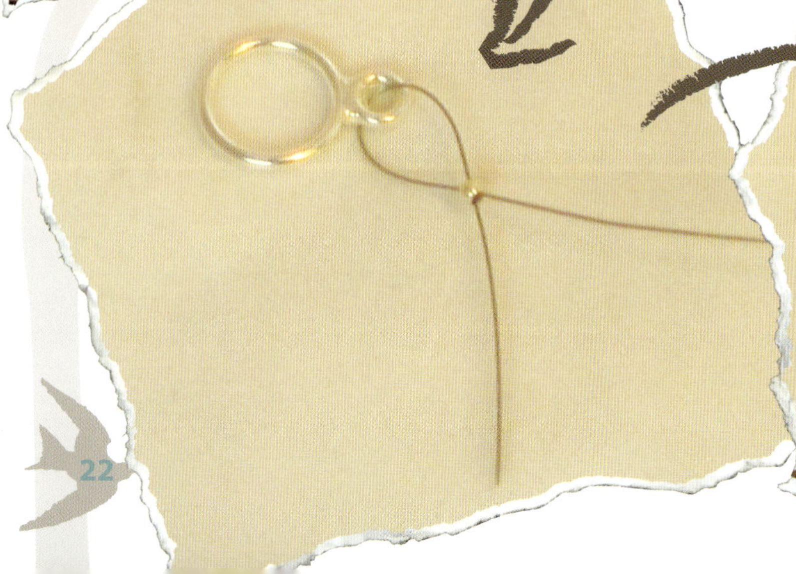

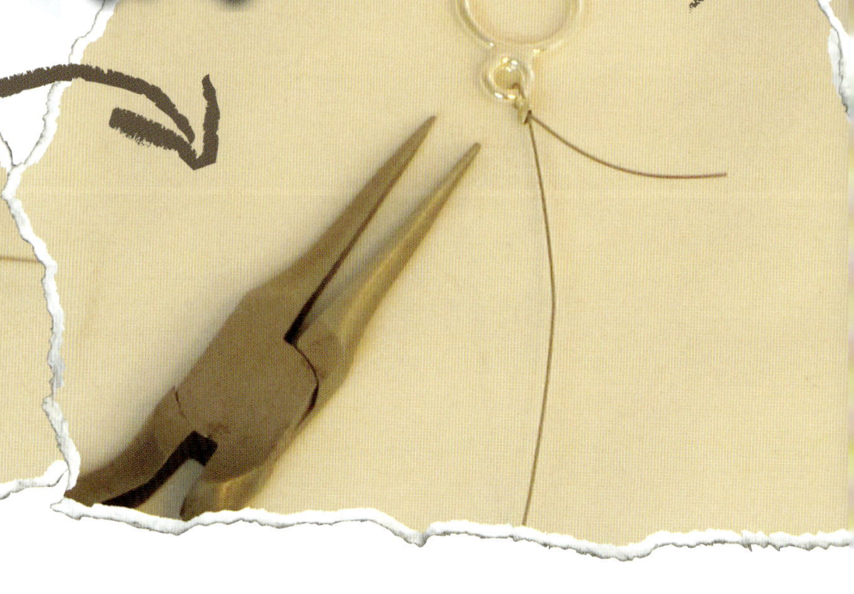

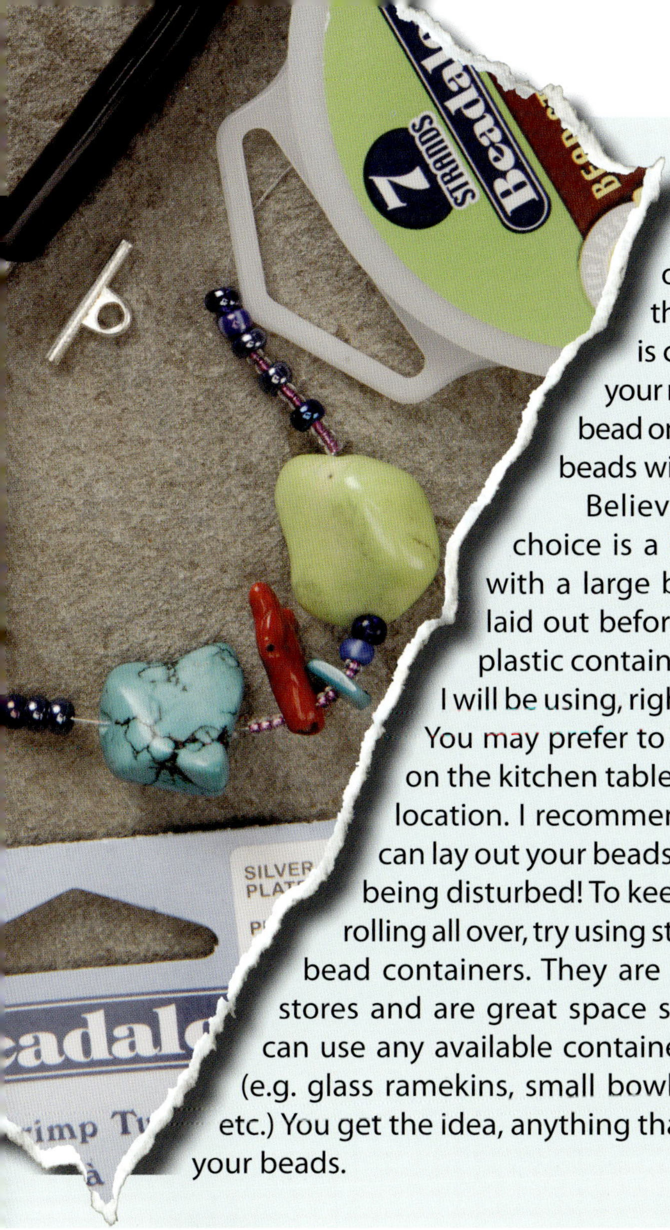

Next, slide a crimp bead several inches onto the open end of the wire, then "thread" the end of the wire through the toggle and back down into the crimp bead until the end of the wire is approximately 1-1/2 inches past the bead. Pull the crimp bead toward the toggle until it is close but not tight to the toggle. Using your needle-nose pliers, crimp (squish) the bead onto the wire. Now, place your chosen beads within arm's reach and begin!

Believe it or not my workstation of choice is a large futon! I sit cross-legged with a large board covered in black velvet laid out before me. On the board, in little plastic containers, are all of the beads that I will be using, right there within arm's reach. You may prefer to set up your workstation on the kitchen table or some other suitable location. I recommend anywhere that you can lay out your beads without them or you being disturbed! To keep your beads from rolling all over, try using stacking, screw-top bead containers. They are available at craft stores and are great space savers. However, you can use any available containers you have around the house (e.g. glass ramekins, small bowls, yogurt tops, container lids, etc.) You get the idea, anything that will allow you easy access to your beads.

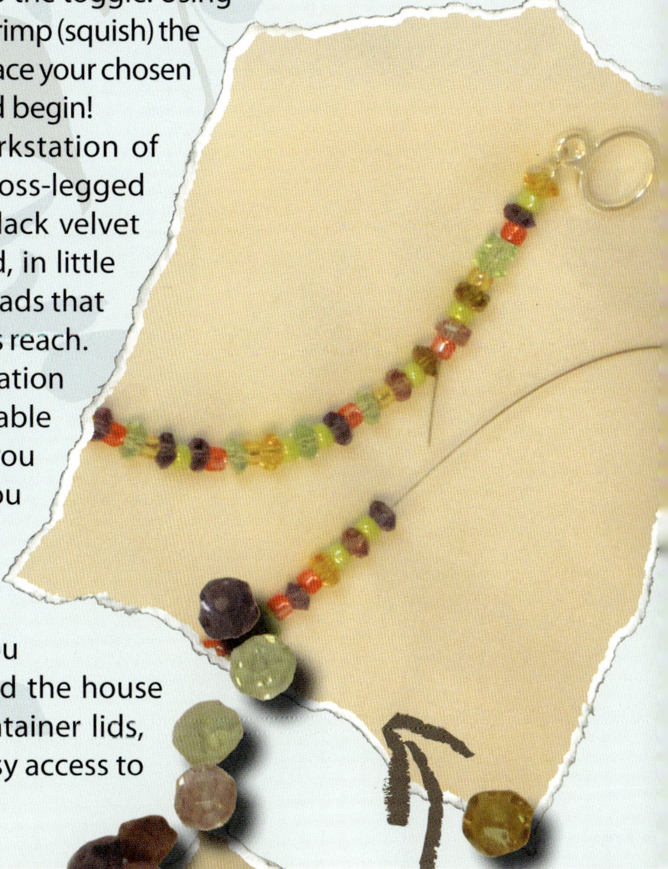

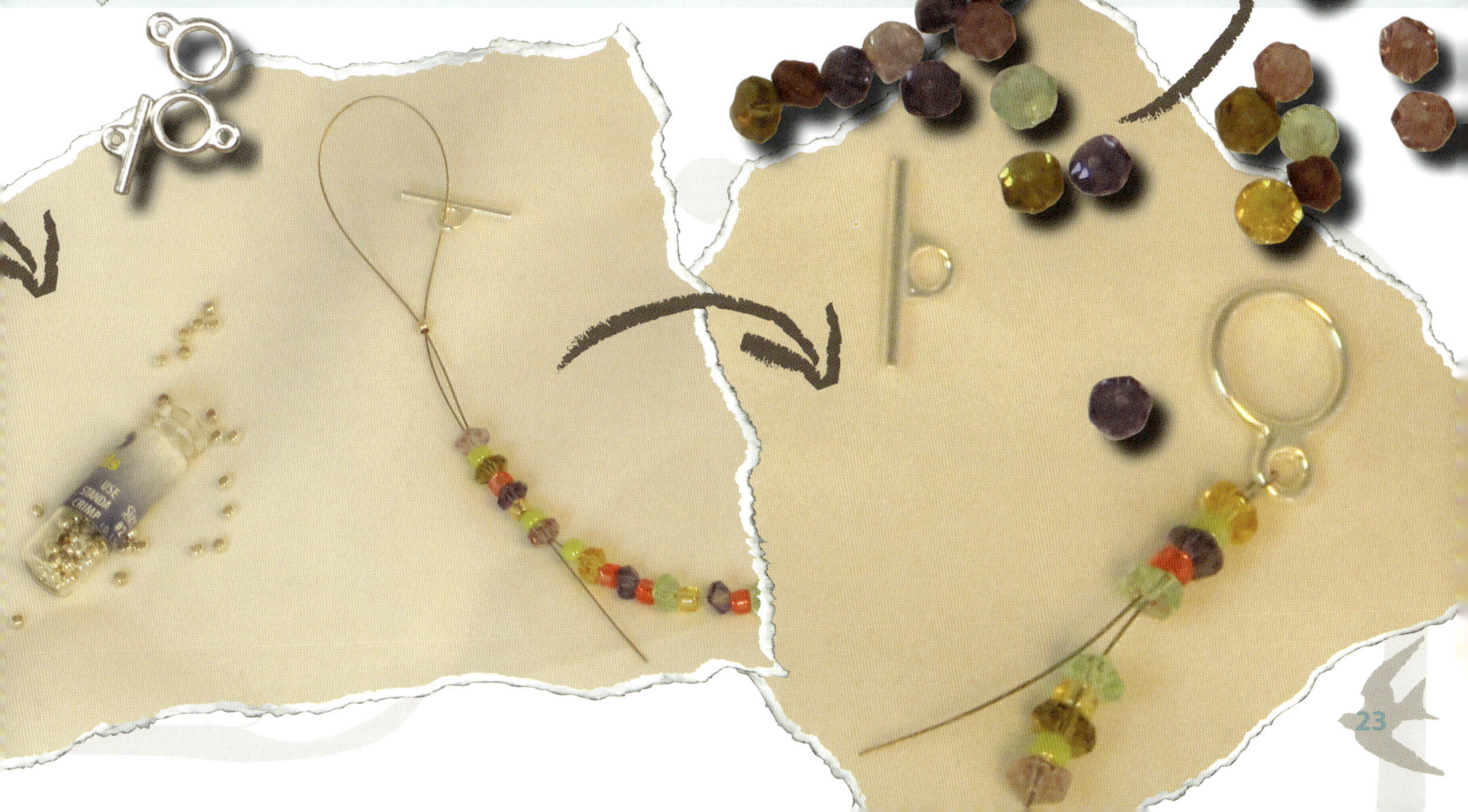

Begin Beading:

The first few beads are important to help strengthen the crimp bead. Make sure that both strands of the wire go through the first few beads. If a bead slips off the short (open) end of the wire during the beading process, don't panic! With a little finesse you can slip it back in! However, this gets more difficult as the project progresses. So be careful near the end. Continue beading until your piece reaches the desired length. You can determine the length by measuring from the first toggle to the last bead (plus a smidge for the other toggle part).

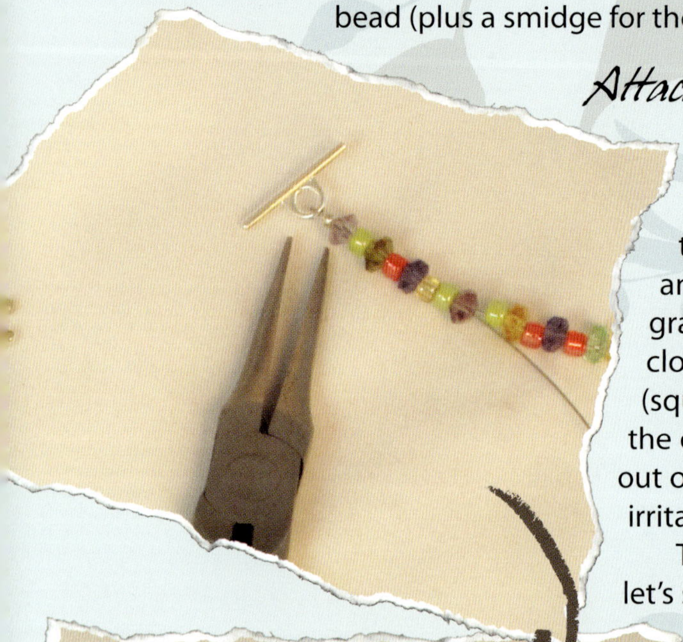

Attaching the Other End of the Toggle:

When your piece has reached the desired length, slide another crimp bead onto the wire, thread the wire through the other end of the toggle, then back through the crimp bead and the last inch or so of beads. Using your needle-nose pliers, grasp the end of the wire and gently pull it until the toggle is close but not tight to the crimp bead. Use your pliers to crimp (squish) the crimp bead. Then, using your wire cutters, cut off the excess wire as close as possible to the last bead it is coming out of. This is important. Otherwise, the wire will stick out and be irritating and scratchy to your skin.

That's how easy it is to make a beaded necklace! Now, at last, let's start your first necklace. (Something more and better!)

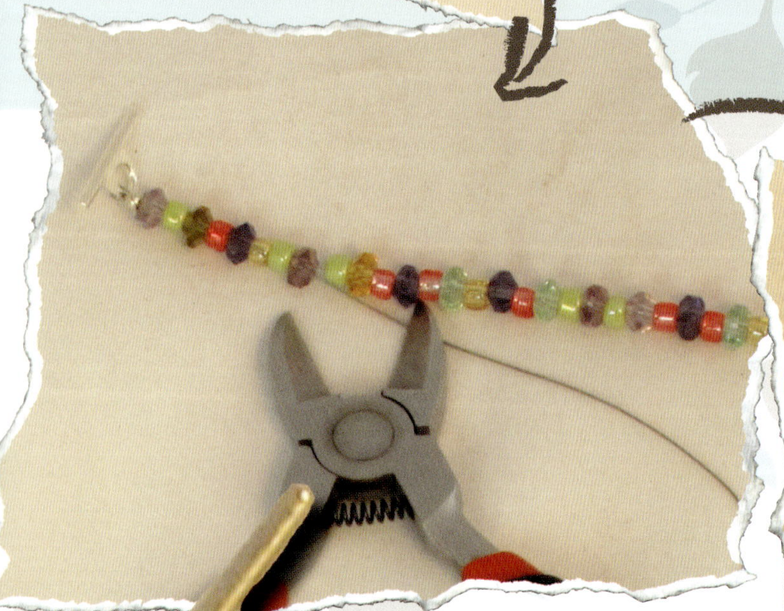

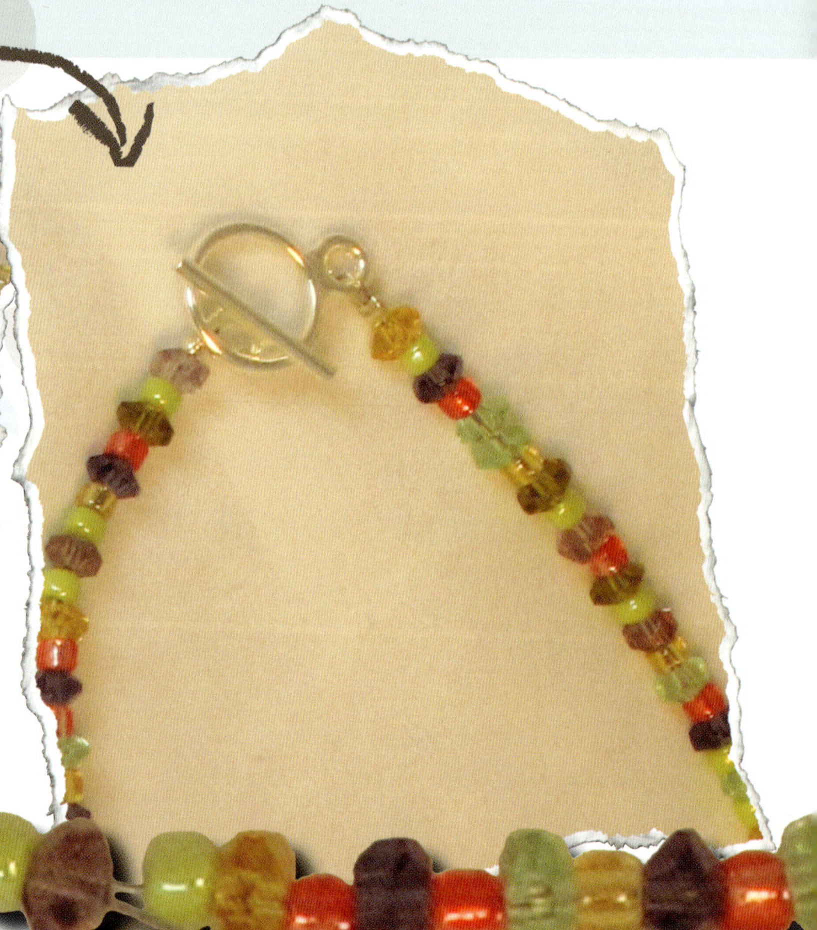

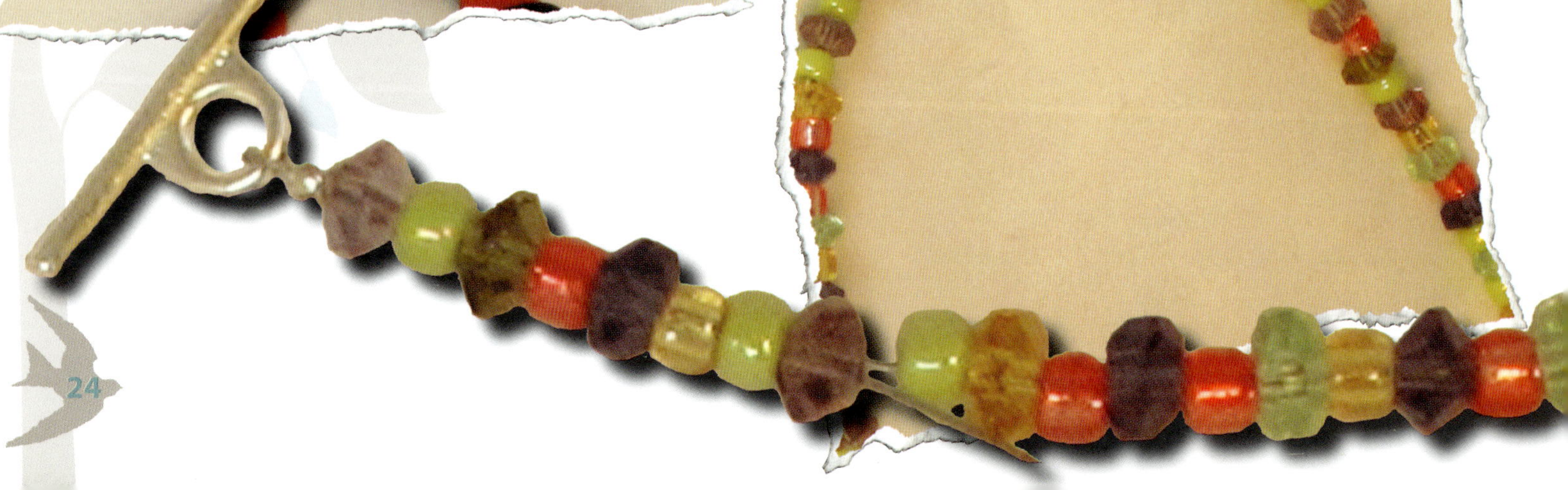

CHAPTER FOUR

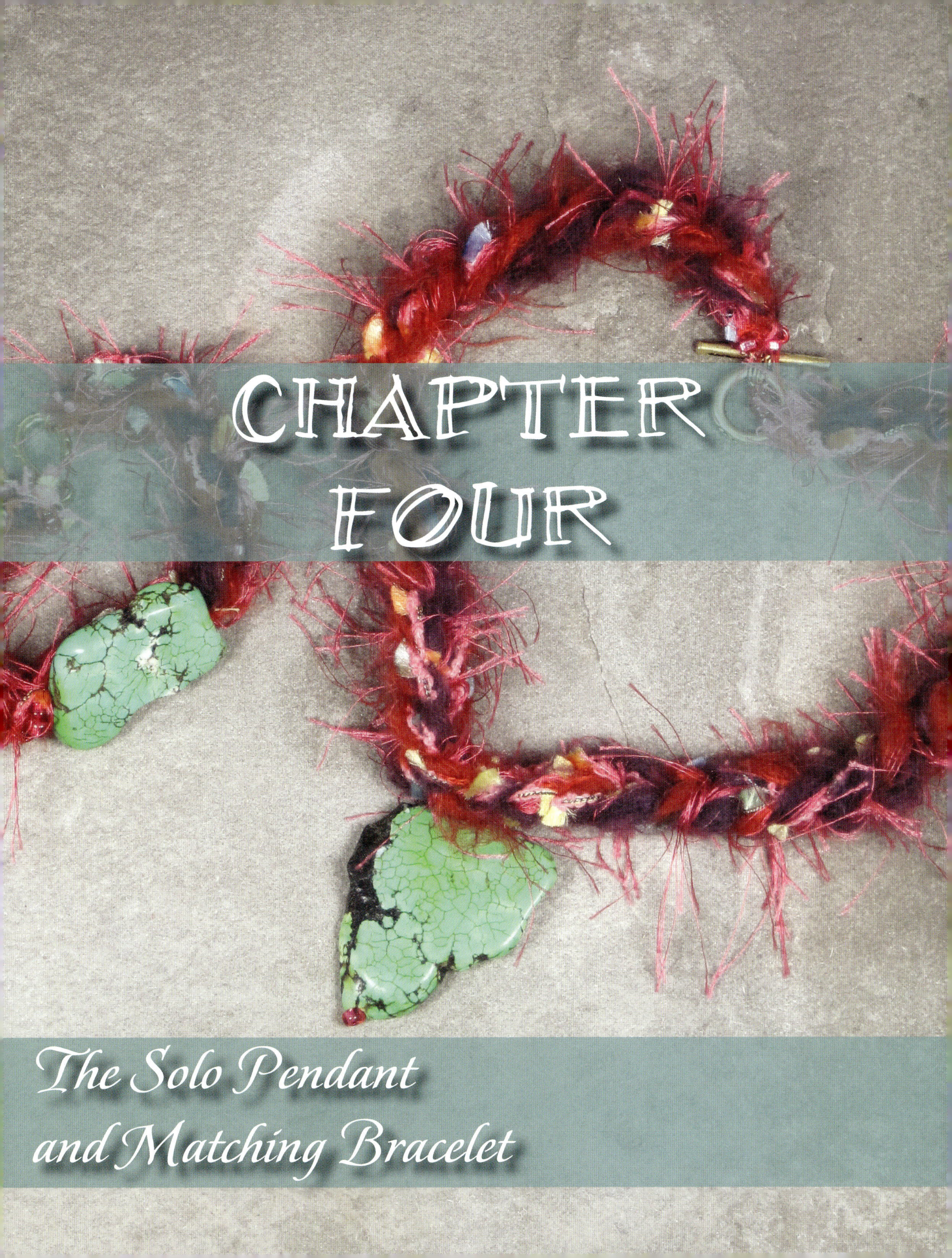

The Solo Pendant and Matching Bracelet

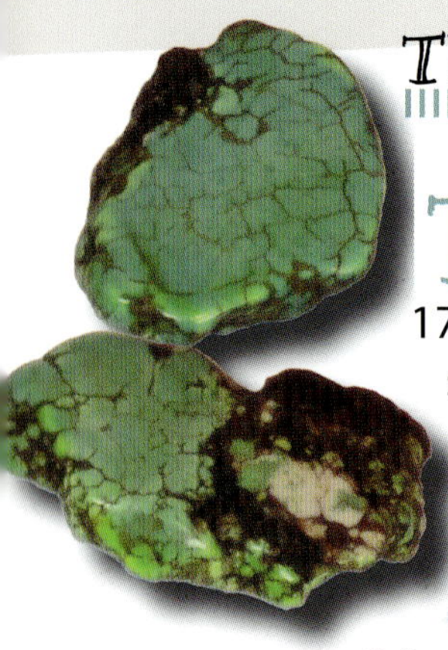

THE SOLO PENDANT

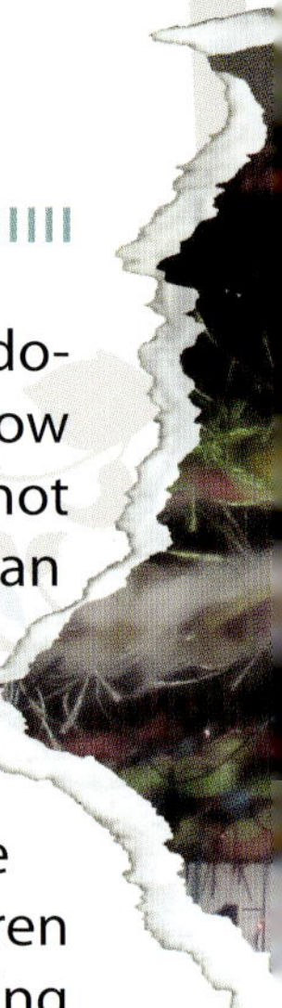

This necklace style evolved from working with my daughter's 4th grade class. After doing many craft projects with my children's classes over the years (my son, Griffin is now 17 and Darla 12), I had grown tired of decoupage. I thought, moms love jewelry, so why not share my new passion? Plus, Mothers' Day was just around the corner, and what mom can resist a stylin' handmade gift from her child? So I offered the children two choices—either a necklace of strung beads, or a crocheted or finger-knitted necklace with a chunky stone hung in the center. Finger-knitting was something that my daughter Darla had done for years. She also knew basic crocheting stitches. I wondered if some of the other girls (and boys!) might also have these skills. The project also required the children learn how to thread a needle and tie a knot. Both basic sewing skills. Not that challenging or thrilling for us adults, but a riveting and satisfying experience for eight-year-olds, and a challenge that put their hand-eye coordination and motor skills to the test! (Yes, I know, threading a needle puts your hand-eye coordination and motor skills to the test! But don't fret, just use your reading glasses!) Off I went to the class room, expecting only a few takers on the crochet/finger-knitting project. Much to my surprise, about three-quarters of the class chose the fiber project. The results were beautiful and unique, and many of the necklaces can still be seen today being proudly worn around town.

So, here goes.

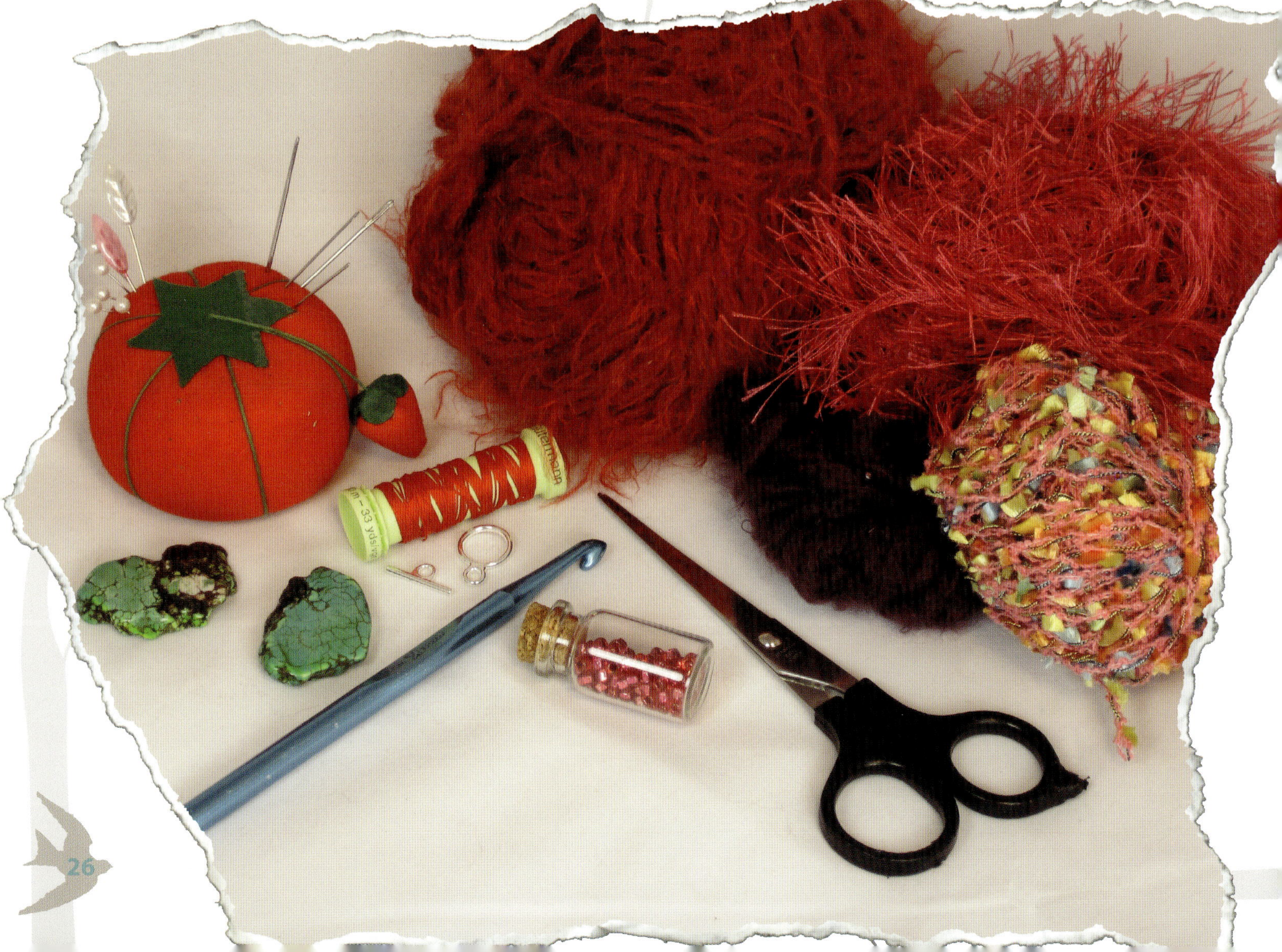

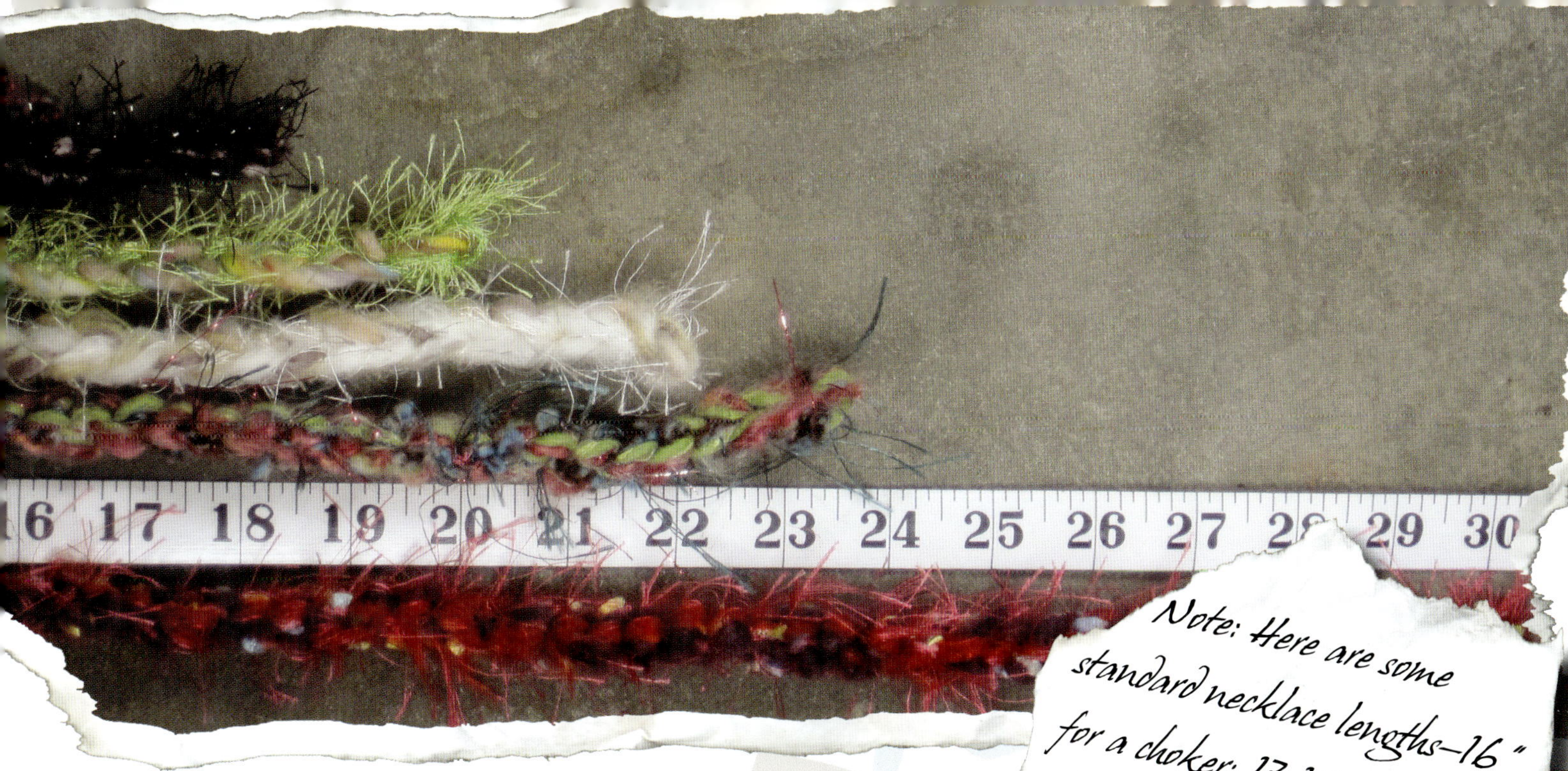

Note: Here are some standard necklace lengths–16" for a choker; 17-18" to reach the collarbone; 20" to reach the center of your sternum; 22" to reach just above your neckline; 24" to reach the center of your chest; and 30" to reach below your chest. (Obviously, these are just estimates, as everyone is shaped differently.)

Tools and Supplies: You will need a medium or large crochet hook; one to four yarns in different colors and textures (dare to make one of them an eyelash yarn!); a sewing needle (the size of which will depend on size of bead holes); thread in a color that best blends with your yarn; a pendant focal piece; size #8 or #9 seed beads; and a sharp pair of scissors.

Choose your pendant: First, choose your pendant. This will help you choose your yarn colors. For this project, I chose a nice chunk of turquoise, which I matched with red/pink/yellow bouclé, a dark purple yarn and a hot pink eyelash yarn. (I love the way hot pinks, reds and purples look against turquoise stones.)

Decide the Length of Your Necklace: Do you want to wear it long over a sweater, or short with a scoop neck? Whatever you chose, crochet a foundation chain to the required length. (We'll call the finished product the "foundation chain.") Because yarns have elasticity, you should crochet your foundation chain an inch or two shorter than you would if it were made of metal, which has no "give." You can always give the chain a little tug to test its stretchiness. (Personally, I never measure, only estimate.) Once the desired length is reached, cut the yarn with the crochet needle still inserted, leaving approximately 5 inches extra. To tie off the end of the foundation chain, hook the excess with the crochet needle and pull it back all the way through. Now you will have a nice knot on the end of your piece! (Otherwise, your end will unravel.) Both ends of the foundation chain should then be trimmed. To prevent the end from fraying and make the knot more secure, use a needle and thread (with a knot on the end!) to make a series of small stitches through and over the knot. Do not cut the thread yet! {A

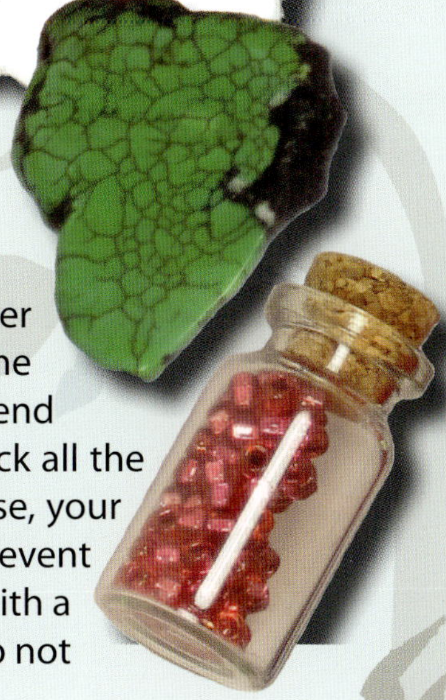

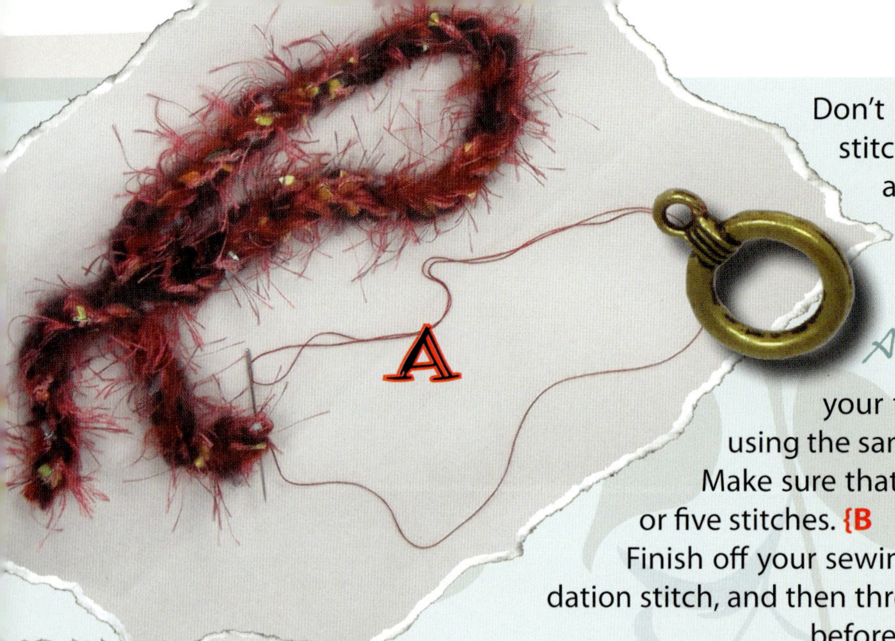

Don't worry too much about the quality of the stitches. They are well disguised by the textures and colors of the yarns. Trim any stray hairs with your scissors.

Attach the Toggle: First, attach the "O" part of your toggle to the end of your foundation chain using the same needle and thread used to finish the end. Make sure that the toggle is secured by using at least four or five stitches. **{B**

Finish off your sewing by sticking the needle through the foundation stitch, and then through the loop created by the excess thread, before pulling taunt. **{C**

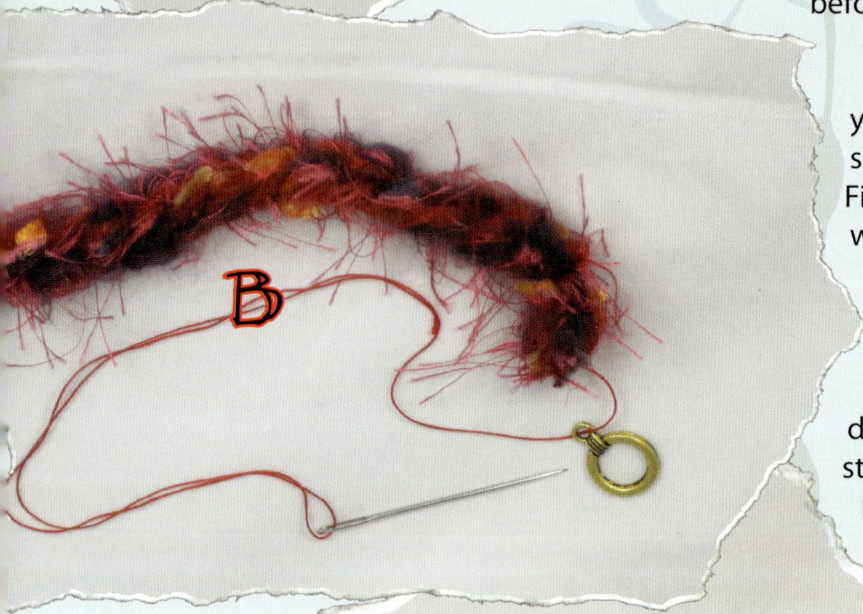

Repeat this several times. Don't cut that thread yet!! I like to add a decorative element to the "O" side of the toggle by creating a "collar" at its base. First, put enough seed beads on the thread to wrap around the foundation chain. Then wrap the seed beads around the foundation chain and put the needle through the first bead and stitch it to the foundation chain. Use several small stitches to secure the "collar" to the foundation chain. Knot off the thread. **{D & E** (If this step is too much for you, it can be skipped. It is rather fussy!) Now you can cut the thread!

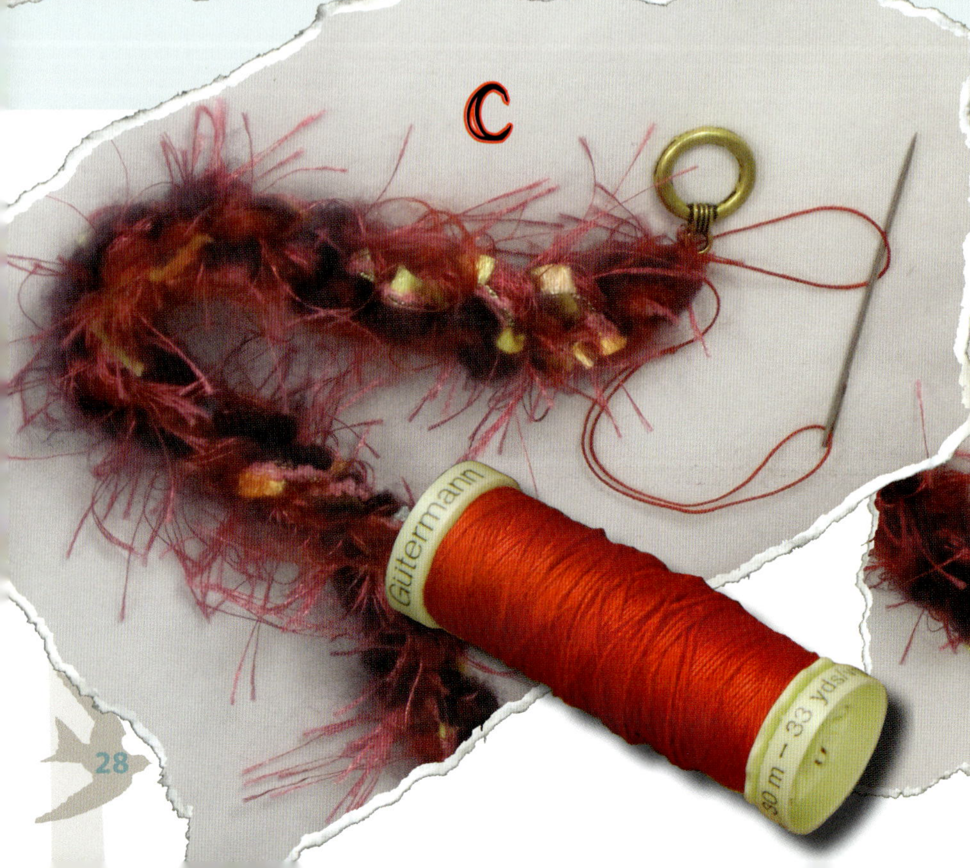

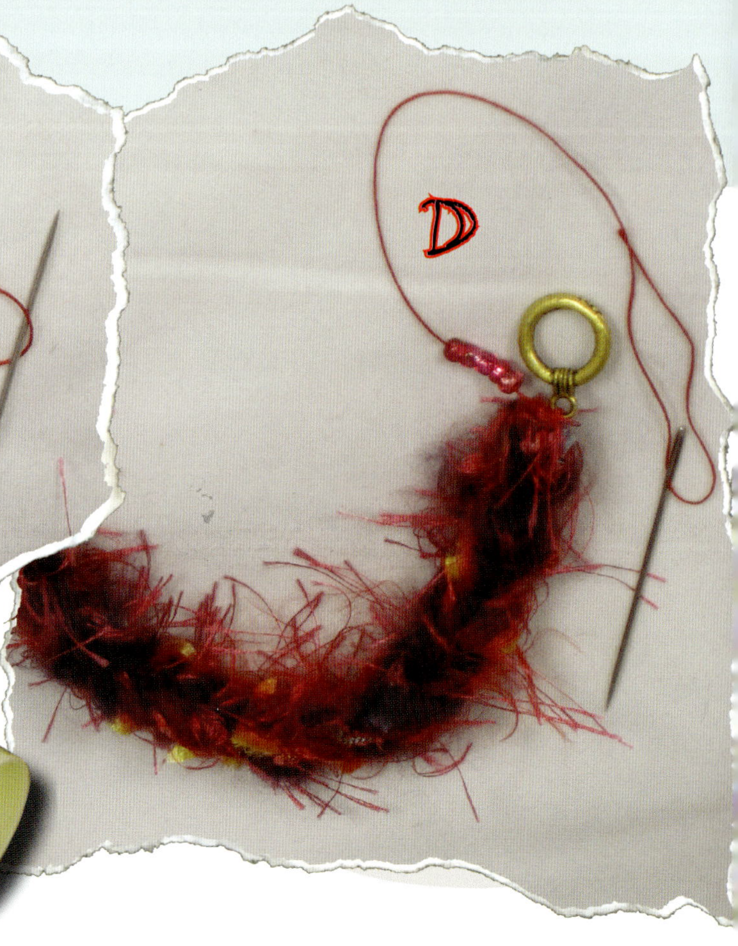

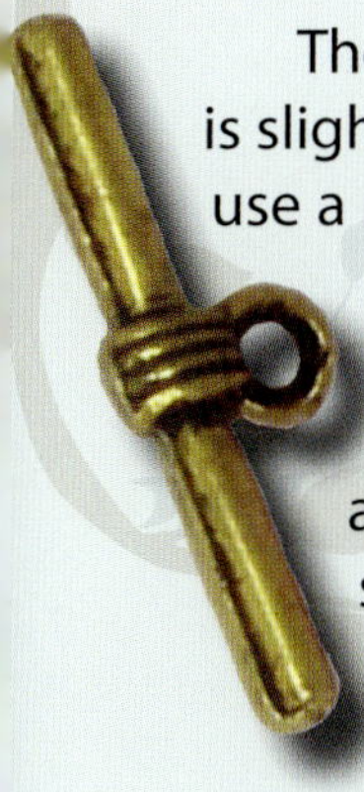

Then attach the "bar" side of your toggle. (The technique is slightly different than attaching the "O" end.) First, again, use a needle and thread (with a knot on the end!) to make a series of small stitches through and over the end of the foundation chain. Again, don't cut the thread! Then, to give the back of the piece a little interest, and to increase the ease of use, thread a few (3 to 5) seed beads onto the thread. Then thread the needle through the eye of the "bar" end of the toggle and back down through the seed beads and into the foundation chain. Thus, the pattern is as follows—thread the needle through the end of the foundation chain, up through the seed beads, through the eye of the toggle, back down through the seed beads and into the foundation chain. Do this two times before knotting off the thread. (The inside of the seed beads might start to get tight, but don't worry.) Finally, you can cut the thread! **{F & G**

Attach the Pendant: First, fold your necklace in half to locate the center point. Secure your thread (with a knot on the end!) to the center point using at least four or five stitches. **{H** (Those pendants can be heavy!)

For pendants with a hole running through the length of the piece, thread the needle through the hole, then through a "stopper" bead (e.g. a seed bead or any other bead that is larger than the hole in the pendent) **{I**, then back up through the hole of the pendant and into the foundation chain.

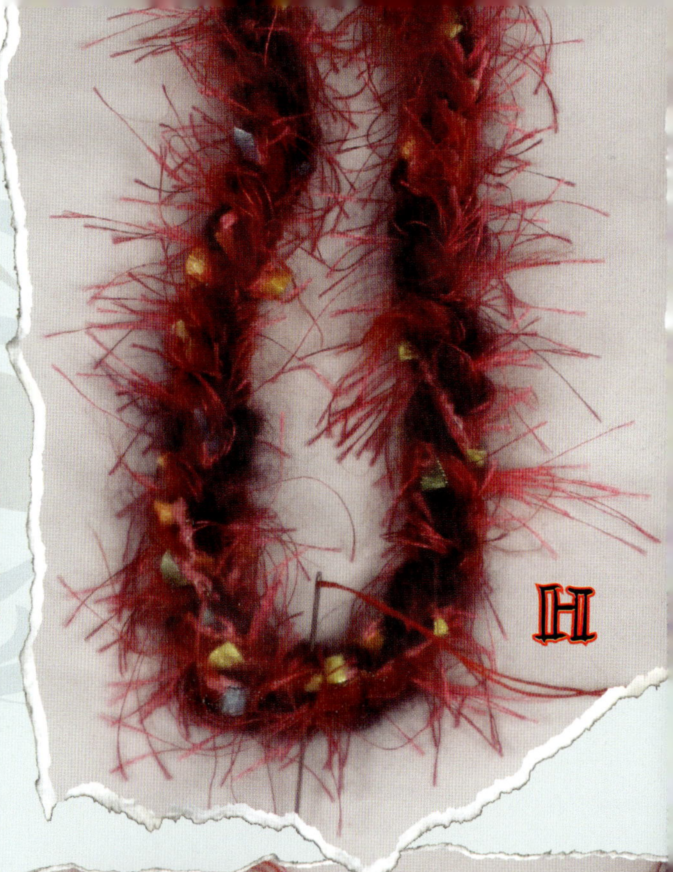

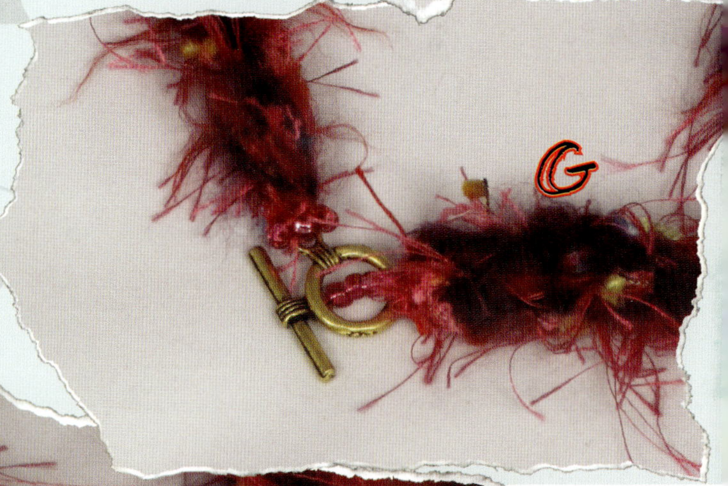

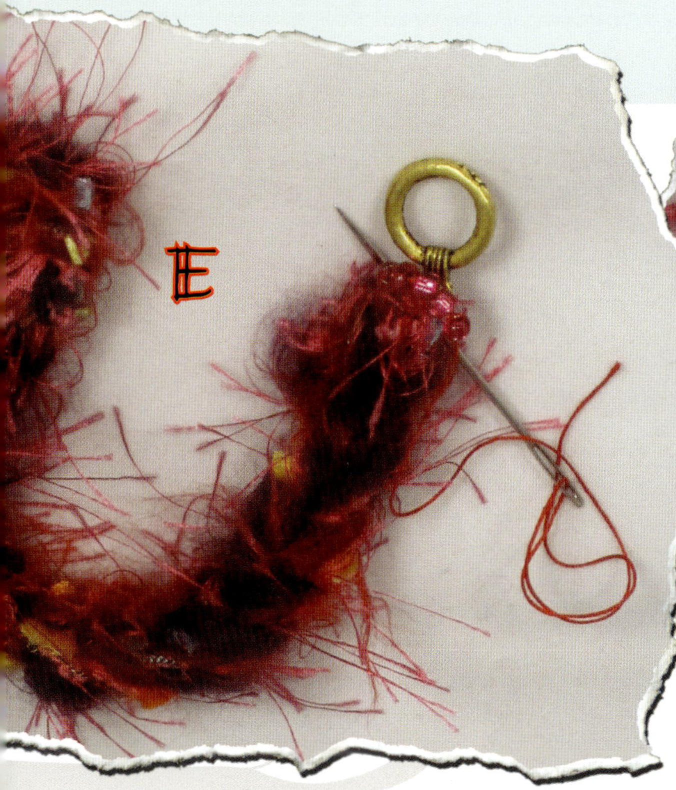

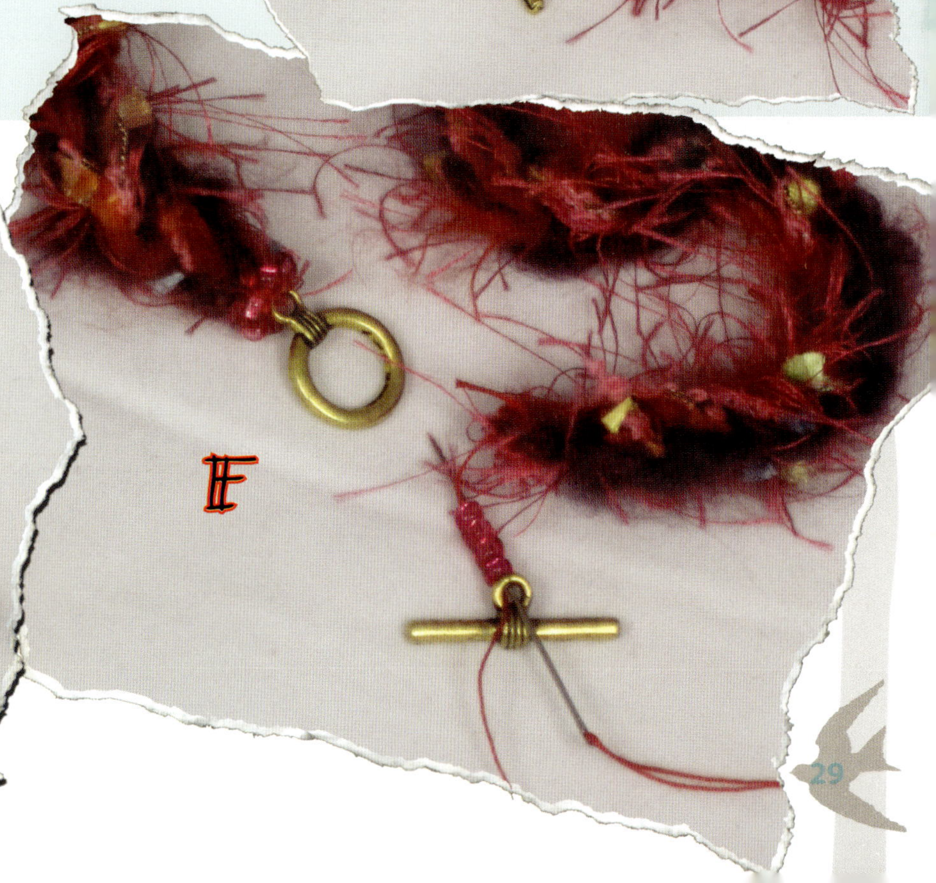

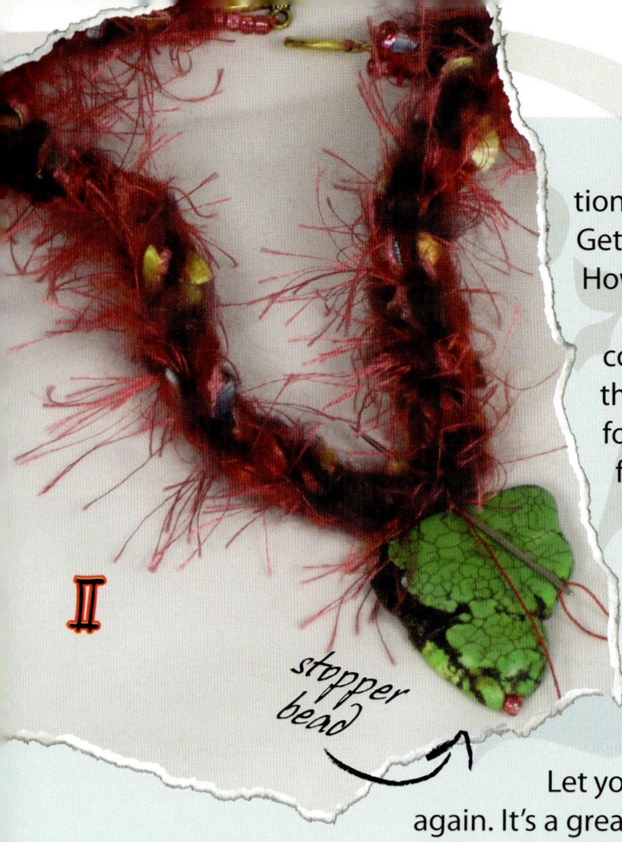

Make sure you pull the pendant as taunt as possible to the foundation chain. Otherwise the pendant will sag and the thread will show. Getting the pendant tight takes some finesse due to the seed bead. However, with a little practice you will soon master the technique.

If your pendant has a hole that runs side to side (like my chunk of coral) you should attach your thread slightly off-center. Then stitch the pendant directly onto the foundation chain. There is no need for the stopper bead this time! Again, pull the pendant taunt to the foundation chain so that it does not sag and no thread shows.

There are many variations for this simple project. Here are a few suggestions. For pendants with the hole running through the length of the piece, try adding five or more "stopper" beads to create a loop at the bottom of the pendant. You can use an even number of the same beads with an "odd" bead in the middle (so that it is centered). You can also try different combinations of beads and chunks. This way, you can add a secondary focal point.

Let your imagination roam free! If you don't like it, just take it out and try again. It's a great way to grow as an artiste.

Had enough yet? I didn't think so! How about a matching bracelet? It's easy!

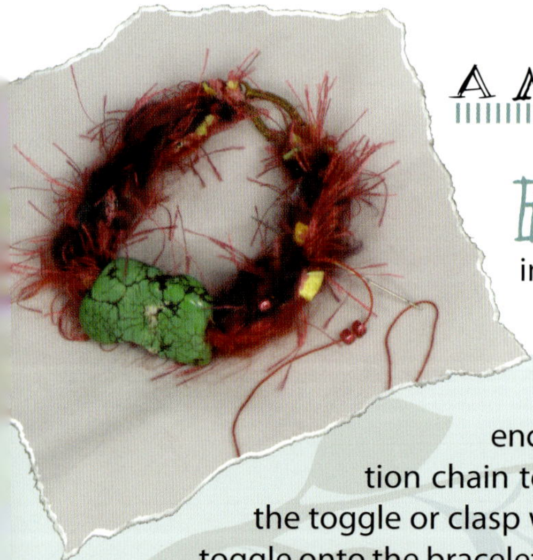

A MATCHING BRACELET

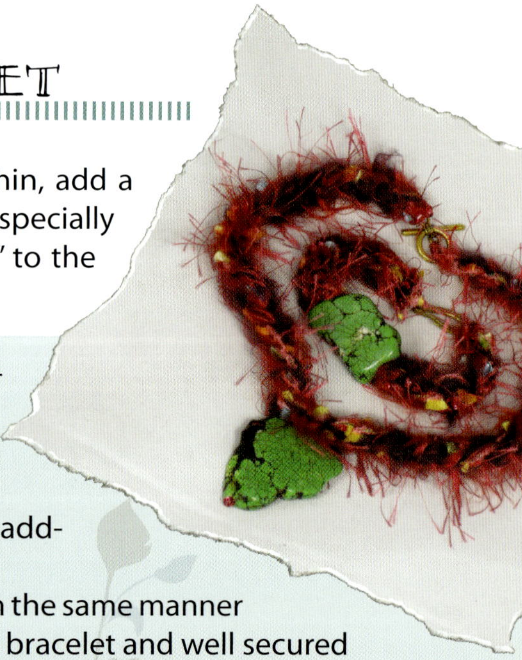

First, if your foundation chain is thin, add a coordinating yarn for heft. This is especially important if you are adding a "chunk" to the bracelet (like I did!).

Second, measure the circumference of your wrist and crochet a foundation chain to the required length. (Remember, the toggle or clasp will add an inch or so.) Then sew the toggle onto the bracelet in the same manner as the necklace, adding decorative frills as you see fit!

Locate and attach the "chunk" on the center of the bracelet in the same manner as the necklace. Again, make sure that the stone is taunt to the bracelet and well secured (if you can, go back through a few times, pulling tight each time).

I like to add a little zing and increase the strength of the bracelet by securing the thread (with a knot on the end!) near the toggle or clasp of the bracelet with a few stitches. Then, with the needle on the good side of the bracelet, add two seed beads to the thread. Then thread the needle back through the foundation chain and back up again at a random point near where the seed beads are already in place. Repeat this for the length of the bracelet. You will feel the stitches adding strength and slightly flattening your foundation chain.

That's it!! Are you ready for the next project? I thought so!

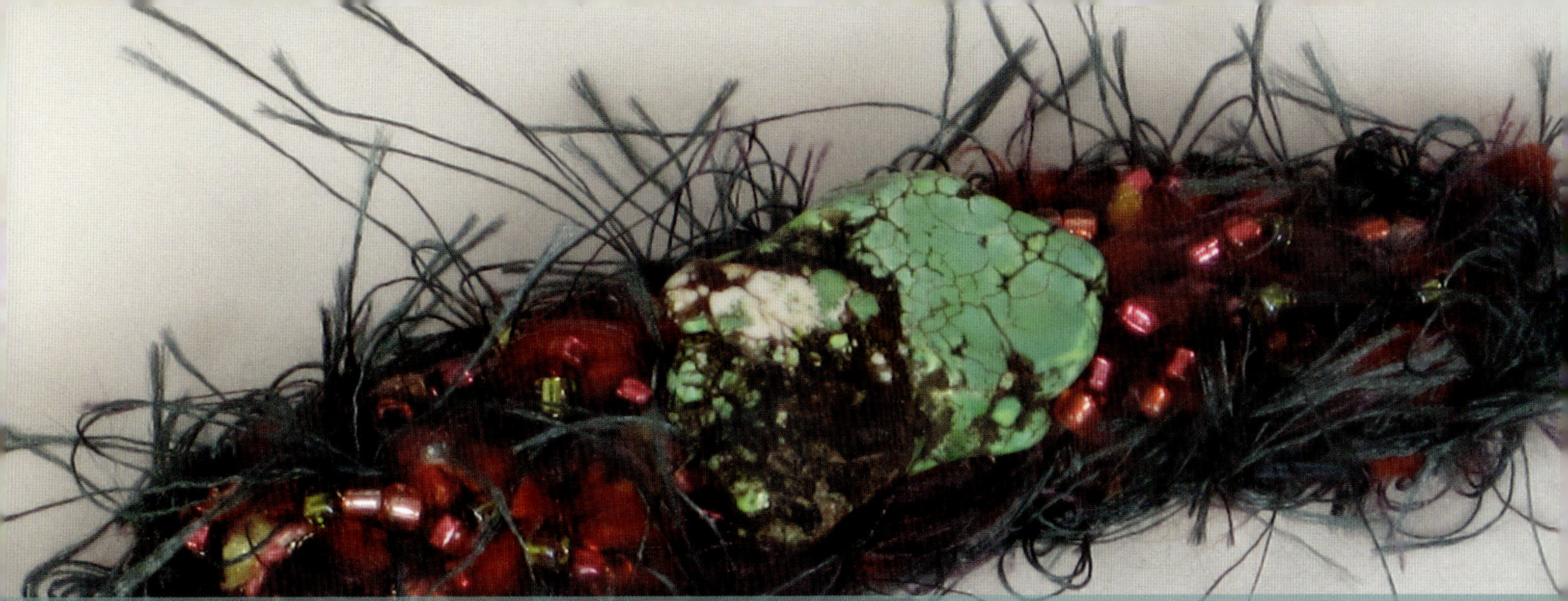

CHAPTER FIVE

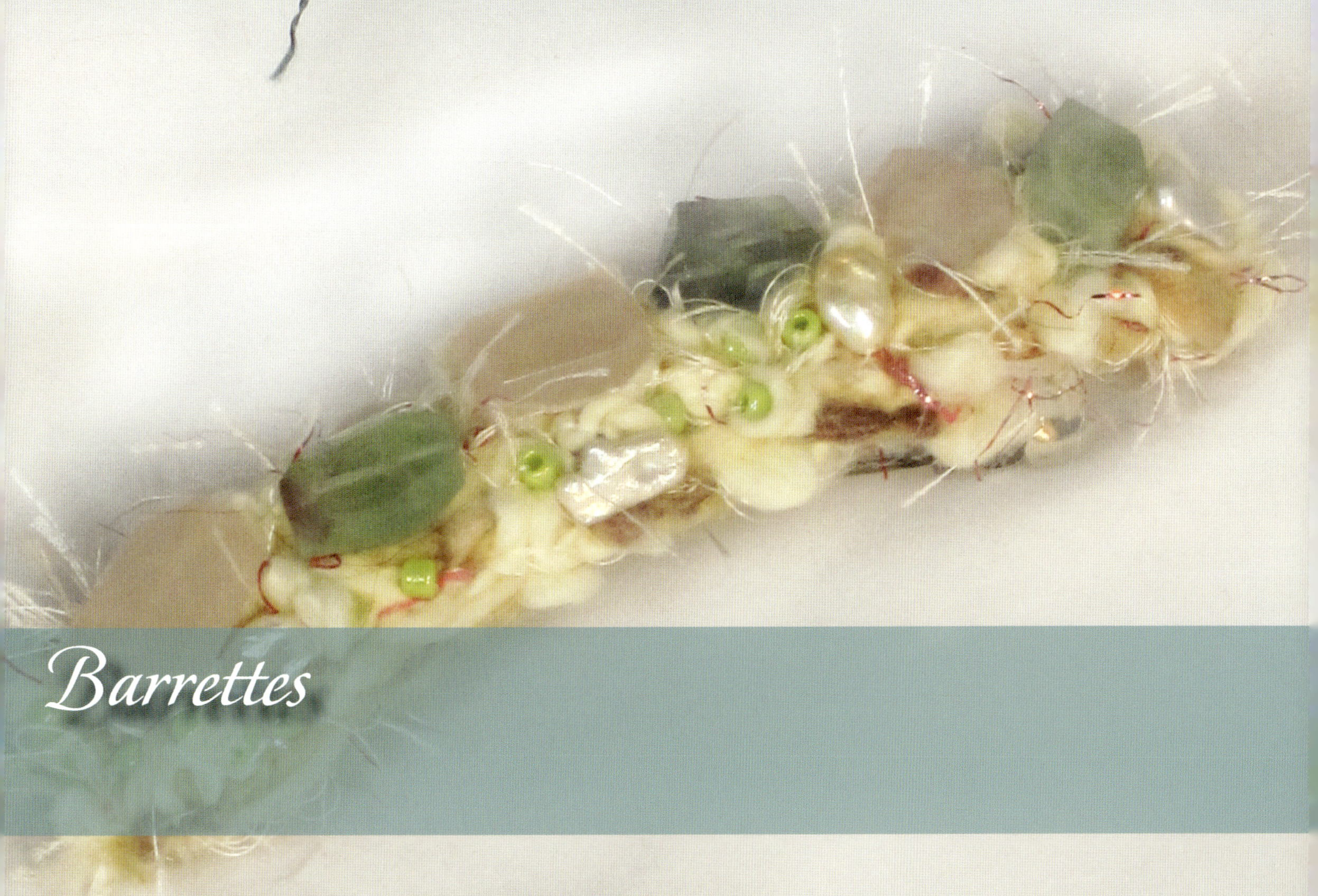

Barrettes

My quest to find special hair clips began about five years ago when I convinced my mother to grow her hair long. Her hair is outrageously thick and beautiful, and now falls halfway down her back (and she's 88!) She often wears it elegantly swept back and clipped. So for birthdays or holidays I like to find her pretty barrettes. The following two styles of barrettes are relatively quick and easy to make.

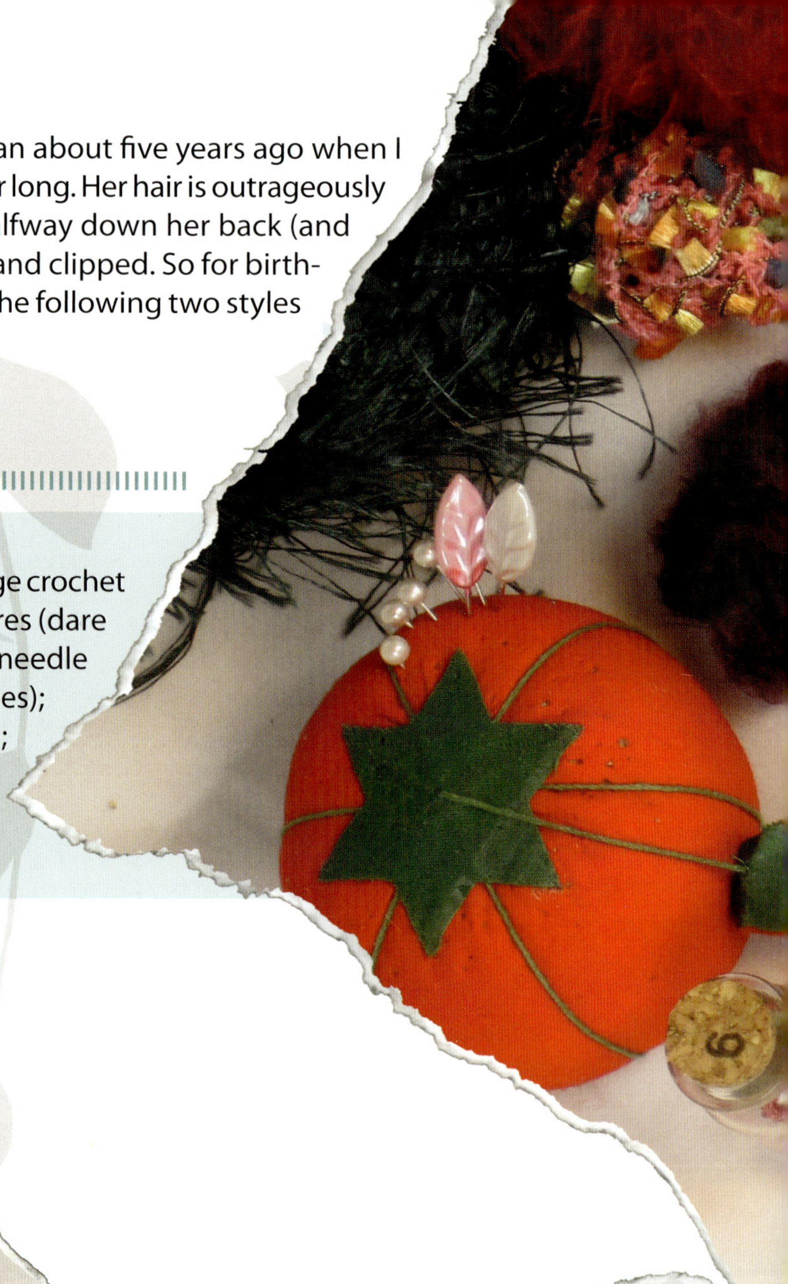

THE FIRST BARRETTE

Tools and Supplies: You will need a medium or large crochet hook; four to six yarns in different colors and textures (dare to make one of them an eyelash yarn!); a sewing needle (the size of which will depend on size of bead holes); thread (in a color that best blends with your yarn); a pendant focal piece; size #8 or #9 seed beads, a sharp pair of scissors, and a barrette base.

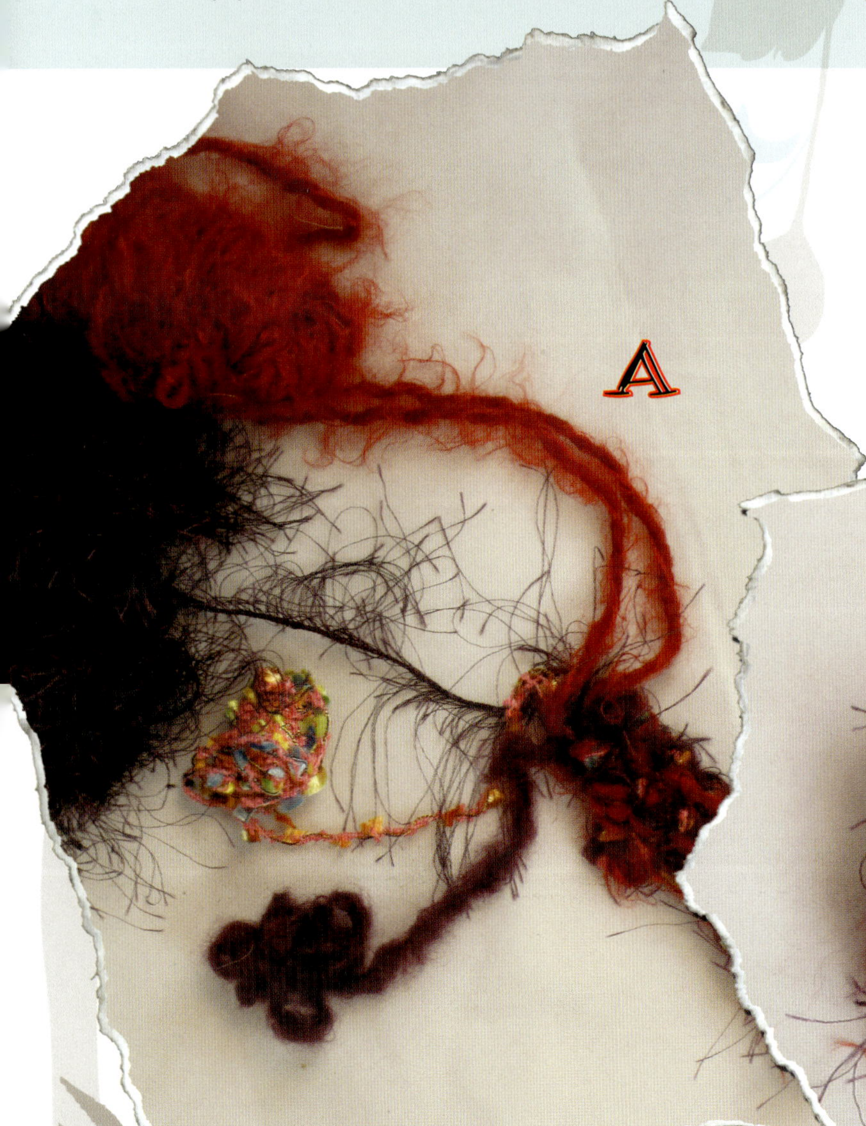

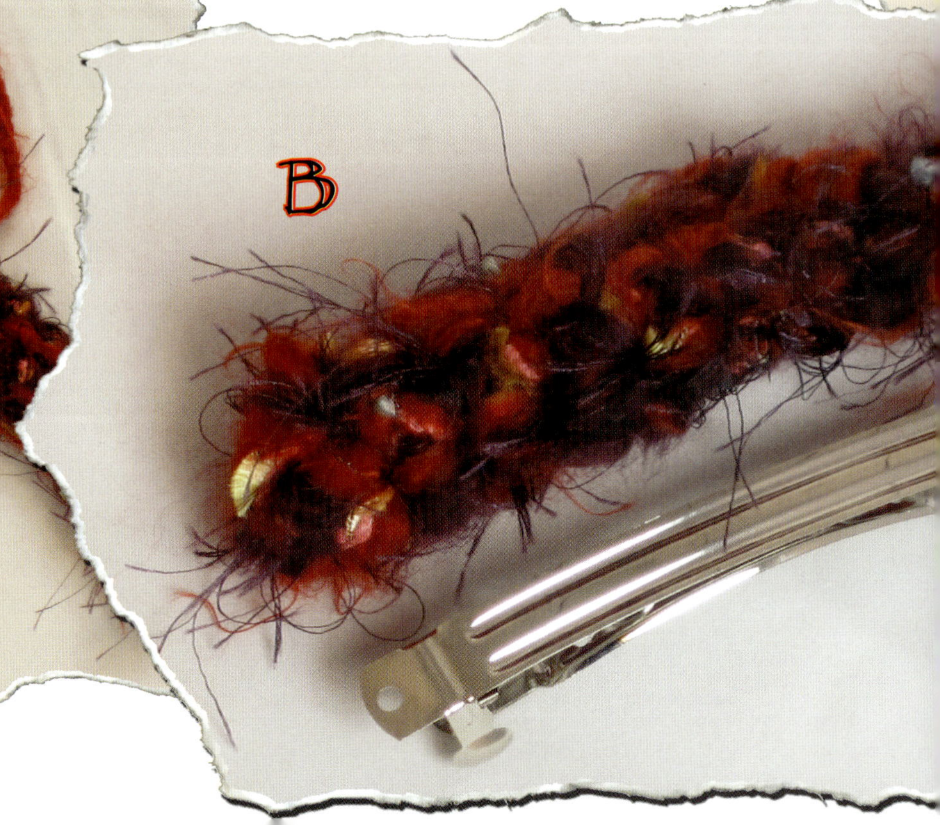

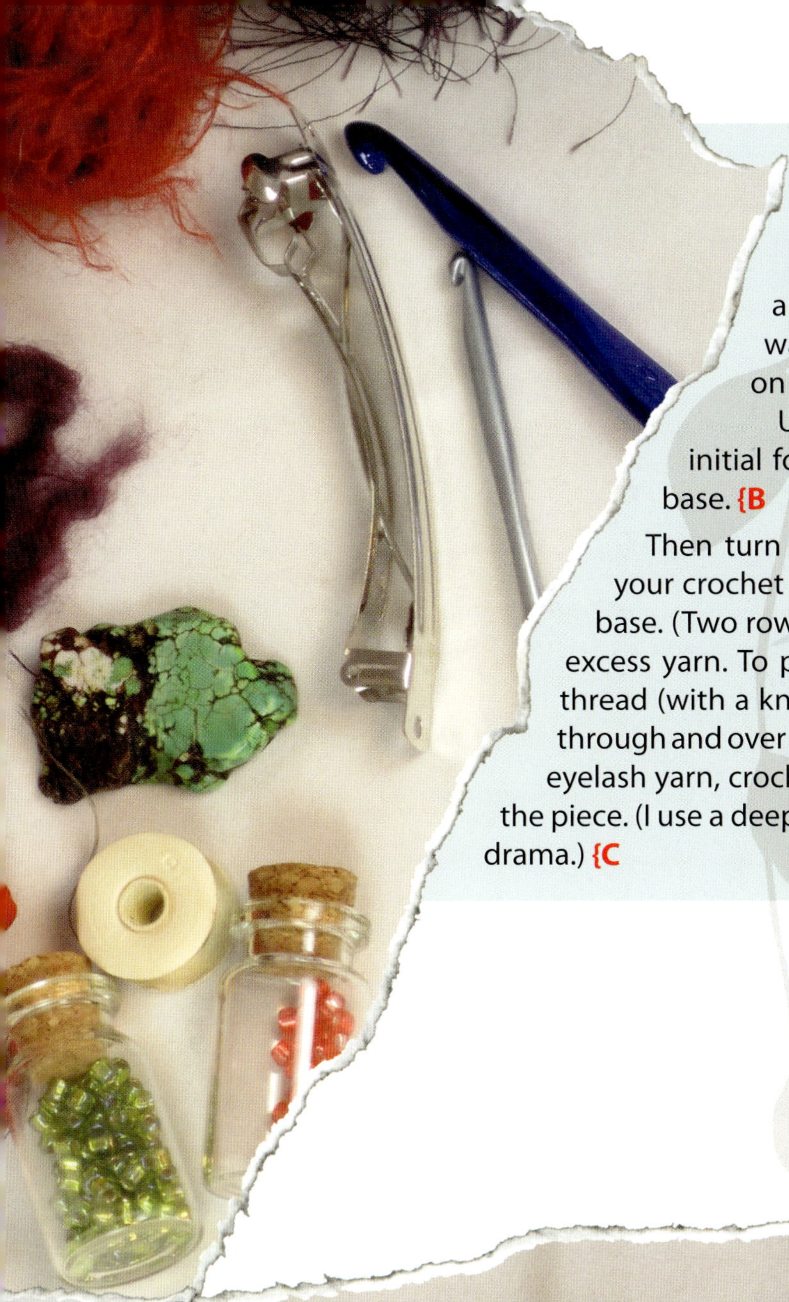

The first step is to make a foundation chain. I chose to work with five strands of yarn—a deep purple angora, a pink/multi-color confetti, a purple eyelash yarn and a rich barn-red angora. I wanted the red color to dominate, so I doubled up on the red yarn, working with two strands. {A

Using your barrette base as a guide, make your initial foundation chain about one inch longer than the base. {B

Then turn around and make a second row. Continue until your crochet strip is at least wide enough to hide the barrette base. (Two rows will probably be enough.) When done, trim the excess yarn. To prevent the ends from fraying, use a needle and thread (with a knot on the end!) to make a series of small stitches through and over the ends until they are bound. Taking a contrasting eyelash yarn, crochet a slip crochet stitch around the whole body of the piece. (I use a deep teal, which, again, I doubled to get lots of eyelash drama.) {C

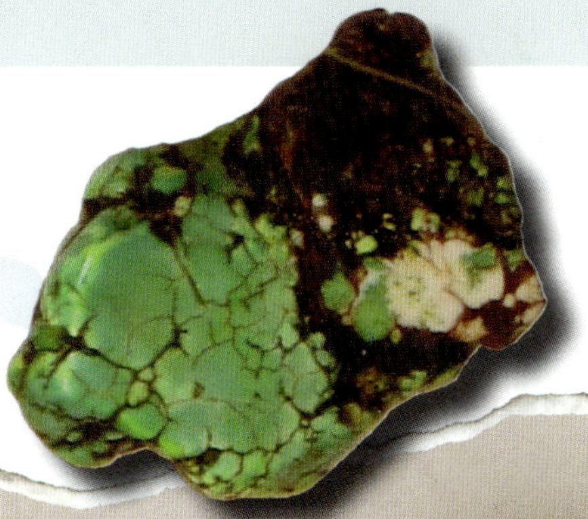

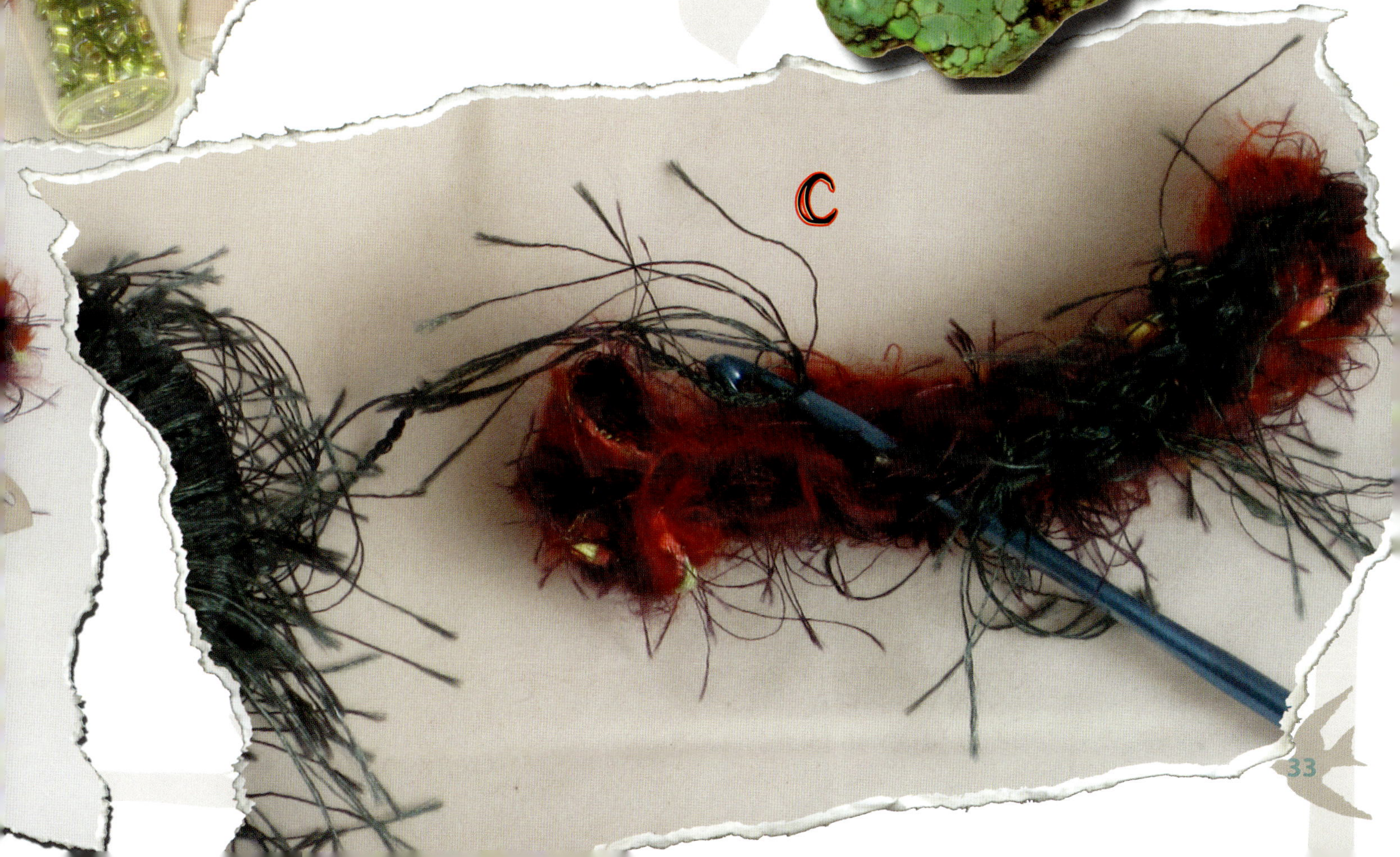

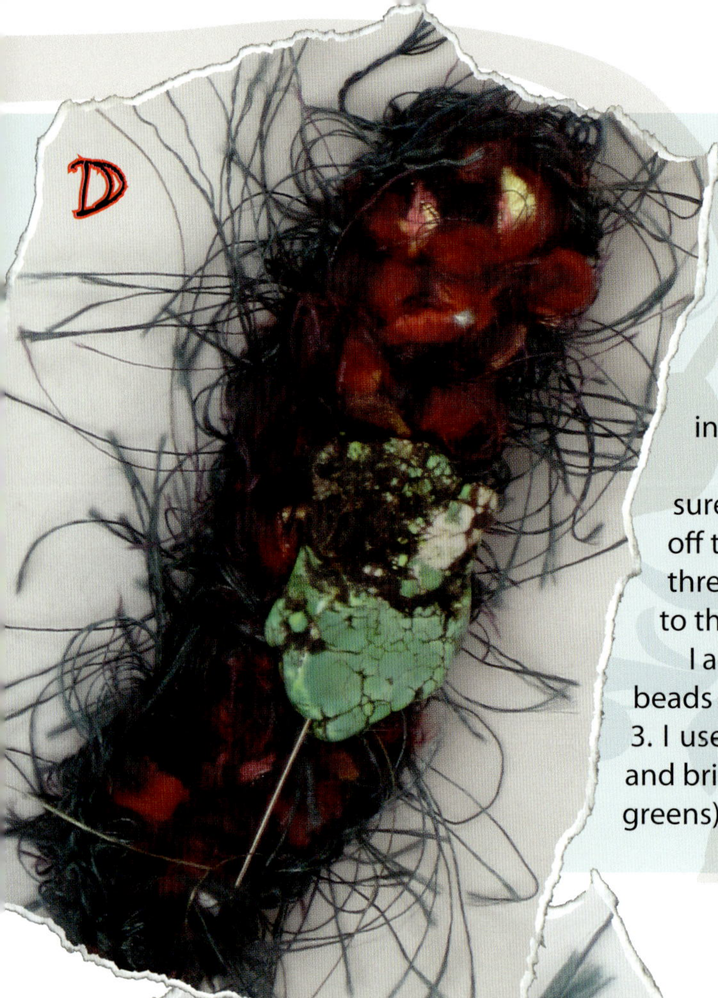

Trim the excess yarn and finish the ends as described above. Your piece should already be looking great! If you want, you could stop right here! For my barrette I chose a nice chunk of turquoise (again!). First, secure your thread to the crocheted strip at the point where your stone is to be located (near the center).

Then put your needle through the stone and then down into the yarn. {D

Repeat this two or three times, tugging each time to make sure that the stone is tight to the crochet strip. When done, tie off the thread at the back with several knots and then cut the thread. When tying off the thread, make sure you keep it tight to the crochet strip or the stone will sag.

I added a little sparkle to my barrette by stitching size 9 seed beads throughout the crochet strip in random groups of 1, 2 or 3. I used colors that both blended with the yarns (the hot pink and bright salmon) and brought out the beauty of the stone (the greens). {E&F

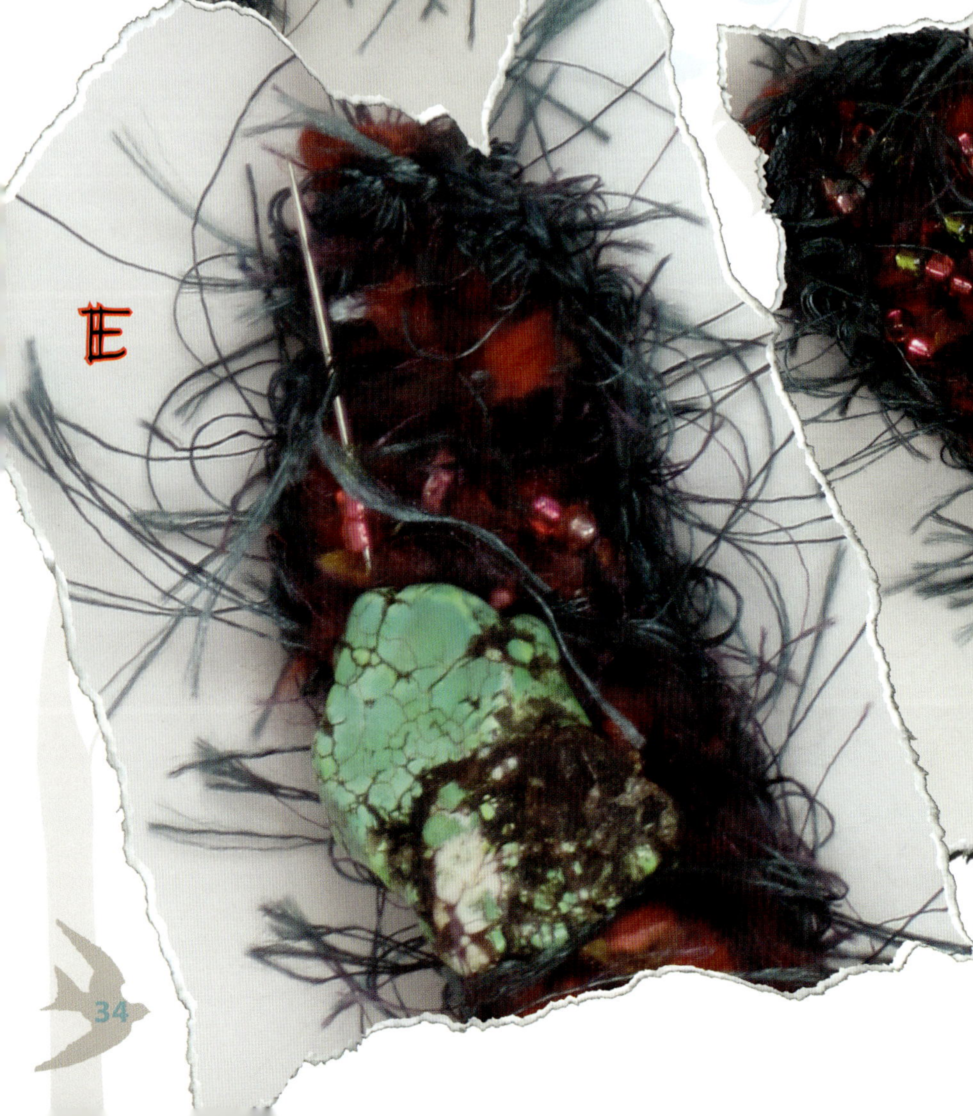

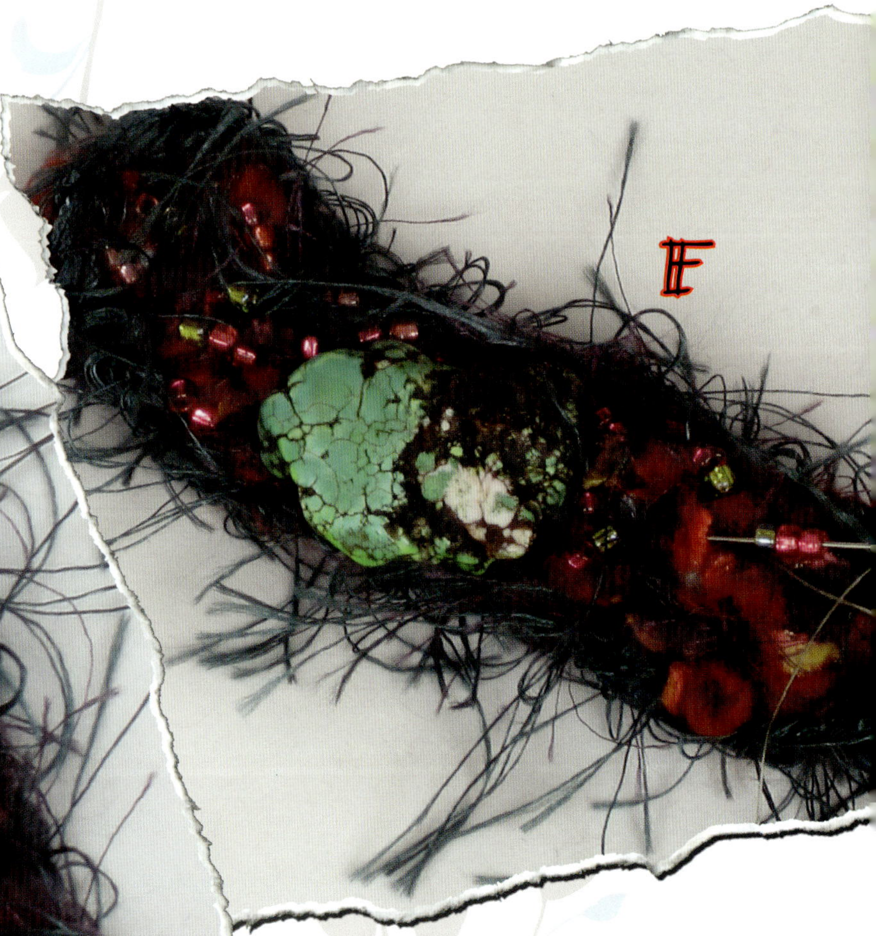

The final step is to attach the metal barrette base. Start by centering your crocheted strip on the metal barrette base. Then stitch down the ends of the crocheted strip to the holes on each end of the metal barrette base. {G

When done, go back and stitch the crocheted strip to the bar of the metal barrette that is flush to the crocheted strip, that is, not to either of the bars that move! {H

Five or six stitches should do. Pulling the crocheted strip tight to the metal base, tie off the end of the thread and cut. That's it! You can try any number of variations on this project. For example, try adding dangly beads hanging down from the bottom of the barrette or outlining the barrette in seed beads. You get the idea. Try new ideas, have fun! Worse case scenario—rip it out and start again!

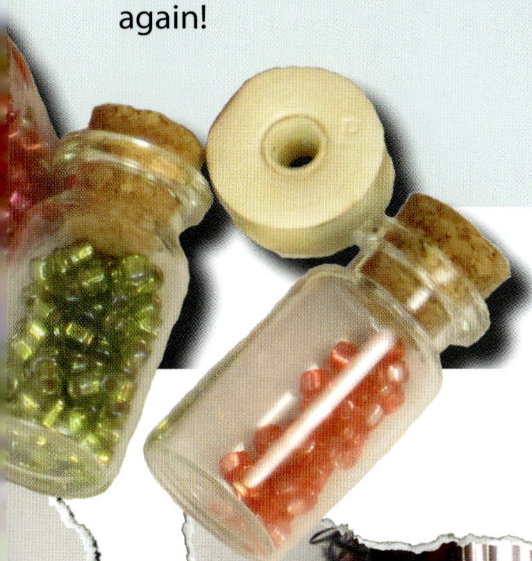

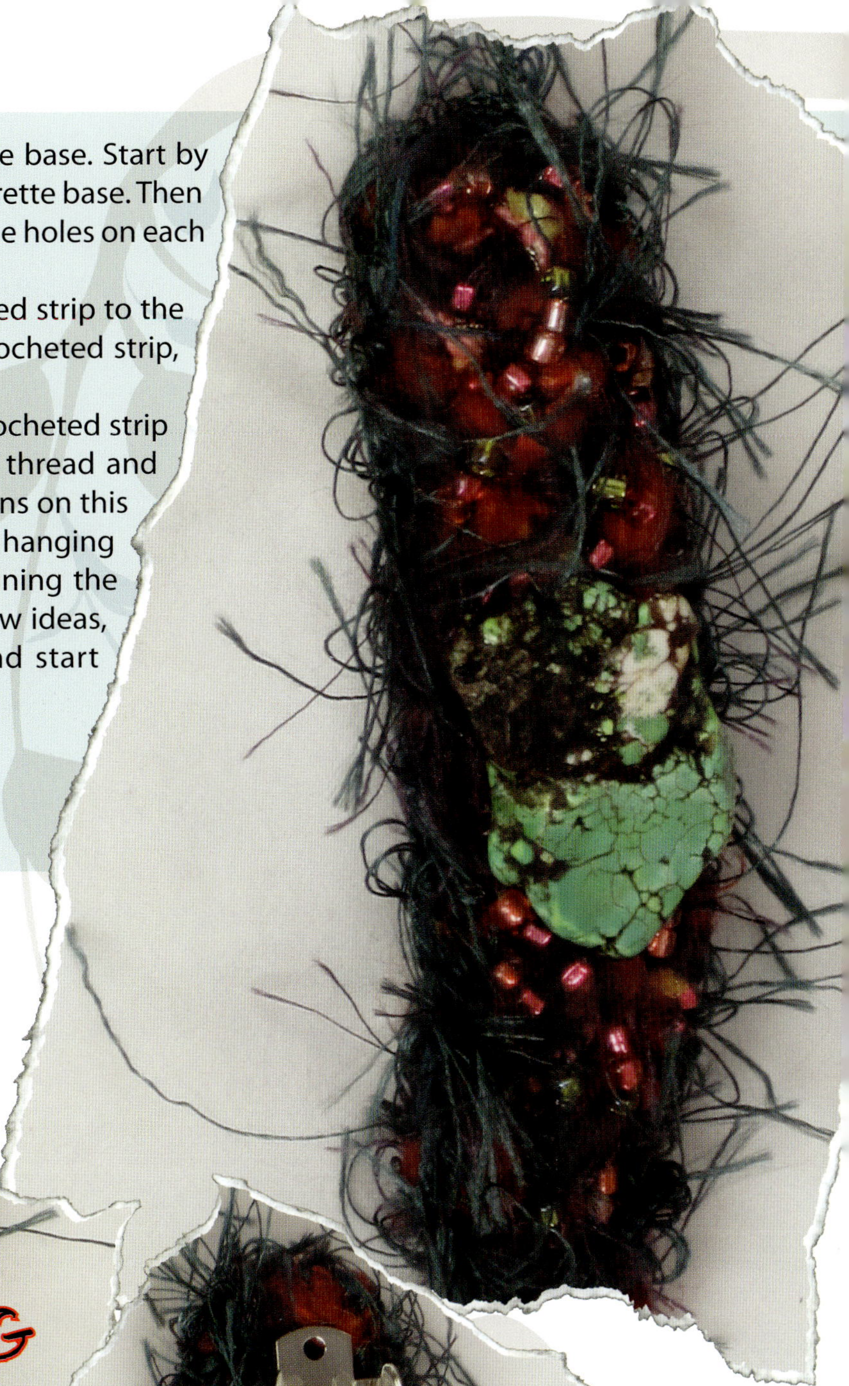

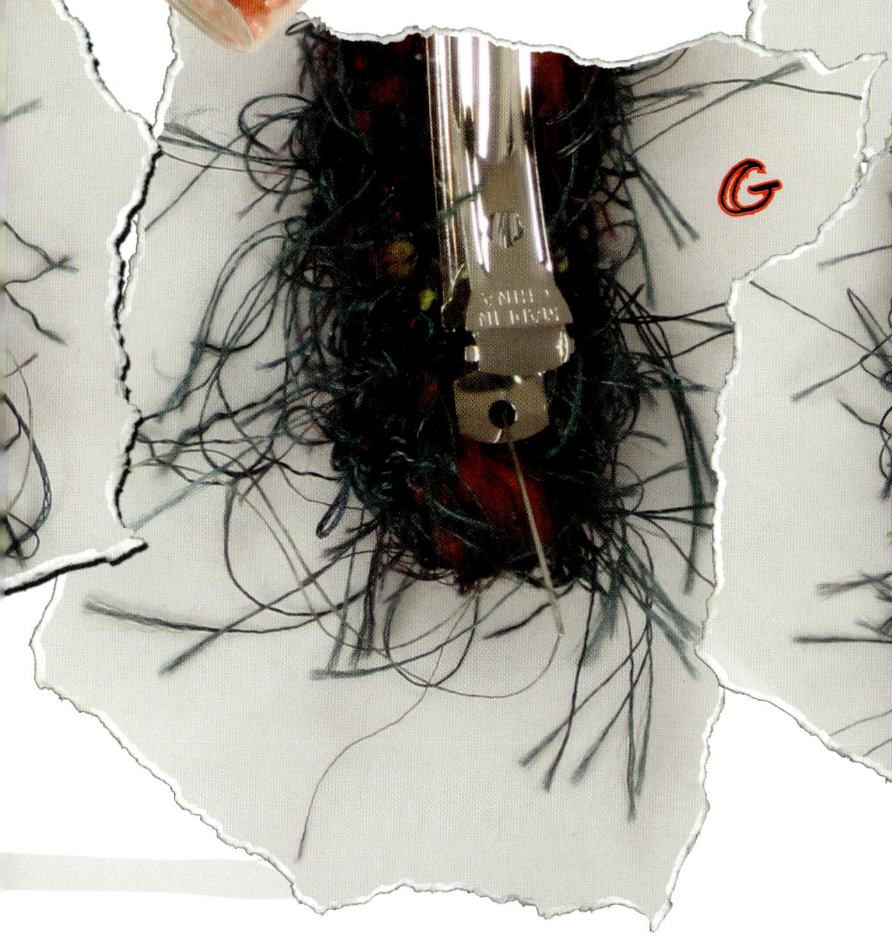

G

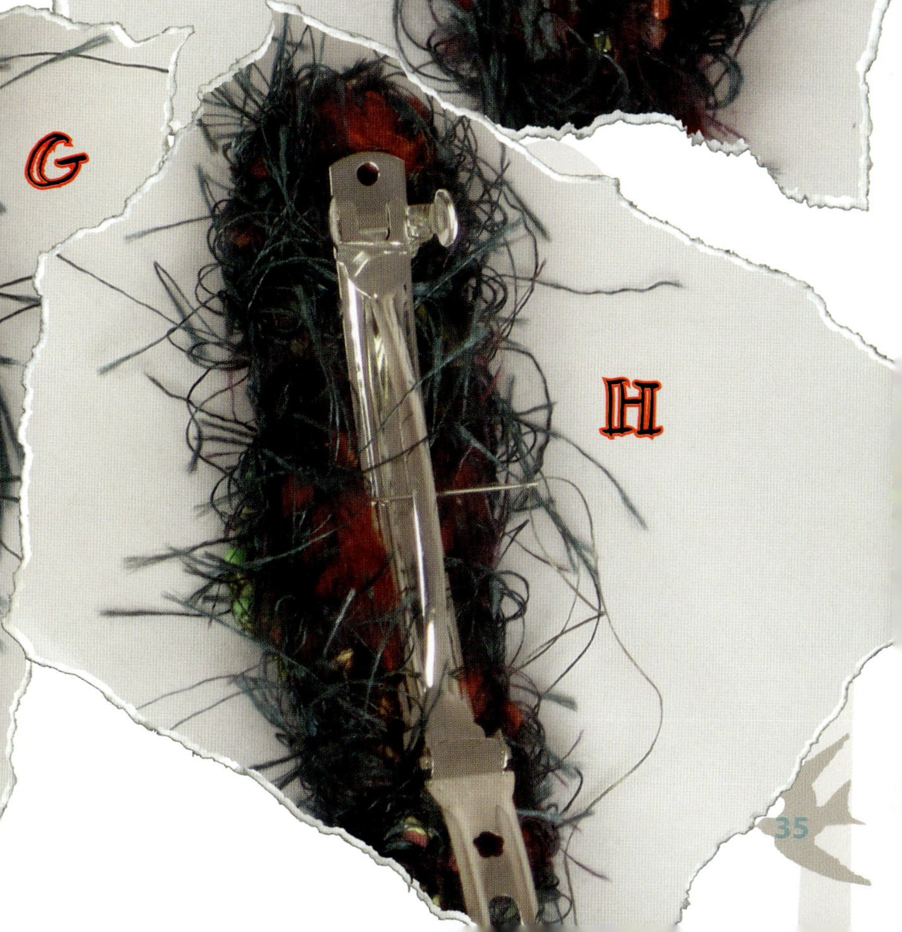

H

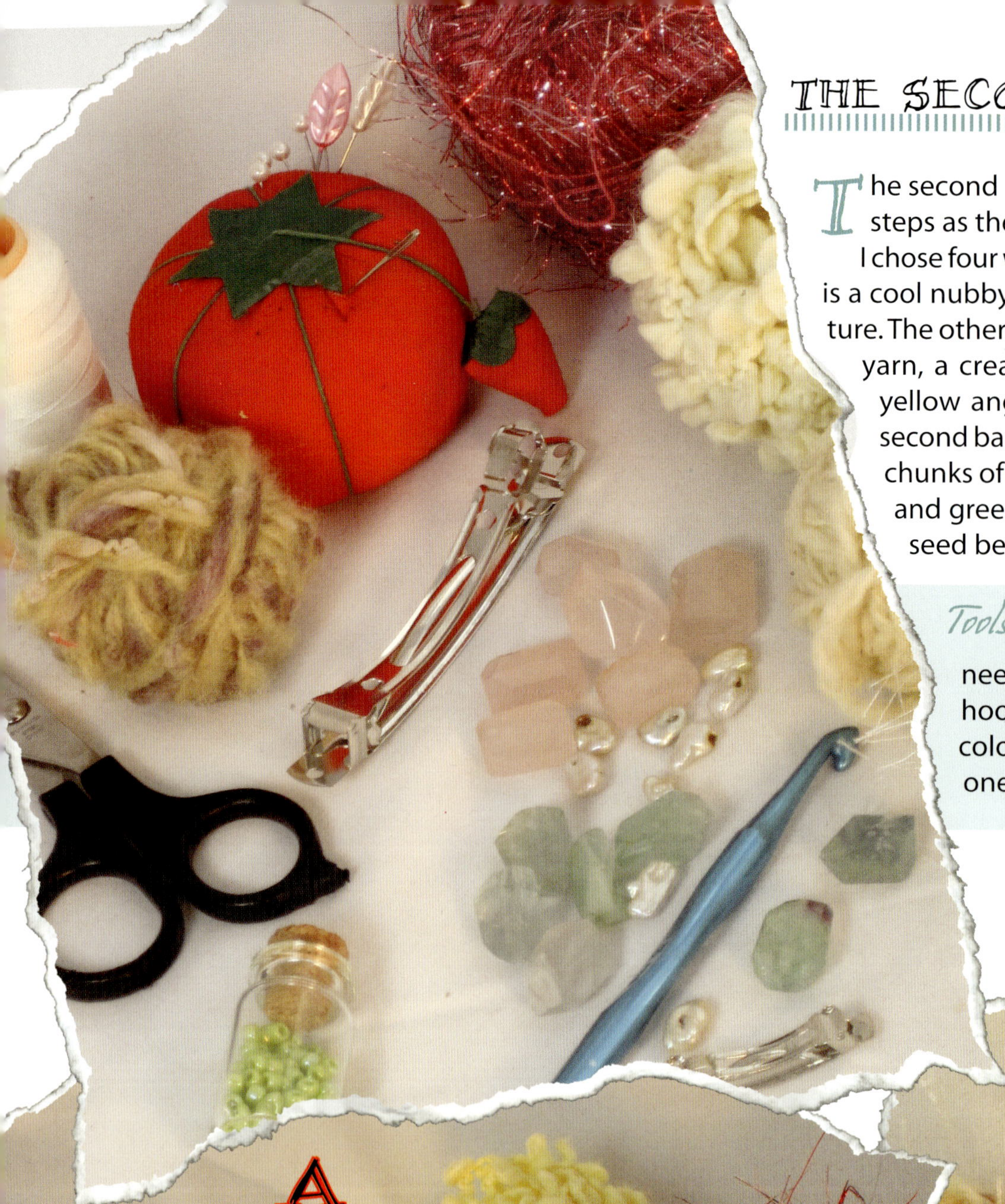

THE SECOND BARRETTE

The second barrette begins with the same steps as the first barrette. **{A & B**

I chose four white and off-white yarns. (One is a cool nubby bouclé that adds a great texture. The others are a metallic fuchsia eyelash yarn, a cream eyelash yarn and a sandy yellow angora.) The overall look of this second barrette is created by the random chunks of gemstones. I used rose quartz and green fluorite with a smattering of seed beads and pearl accents.

Tools and Supplies: You will need a medium or large crochet hook; four to six yarns in different colors and textures (dare to make one of them an eyelash yarn!); a

A

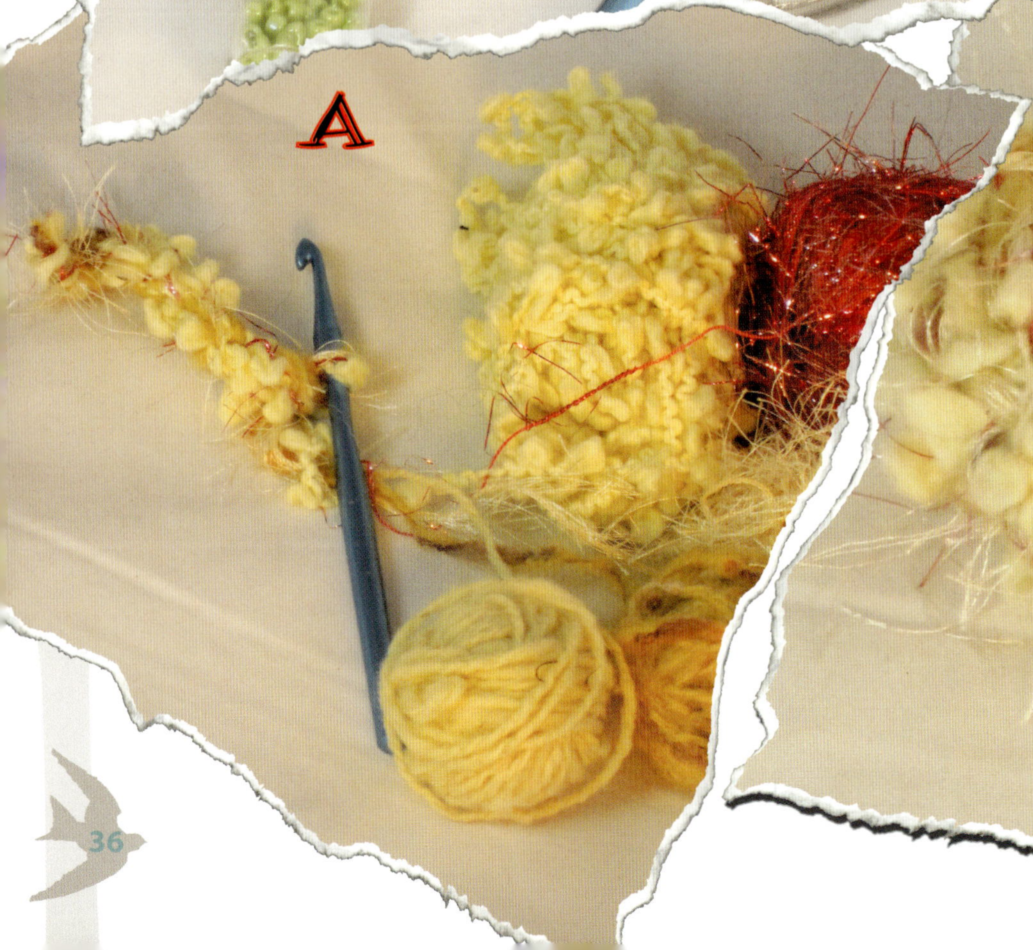

B

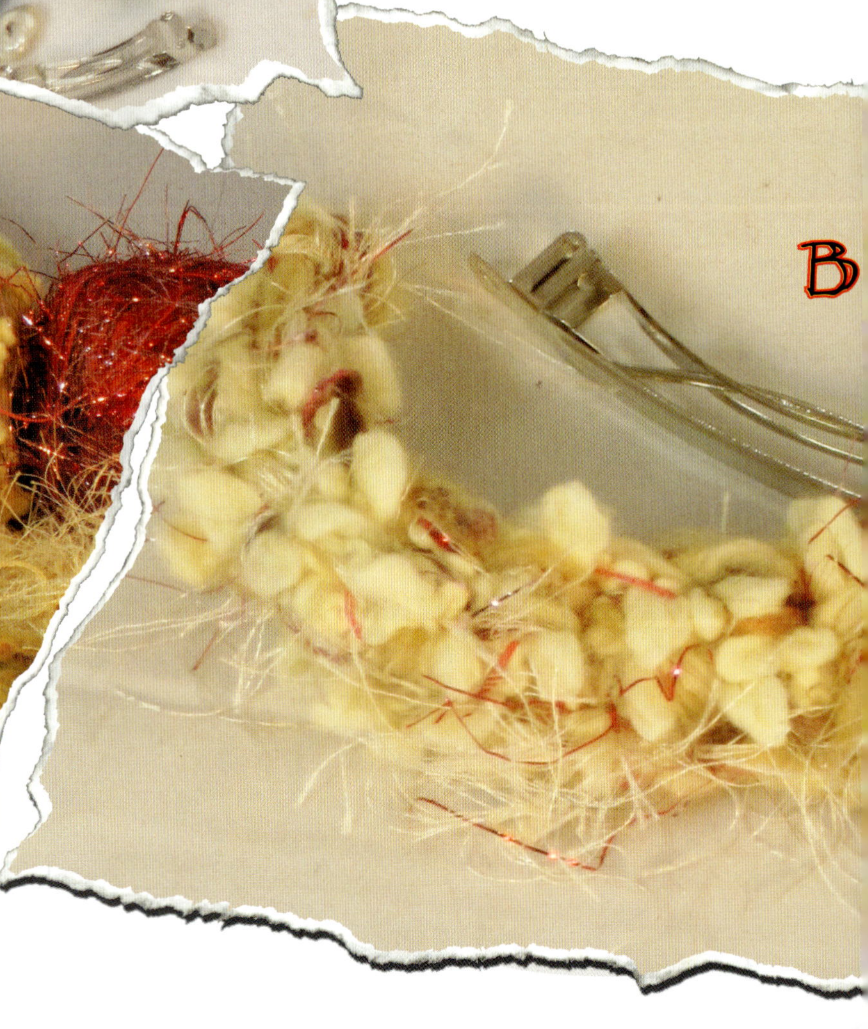

'ote: Sometimes the holes in the pearls are too small for the eedle. When this occurs, I remove the needle from the thread nd put the thread through the pearl without the needle. I then ut the needle back onto the thread and continue. This takes a ttle patience. However, it's worth it.

sewing needle (the size of which will depend on size of bead holes); thread (in a color that best blends with your yarn); assorted gem stones and pearls; size #8 or #9 seed beads, a sharp pair of scissors, and a barrette base.

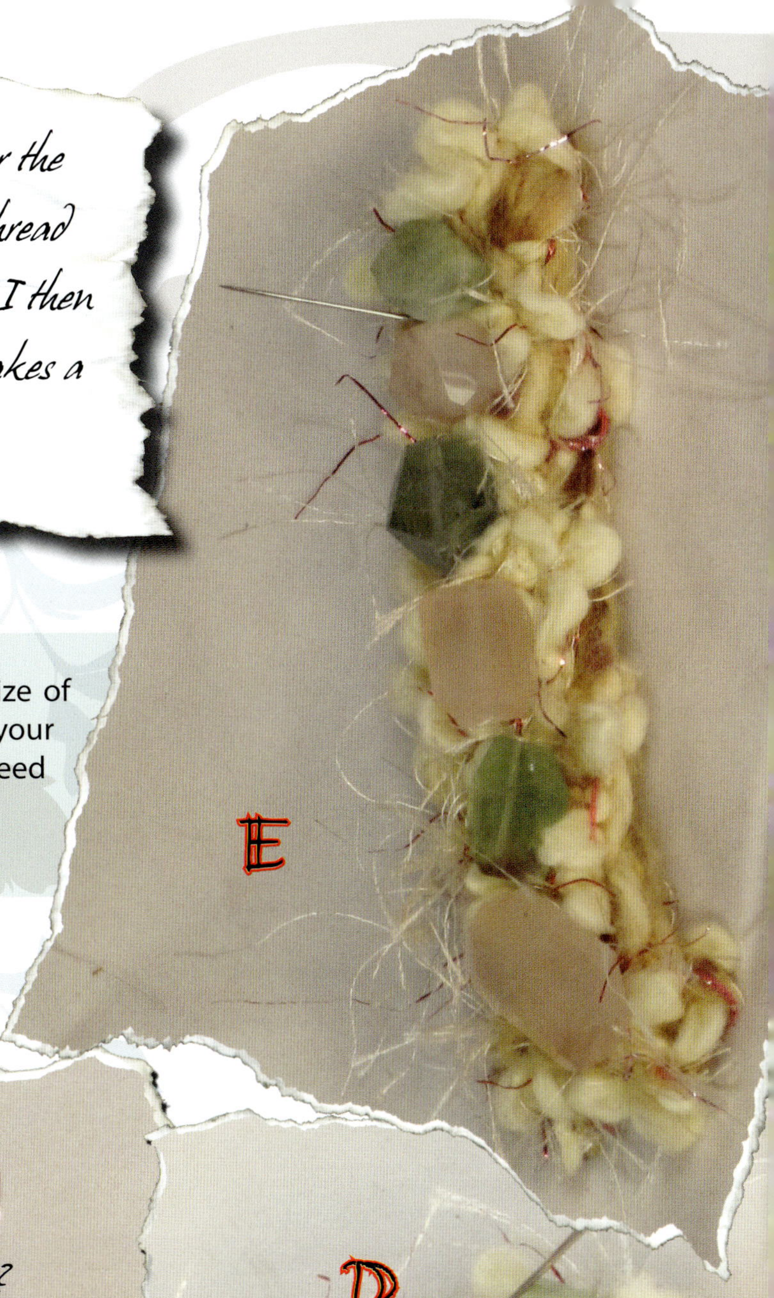

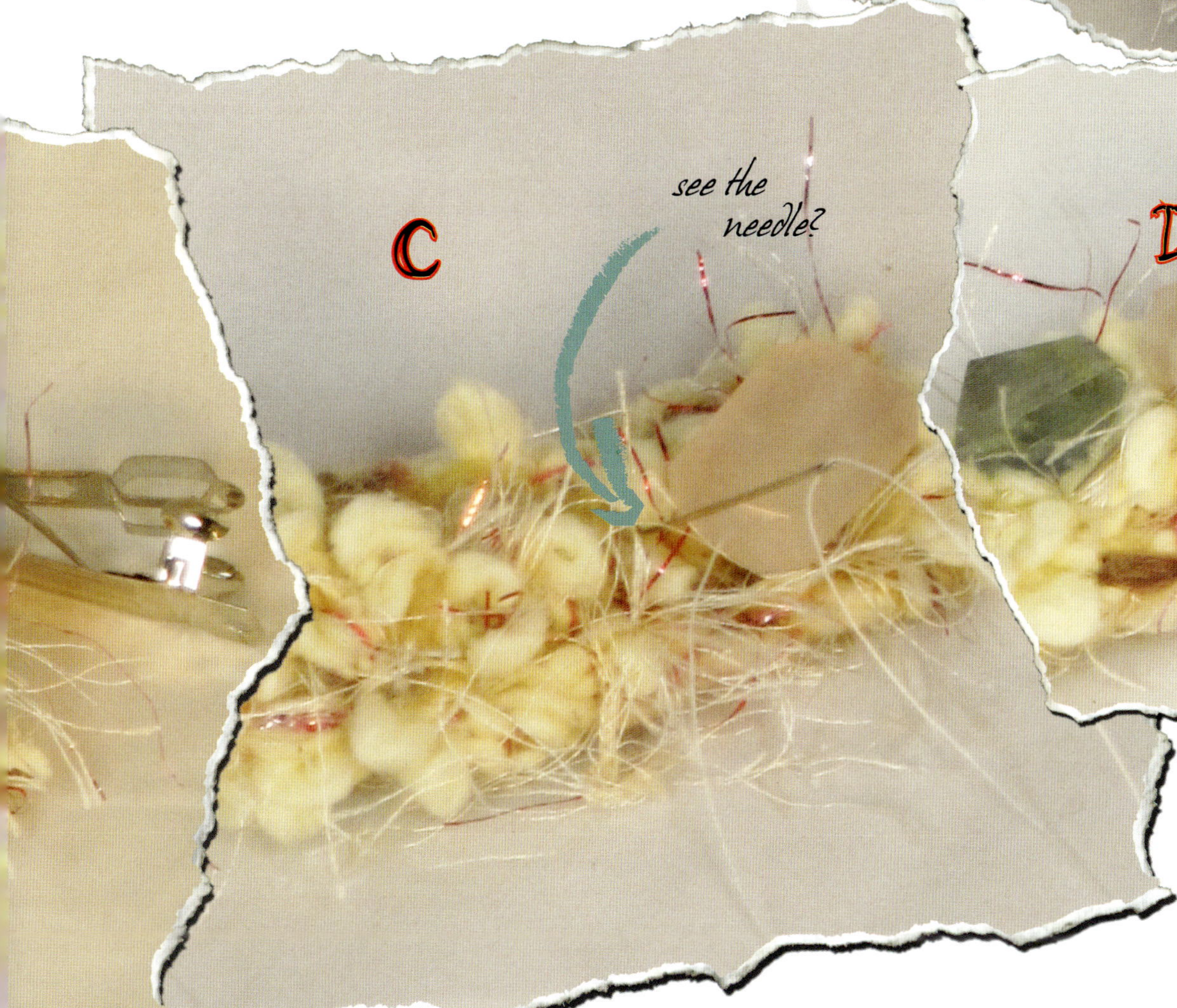

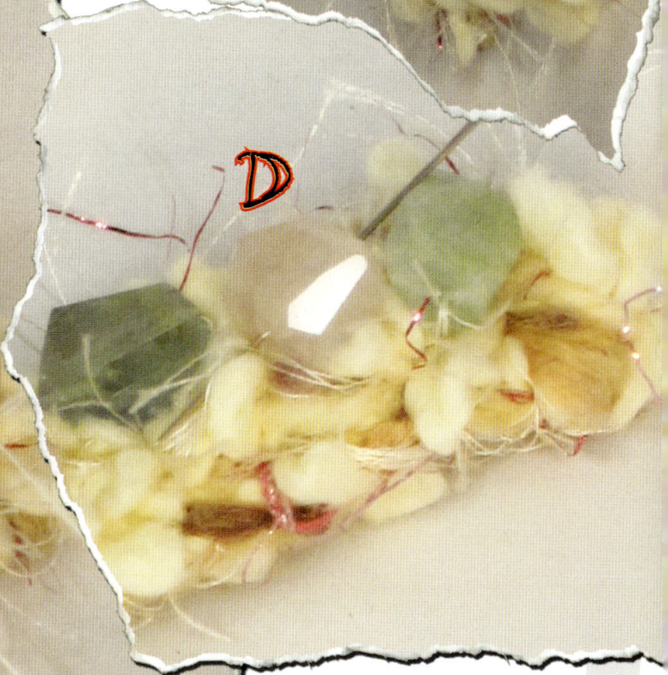

First, starting at one end, sew your gemstones on to the crocheted strip in a gently meandering pattern. The effect should be scattered and casual, not a perfect line. Alternate the stones as you work your way across. Make sure that you pull each stone tight before proceeding to the next. {C, D, & E

When done, securely knot the thread and cut. Then go back and, again starting at one end, randomly stitch seed beads and pearls onto your barrette. {F & G

To finish, sew the finished crocheted strip onto the metal clip as described above, on page 35.

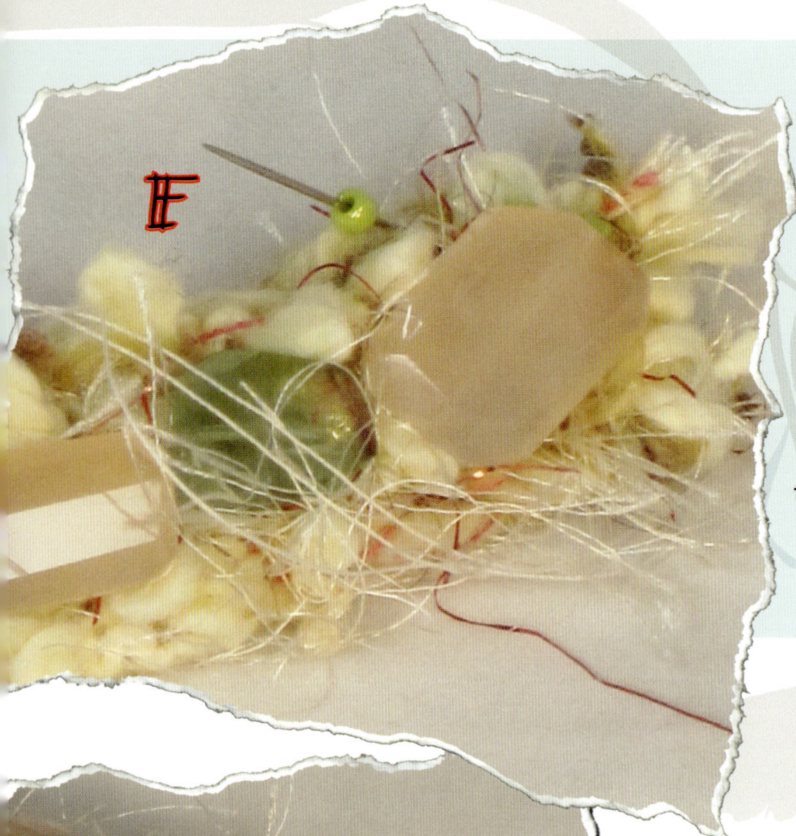

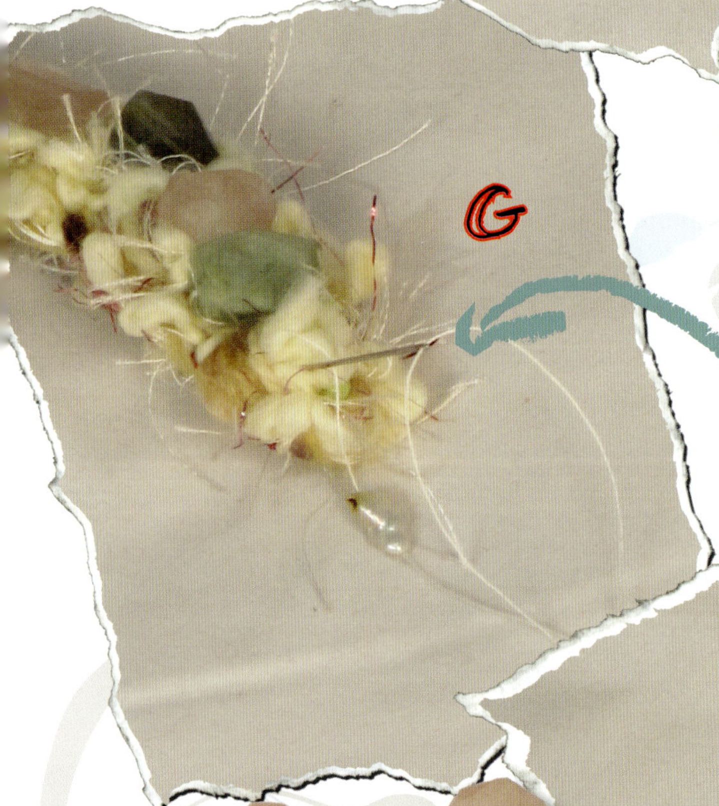

see the needle?

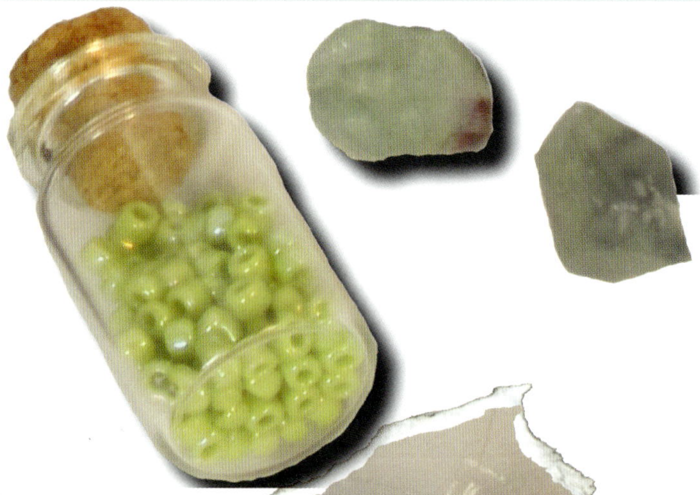

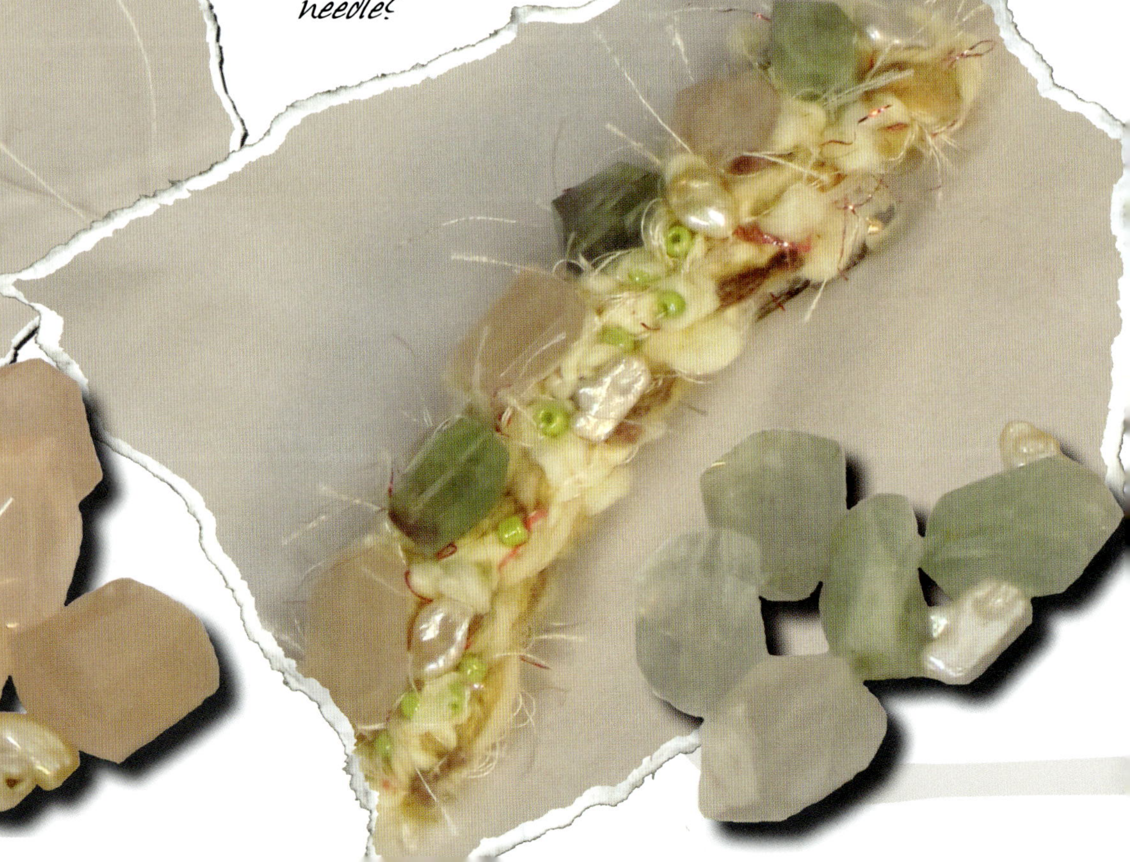

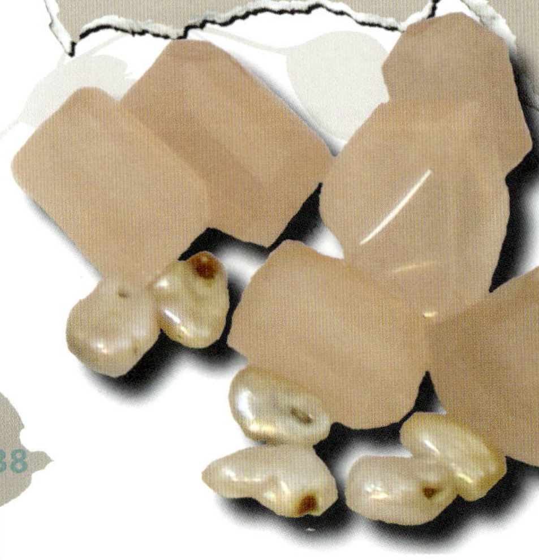

CHAPTER SIX

Earrings, Earrings, Earrings

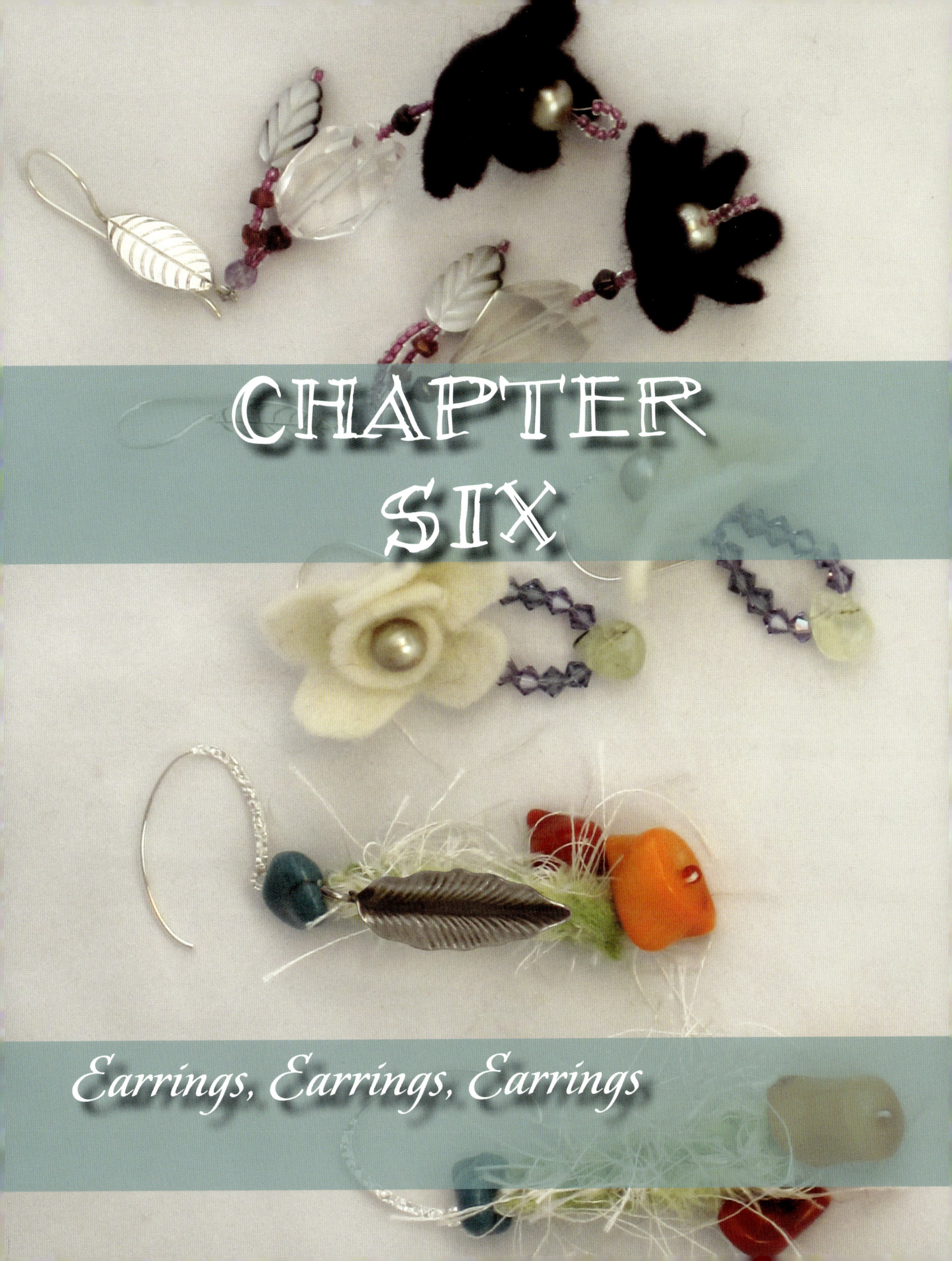

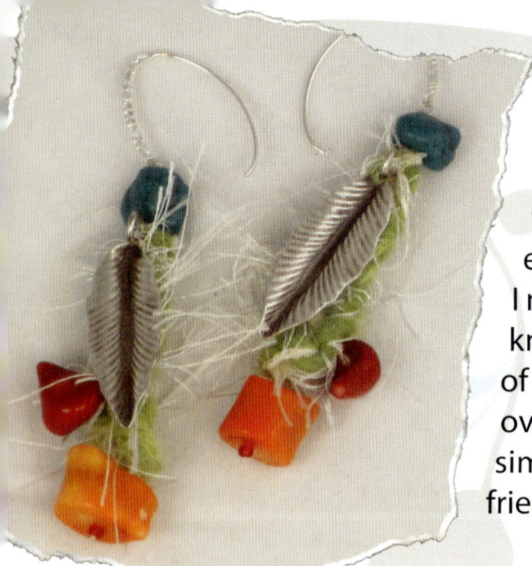

I love earrings! They are probably my favorite adornment. Since I was teenager, I've never left home without them. I have worn everything from funky giant peacock feathers to simple, classic diamond studs. Of the earrings I make, my favorite are the "shoulder dusters" (you know, long enough to reach your shoulders). Sort of Carmen Miranda meets Pocahontas. To avoid overwhelming people, I always wear them with simple attire. Here are three styles loved by my friends and me.

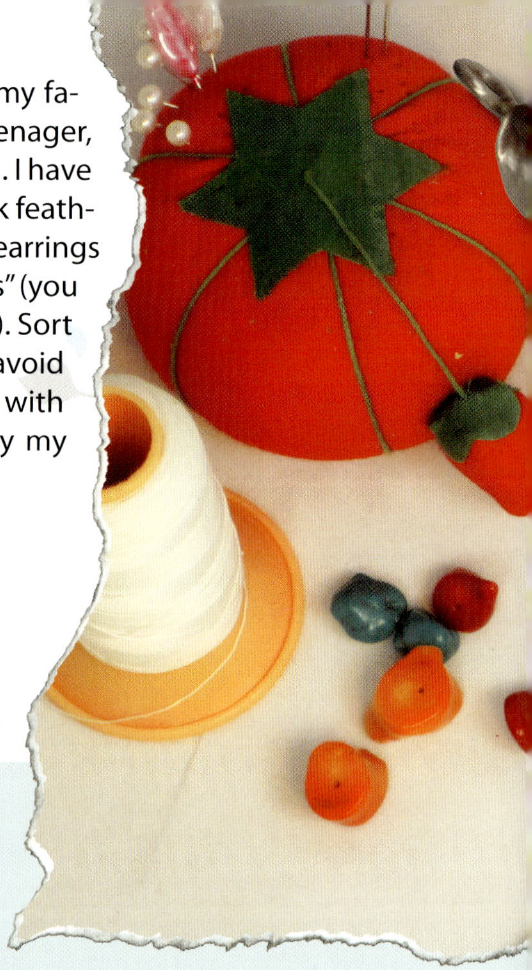

EARRING DESIGN #1
(a.k.a. "The Fishing Lure")

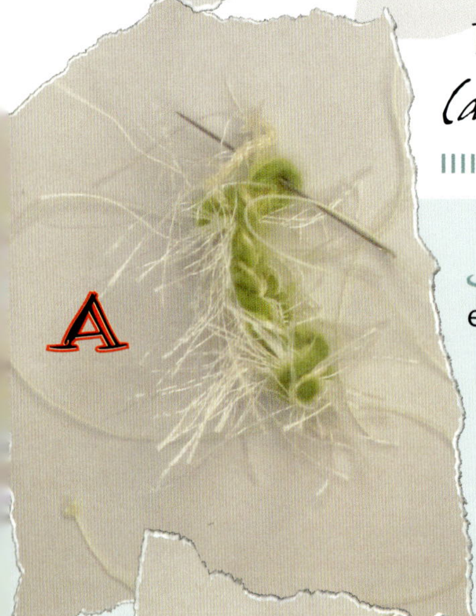

Supplies: Green angora yarn and off-white eyelash yarn; two orange and two red coral beads; two turquoise beads; two large pounded earring wires (I used a "fish" hook style, although any style will do); two silver leaf or feather charms; a small crochet hook; a needle and thread; and scissors.

Start by making a foundation chain 4 or 5 chains long (depending on how long you want the earrings). Finish one end by using a needle and about 12 inches of thread (with a knot on the end!) to make a series of small stitches through and over the ends until they are bound. Do not cut the thread yet! {A

When finished, pull the thread through the turquoise bead, then through the hole of the earring wire, then back down through the turquoise bead and back into the foundation stitch near when you began. {B&C

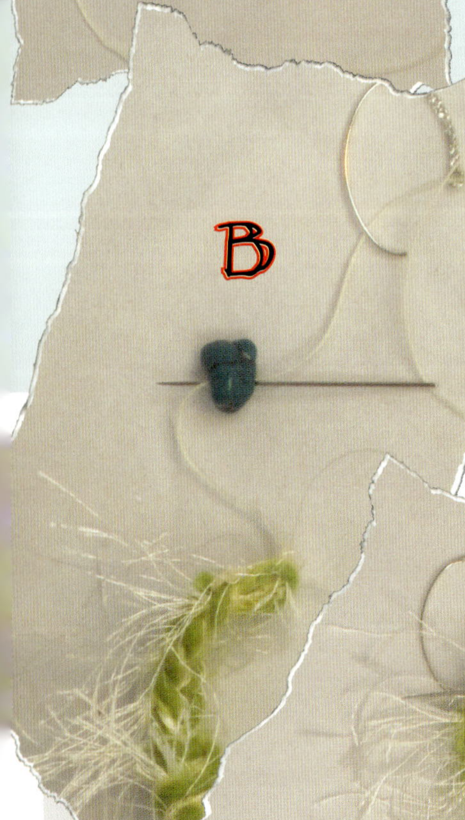

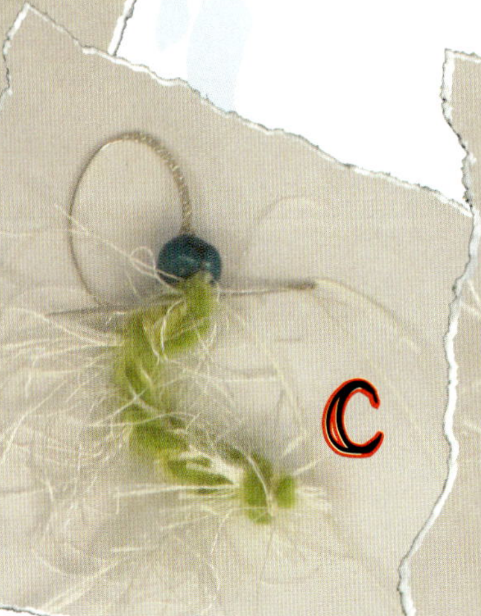

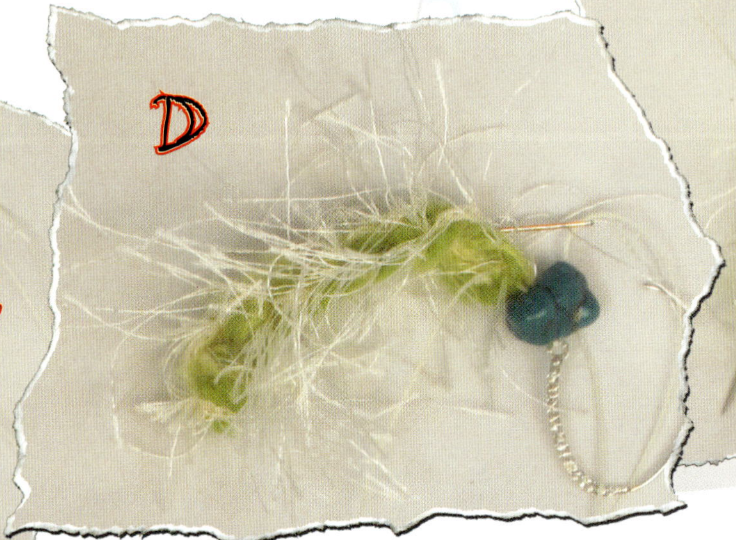

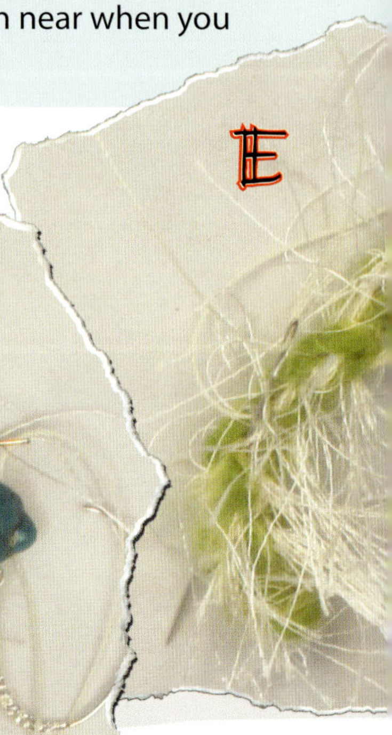

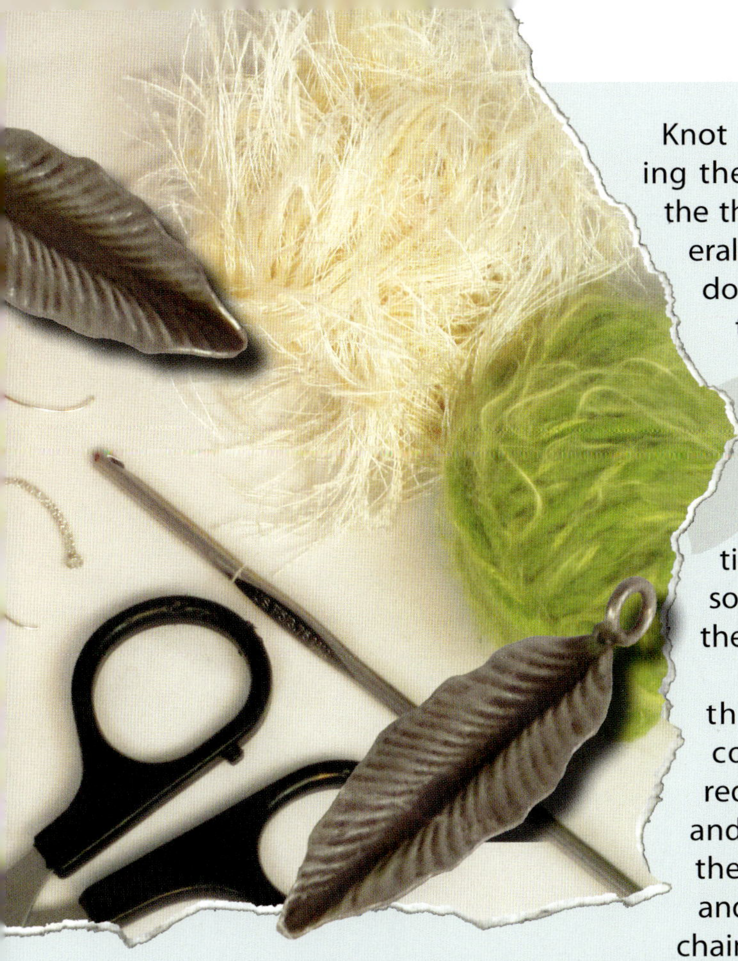

Knot off the thread after pulling the bead snug. Do not cut the thread yet! Next, using several stitches, "weave" the thread down the length of the foundation chain to almost the other end. **{D&E**

Stitch the red coral bead onto the foundation chain near the end. **{F**

Next, pierce the foundation chain with the needle so that the point comes out the end. **{G**

Then thread it through the orange coral bead, then the red seed stopper bead, and then back through the orange coral bead and into the foundation chain. **{H**

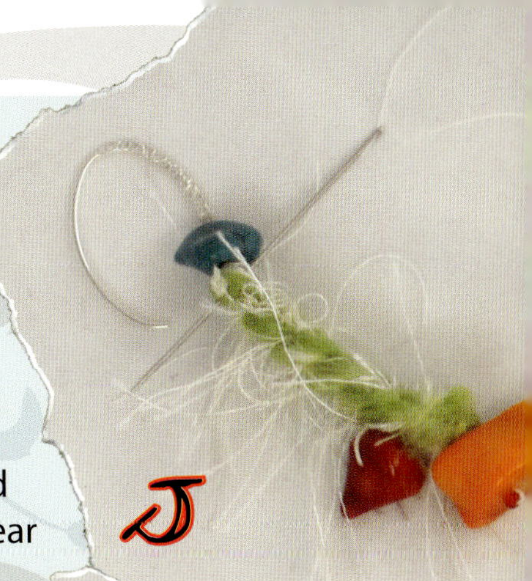

J

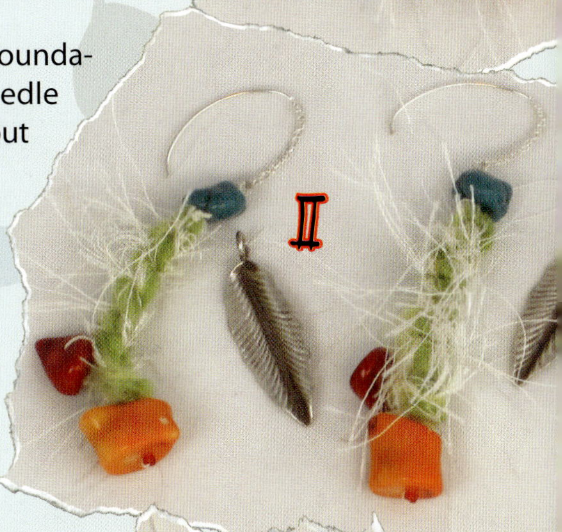

I

Knot the thread securely. It is now safe to cut the thread! As a finishing touch, and to give the piece a Native American flavor, you can attach a silver leaf or feather near the top (at the base of the turquoise bead). **{I & J** Make sure it is oriented correctly (i.e. facing out when the earrings are being worn) and hangs "naturally."

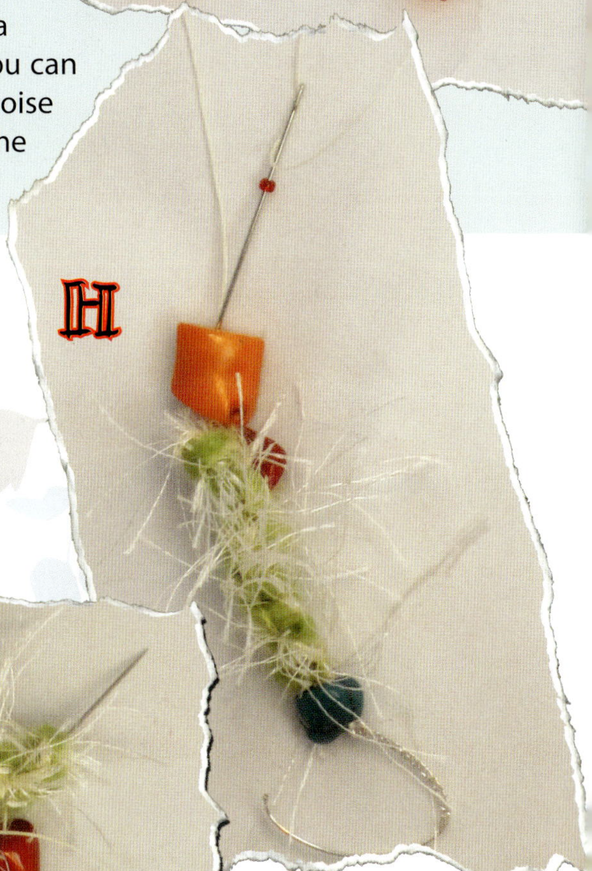

H

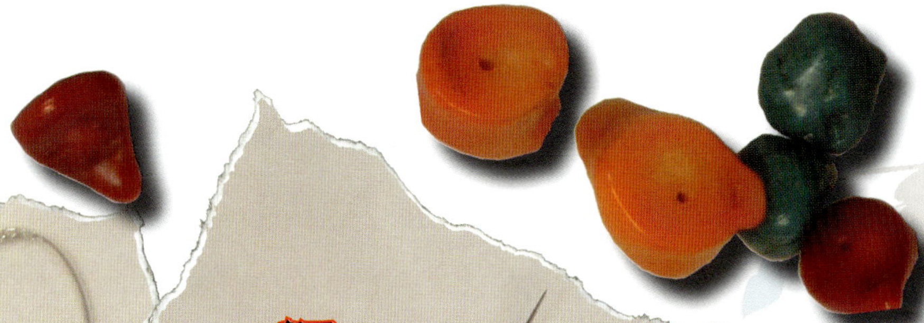

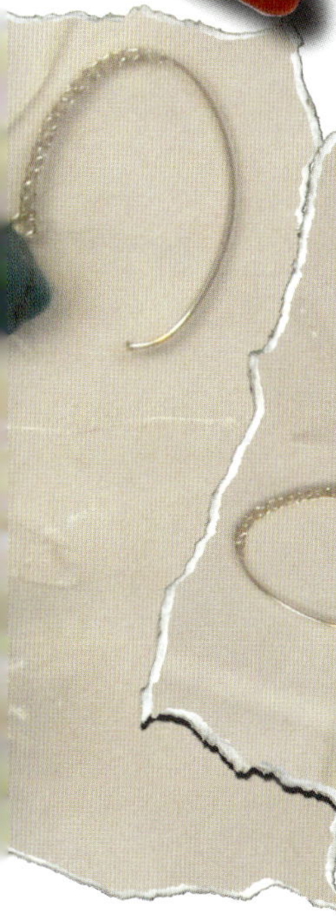

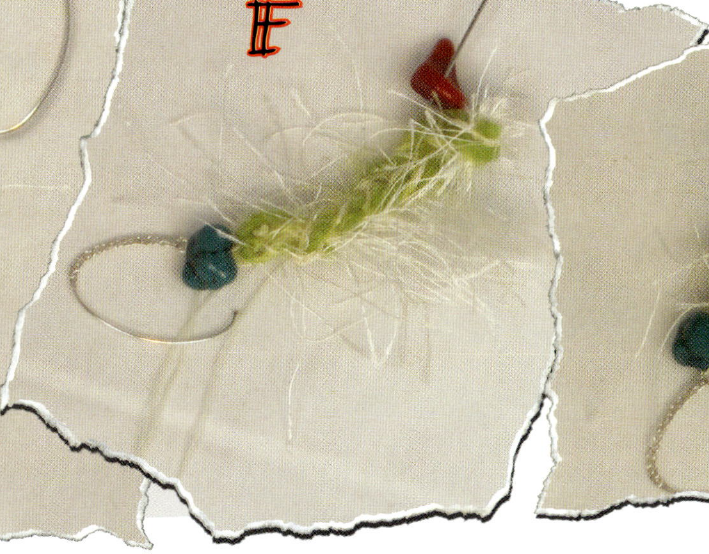

F

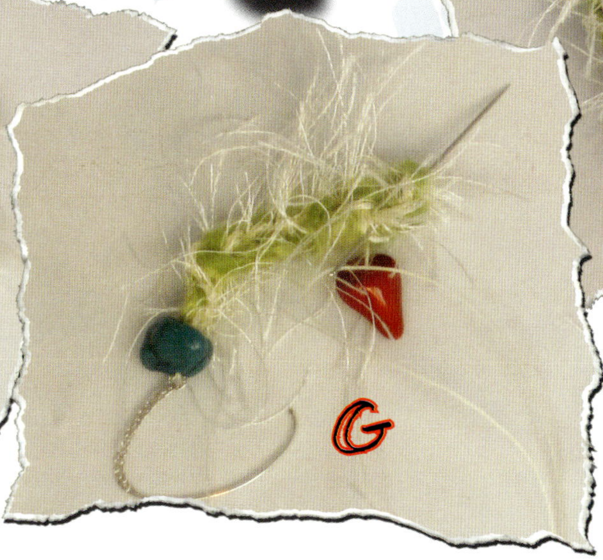

G

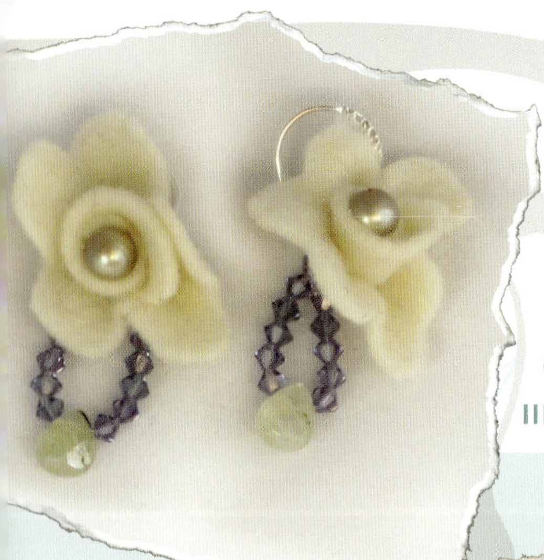

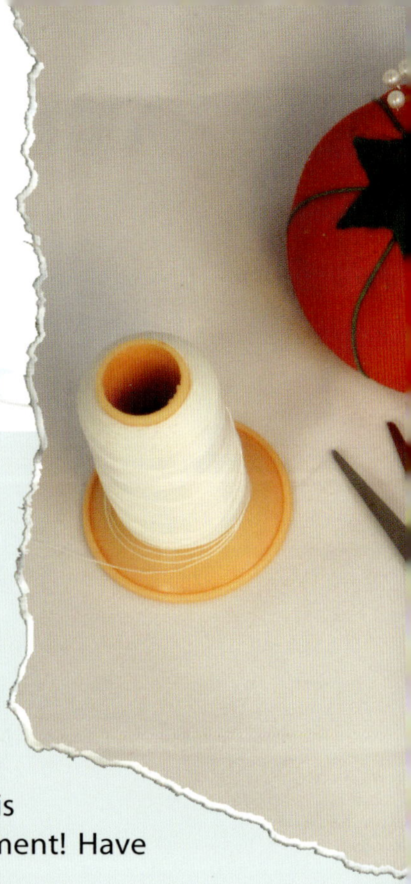

EARRING DESIGN #2
(a.k.a. "The Lovely Felt Flower")

Tools and Supplies: Two off-white "rose" felt flowers (see Basic Skills chapter); two medium size round pearls; 24-32 Austrian crystal beads (small); pear-shaped glass or stone bead; small pounded earring wire (I used a "fish" hook style, although any style will do); a needle and thread; and scissors. (I used an off-white because it is classic and matches everything. However, this style works with any color. Experiment! Have fun! Go wild!)

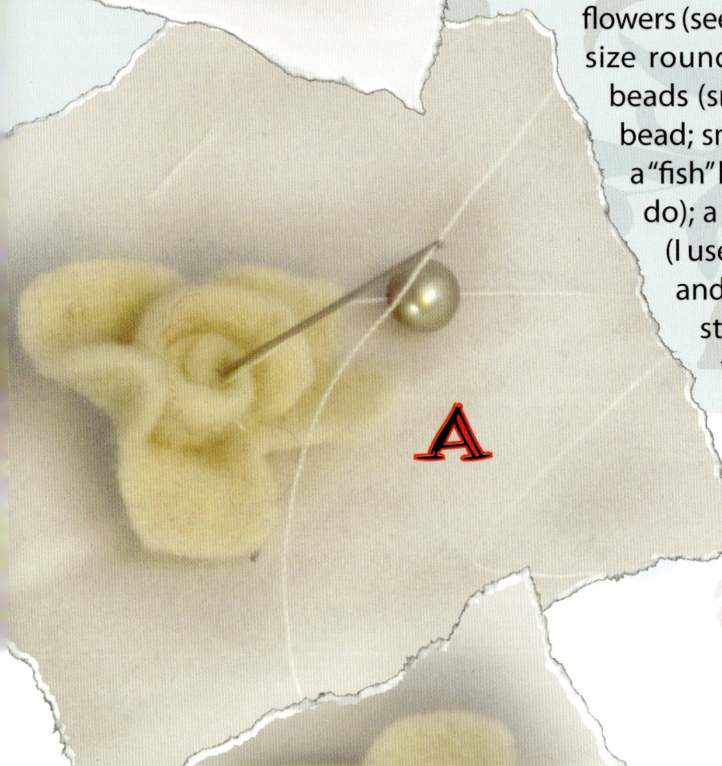

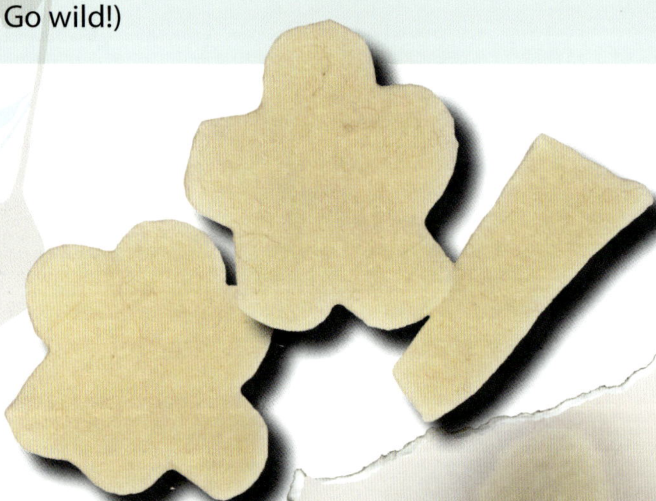

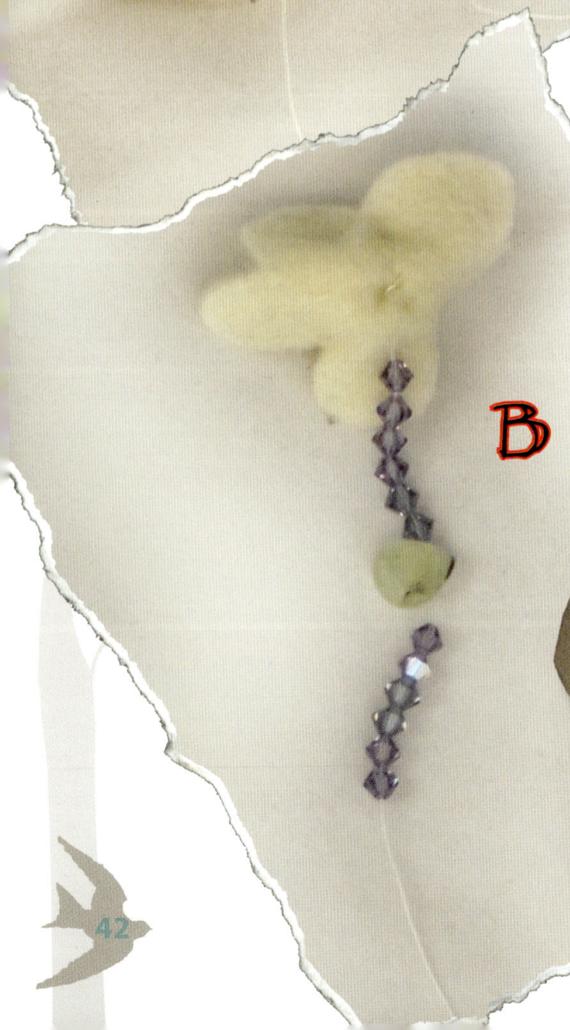

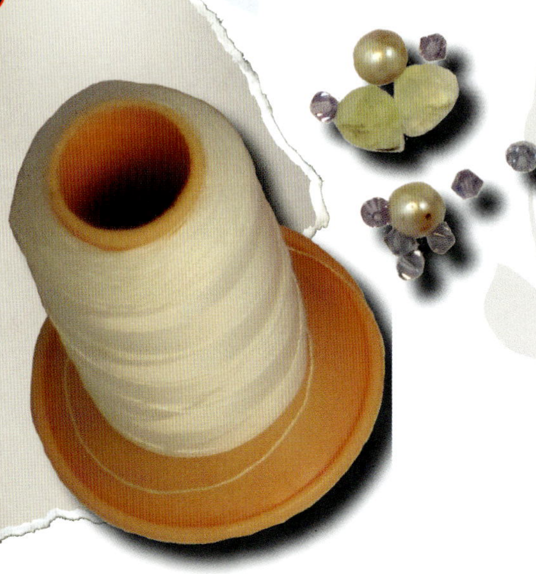

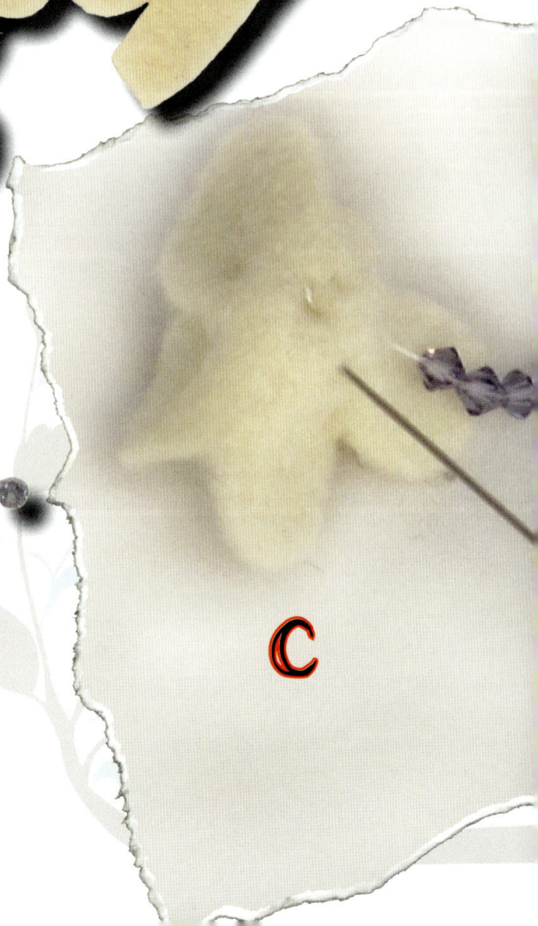

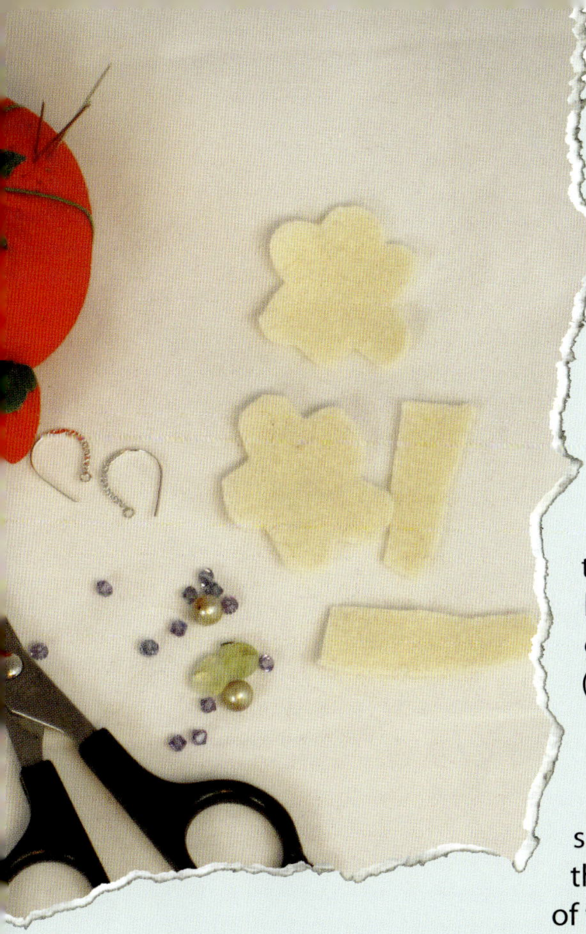

Using a needle and about 12 inches of thread (with a knot on the end!) pierce the center of your felt rose through the front and pull until the knot catches. (This make take a couple of tries.) Pierce the needle through the back center of the rose to bring the thread to the front center. Using the needle and thread, attach the pearl at the very center of the front of the rose **{A**. (Sometimes the hole of the pearl is too small for the needle. If this occurs, remove the needle from the thread, thread the pearl by hand, and then re-attach the needle.)

The needle and thread should now be at the back of the rose. Tweak the pearl so that the thread does not show. Pull the thread snug and tie a knot. Do not cut the thread yet! Make a "swag" by stringing 6 or so Austrian crystal beads, then the pear shaped glass or stone bead, and then 6 or so more Austrian crystal beads. (Make sure the number of crystal beads on each side is the same, or the pear-shaped bead will not be centered.) Then re-attach the thread onto the rose near where it exited. **{B&C**

Secure with a couple of stitches before attaching the earring wire to the back of the rose. **{D&E**

When attaching the earring wire, put a few stitches up the shaft of the wire to help prevent the rose from "drooping." You're done!

E

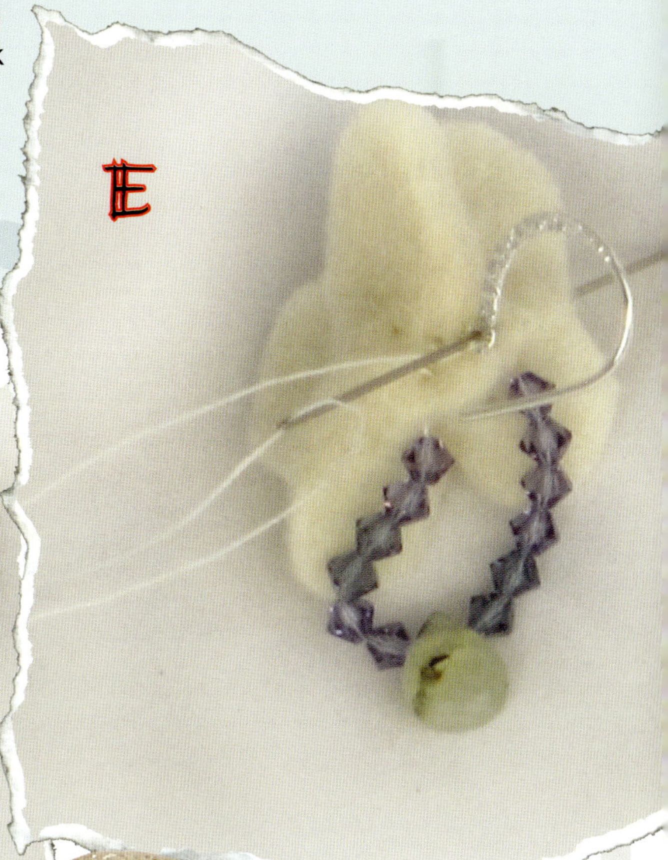

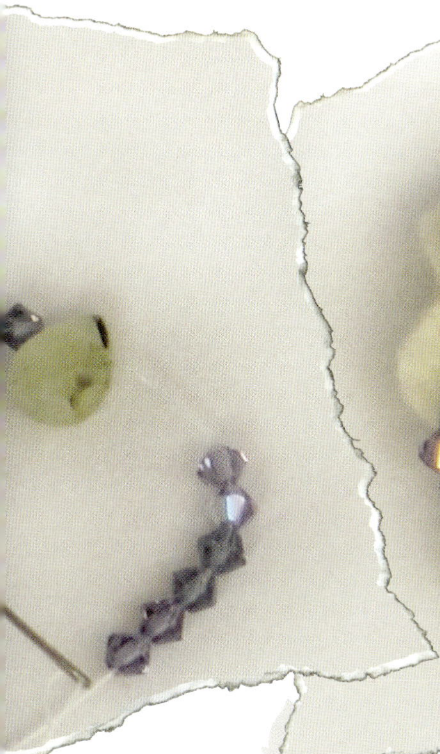

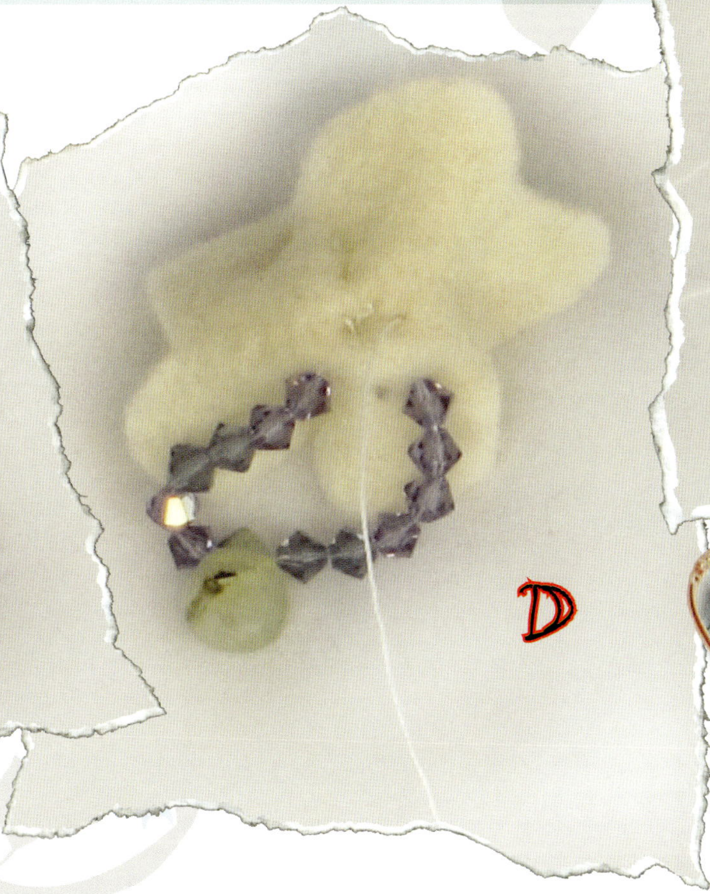

D

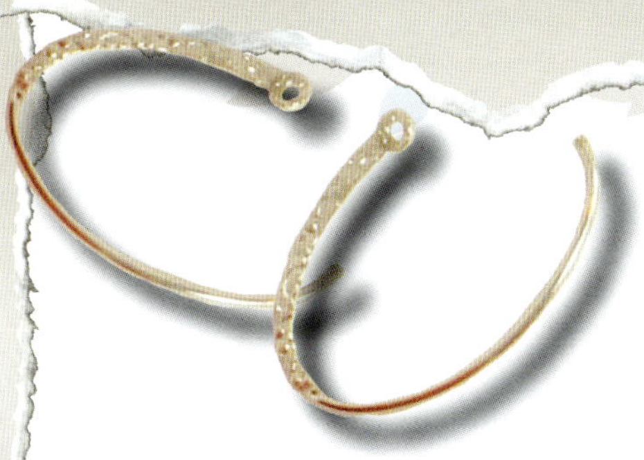

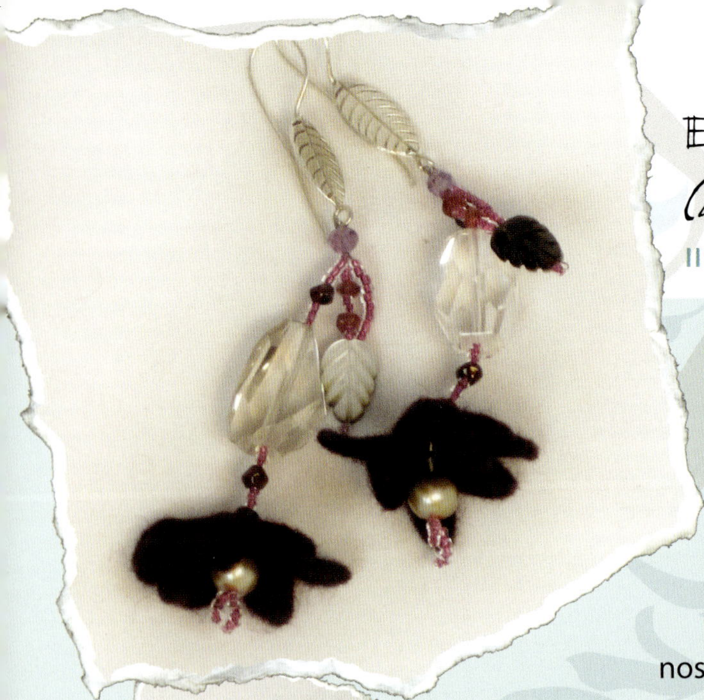

EARRING DESIGN#3
(a.k.a. "The Hanging Flower")

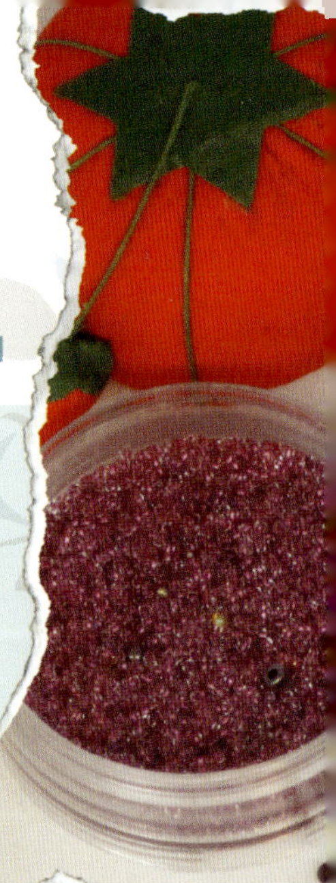

Tools and Supplies: Two burgundy "daisy" felt flowers (see Basic Skills chapter); many tiny raspberry seed beads; 12 pieces of garnet (#9 seed beads may be substituted); irregularly faceted quartz; two mother of pearl or glass leaves; earring wire; two medium sized round pearls; fine beading wire; 4 crimp beads; wire cutters; a needle; and needle nose pliers.

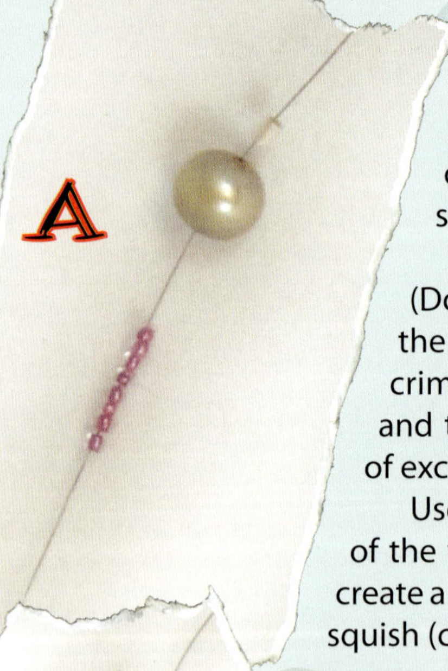

A

Using about a foot of beading wire, and holding it so that the beads will not fall off, string the following items in the following order—a crimp bead; a pearl; and 8 raspberry seed beads. {A

Scoot the items toward one end of the wire. (Don't push them off!) Take the now short end of the wire (i.e. the end which is furthest from the crimp bead) and pass it back through the pearl and the crimp bead, leaving only a short amount of excess. {B

Use your needle nose pliers to pull the short end of the wire until it is snug and the threaded beads create a mini-swag or loop with no wire showing. Then squish (crimp) the crimp bead. {C

Thread a needle onto the open (long) end of the wire and pierce the needle through the front center of your felt daisy. {D

Note: The quantities in this description are designed to match the sample earrings and to be proportional. They need not be followed exactly. However, the bead count must be the same for both sides of your earrings or they won't match. So keep track!

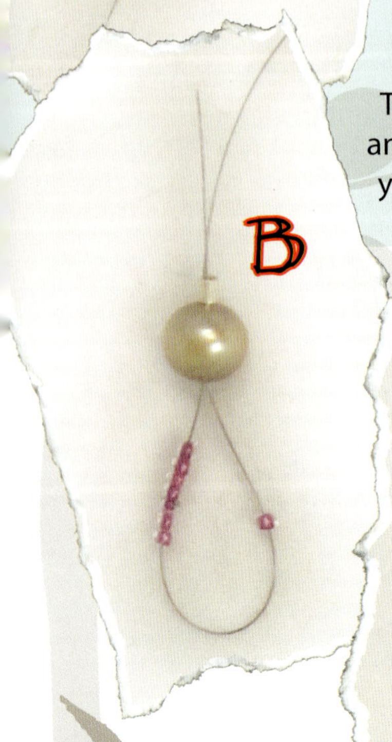

B

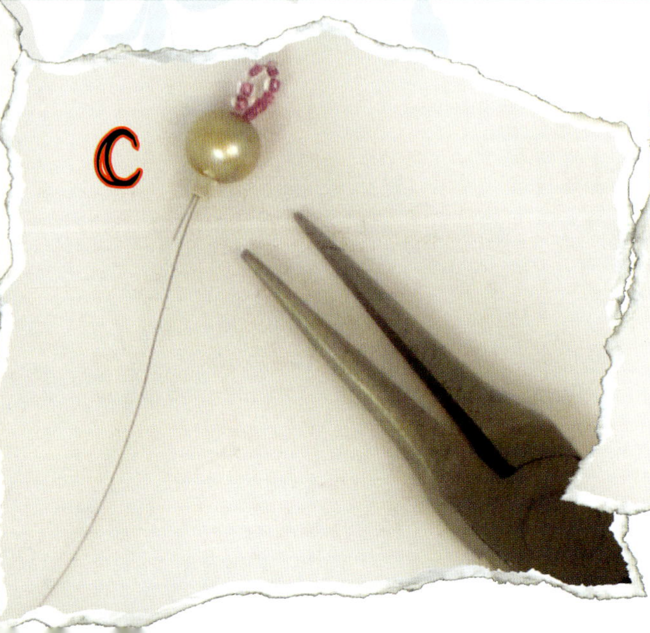

C

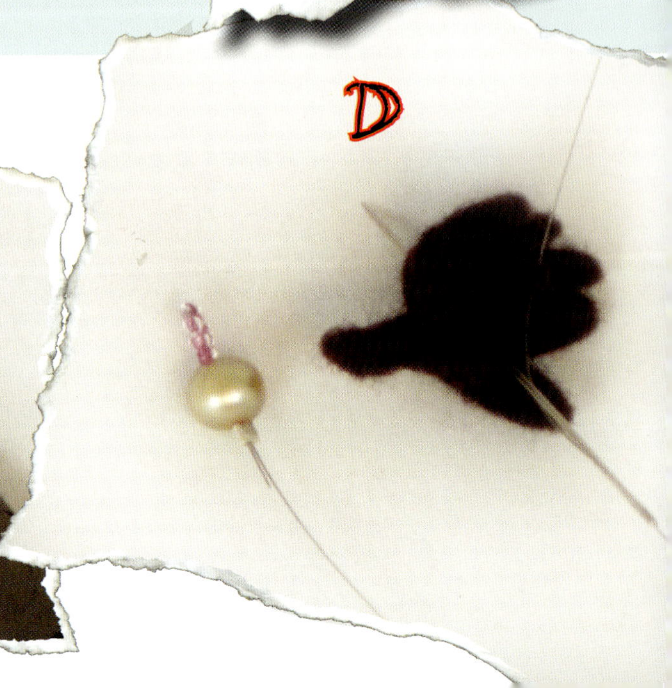

D

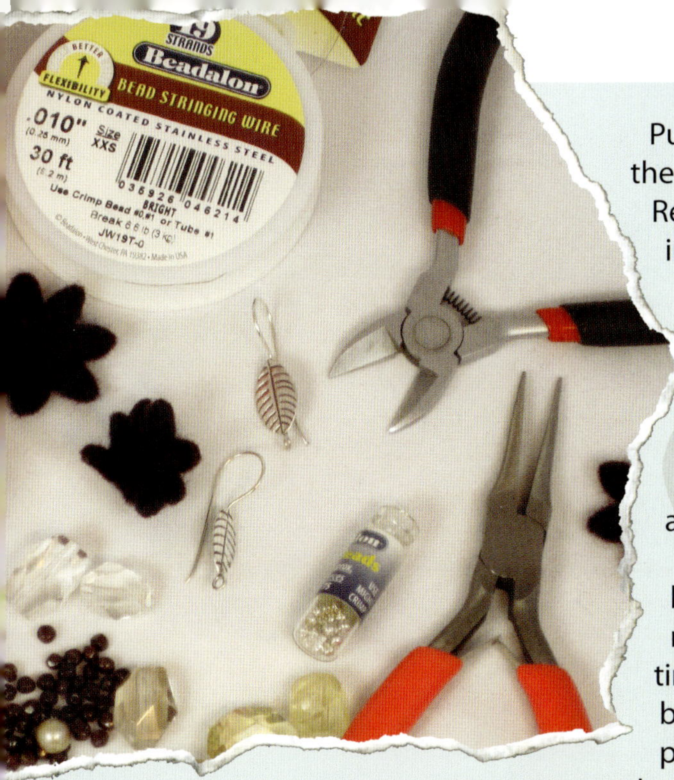

Pull the wire until the pearl is nestled snugly in the center of the daisy. The wire is now coming out of the back of the flower. Remove the needle. String items onto the wire in the following order—a piece of garnet; 3 tiny raspberry seed beads; another piece of garnet; 3 more tiny raspberry seed beads; one of the irregularly faceted pieces of quartz; 3 more tiny raspberry seed beads; another piece of garnet; 3 more tiny raspberry seed beads; and another piece of garnet. **{E&F**

Then thread the wire into the "eye"of the earring wire and back down through the last piece of garnet. **{G**

To make your "petal," string onto the wire 2 tiny raspberry seed beads; another piece of garnet; 3 more tiny raspberry seed beads; a mother of pearl or glass leaf; and 1 tiny raspberry seed bead (as a stopper). Then thread the wire back up through the leaf. Pull the items snug on the wire. Then string 9 tiny raspberry seed beads. **{G**

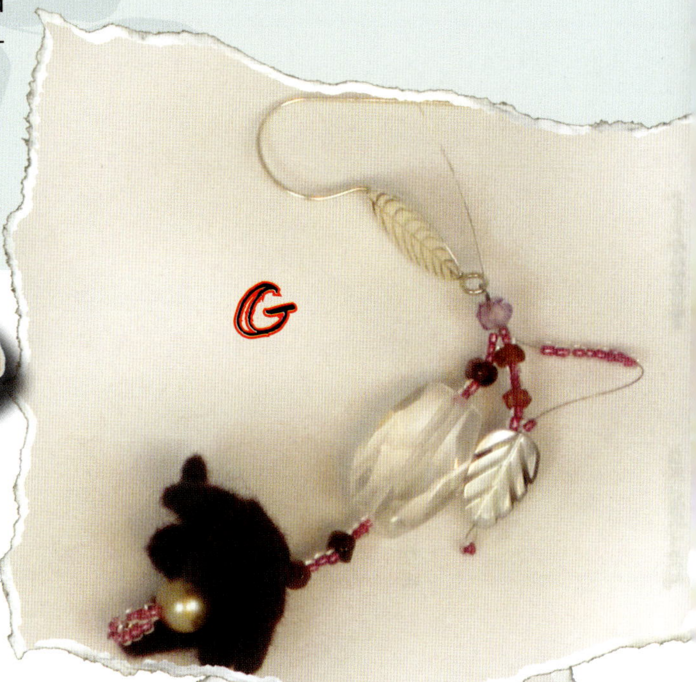

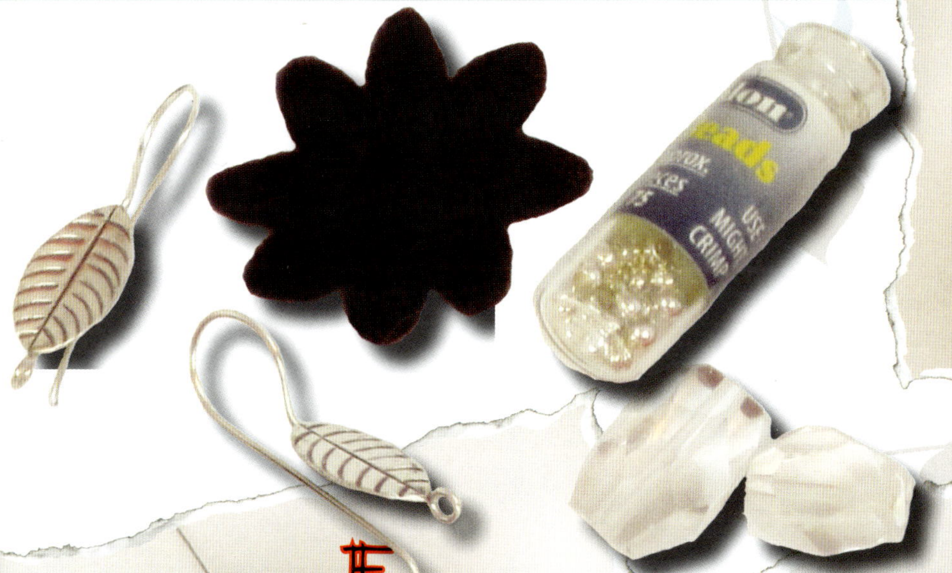

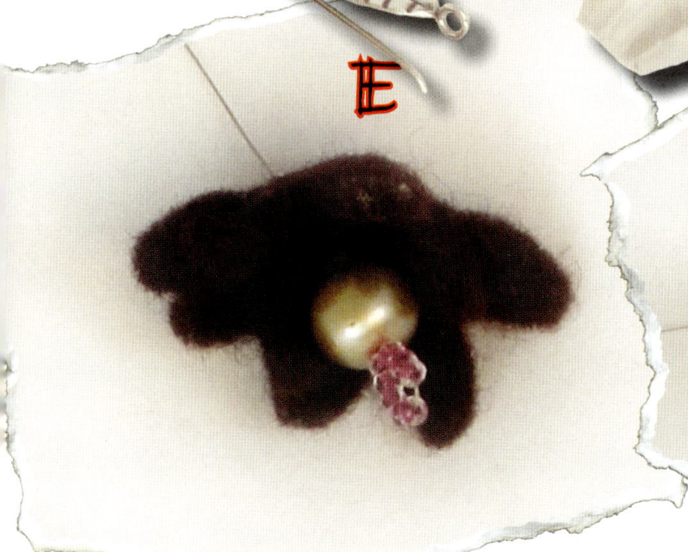

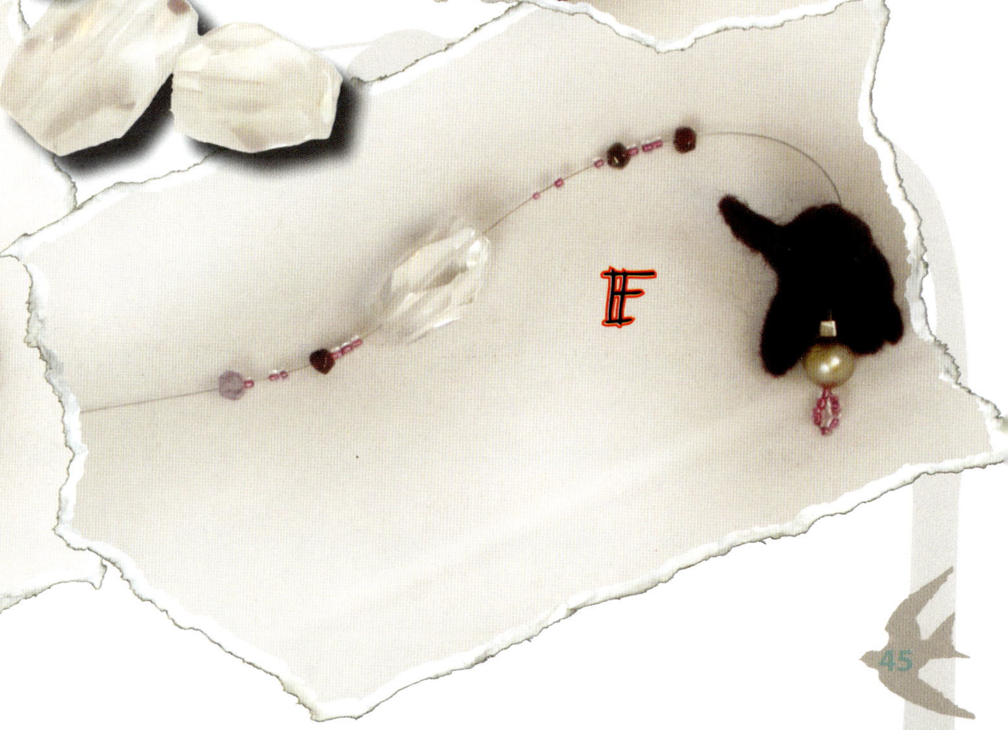

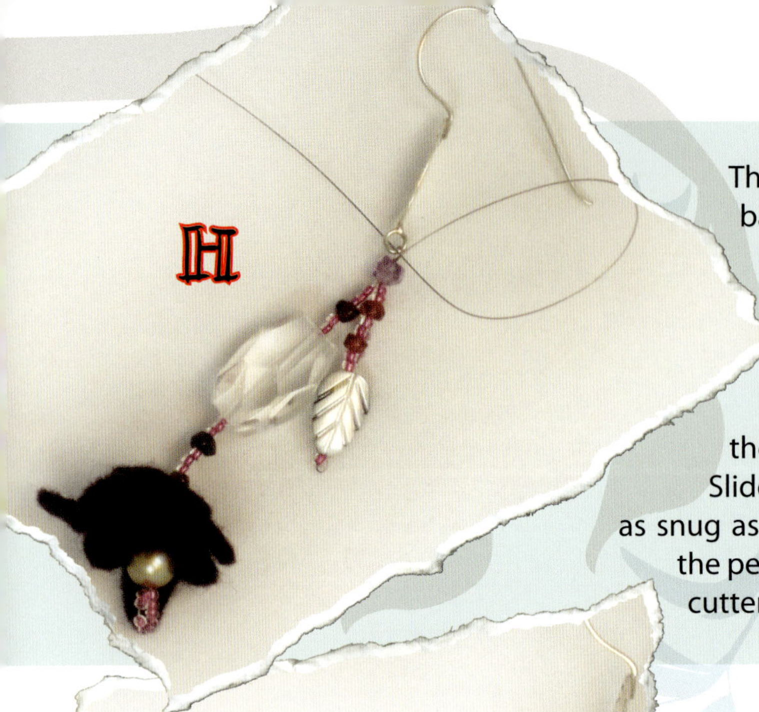

Thread the wire back up through the piece of garnet {G; back through the "eye" of the earring wire and back down through all of the beads, etc. leading to the felt daisy. (This will take some massaging. Be patient.) {H&I

The end of the wire should now be poking out between the last garnet and the felt daisy. Thread the needle onto the wire and bring the wire back to the front center of the felt daisy. {J

Slide a crimp bead onto the wire and bring the crimp bead as snug as possible to the felt flower (so that it is concealed by the pearl). Finally, squish (crimp) the crimp bead and use wire cutters to trim any excess wire {K. Violà.

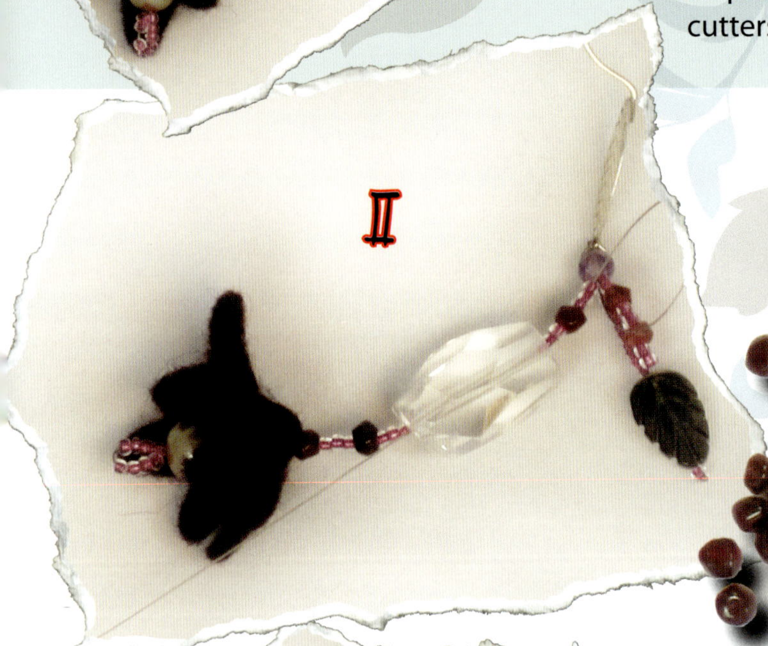

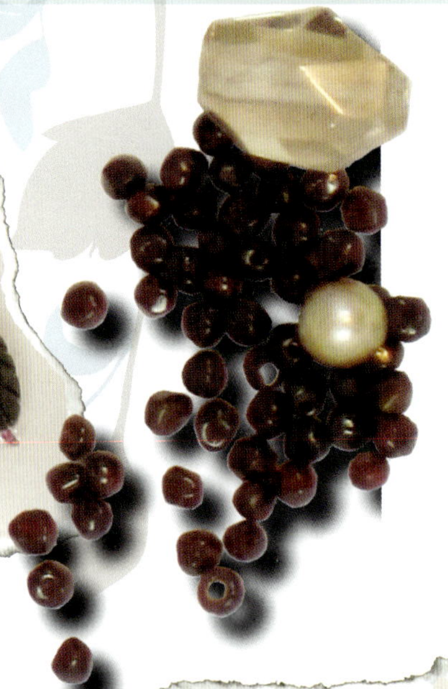

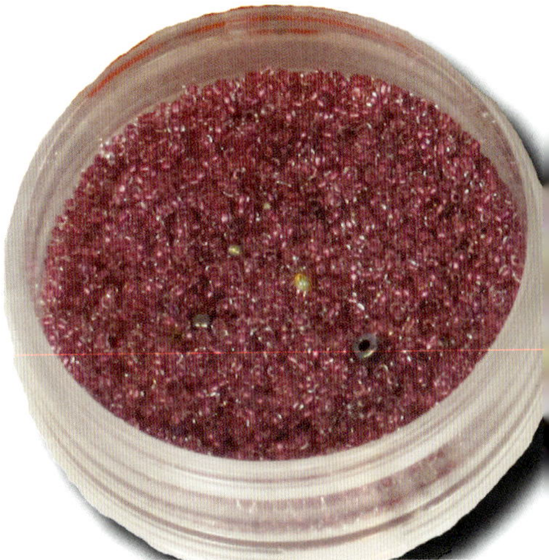

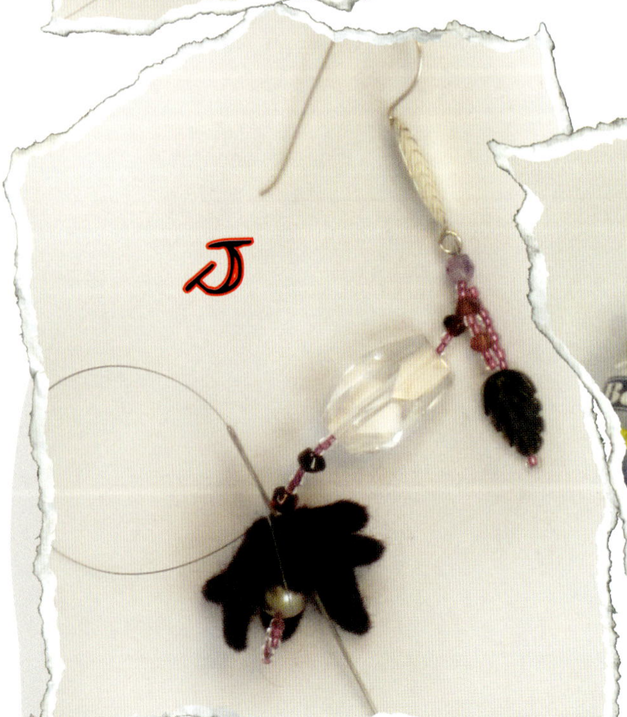

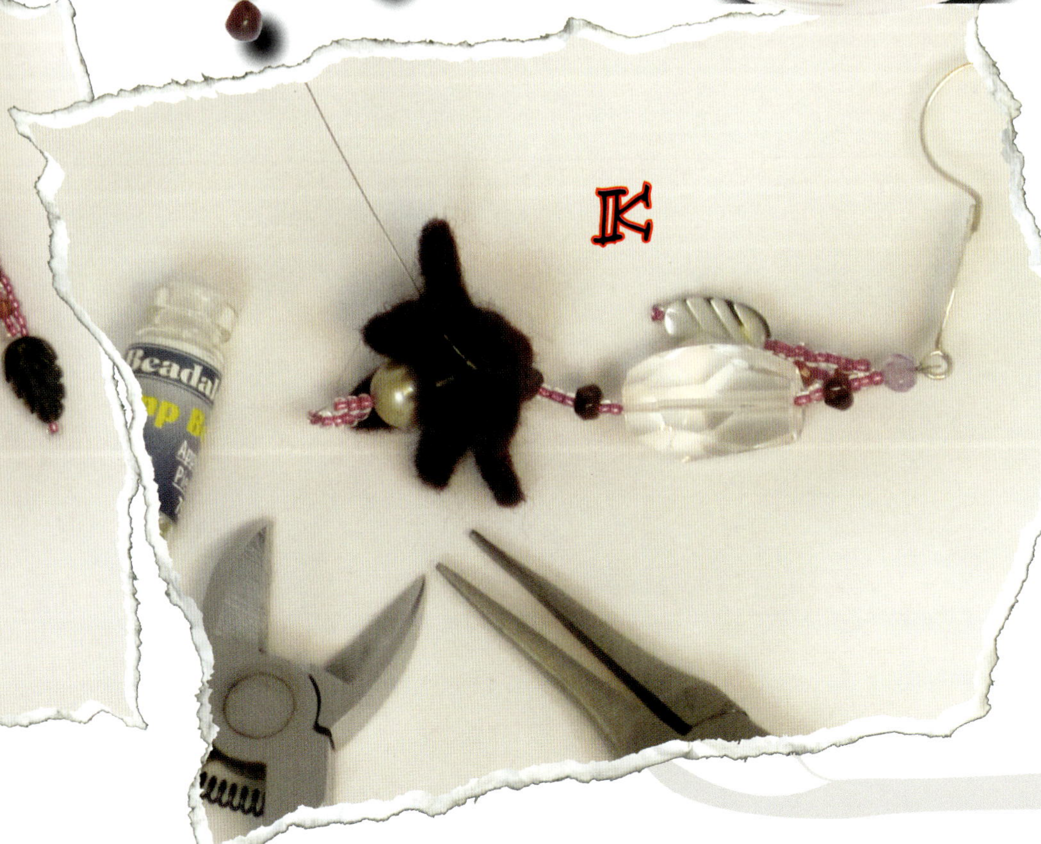

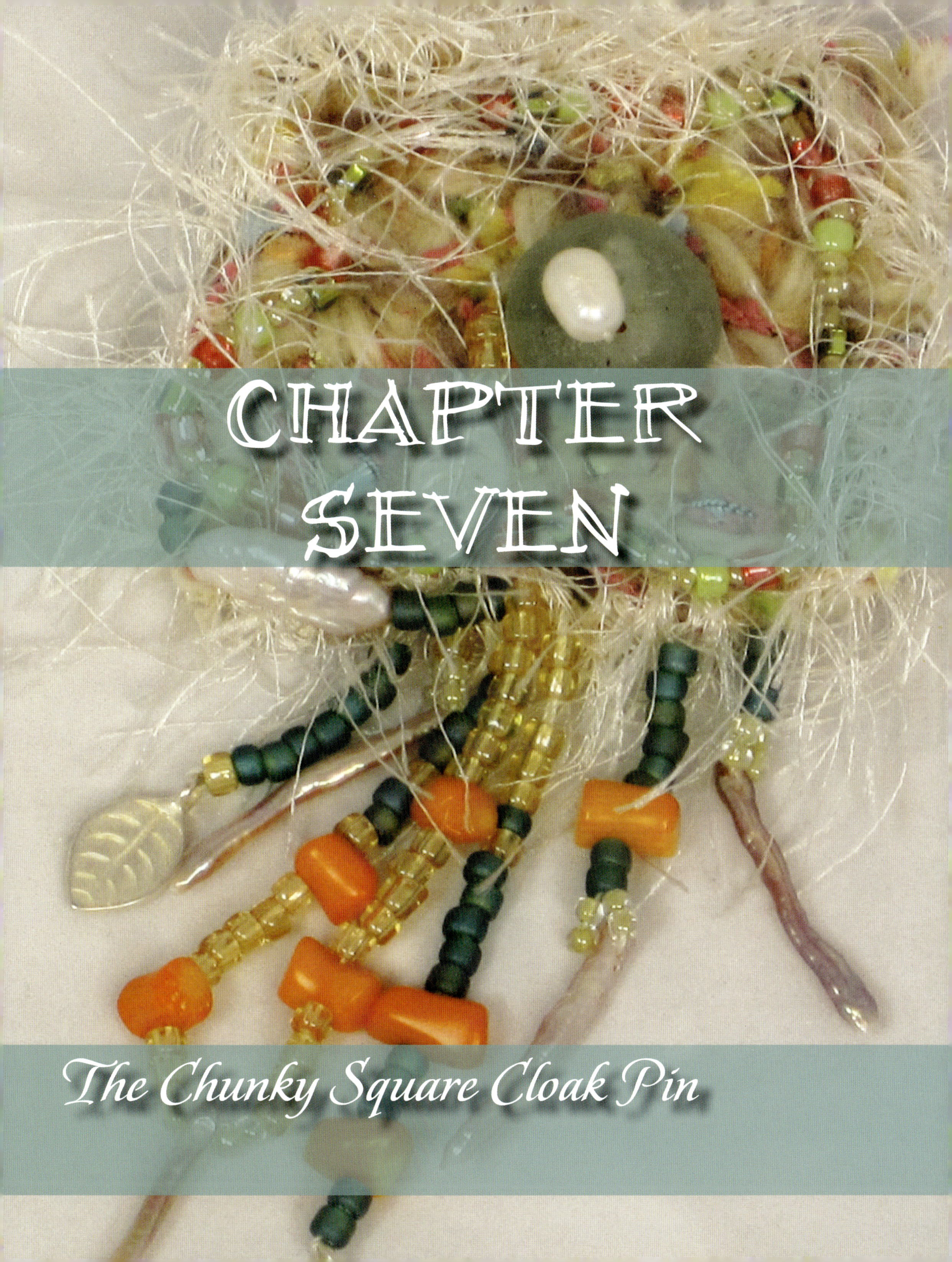

Chapter Seven

The Chunky Square Cloak Pin

CLOAK PIN
(A Five Stitch Cloak Pin)

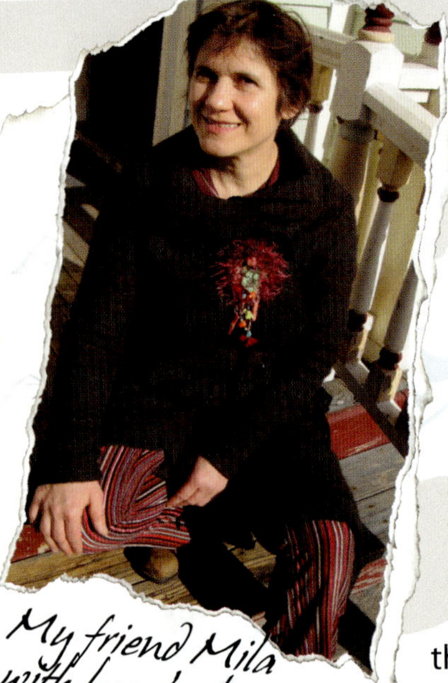

My friend Mila with her cloak pin

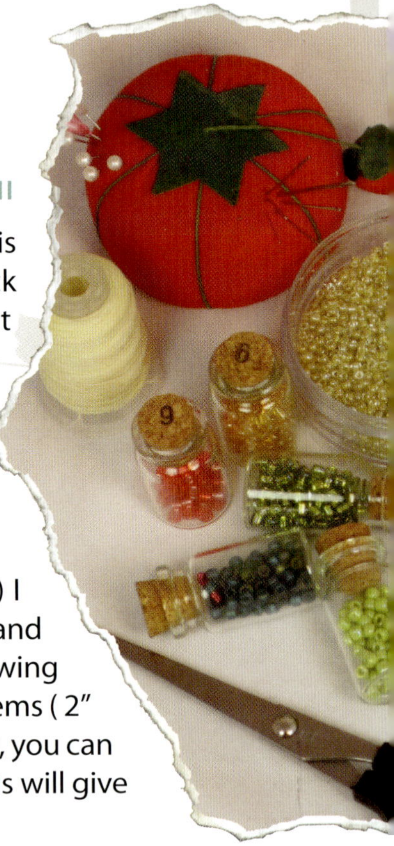

My dear friend Mila was the inspiration for this project. She has this fabulous, arty, black boiled wool wrap coat that is the perfect canvas for a big fuzzy colorful brooch, so I experimented and made a few. They looked great, and were unique and lots of fun to wear. (Mila got the first!) However, these brooches are not limited to winter coats and bulky sweaters. They also look great pinned to a shawl or a scarf. I use a kilt pin for the closure. (You know, the really big ones that look like a diaper pin without the little yellow ducky!) I like using a kilt pin because it is very secure and substantial, and has a no-nonsense feel. You can find them for sale at large sewing stores like Joanne's Fabrics (3") or online at Fire Mountain Gems (2" or 3"). If the large-size brooch has too much attitude for you, you can use less stitches. We will begin with a five stitch brooch. This will give us a more typically-sized (but still large) pin.

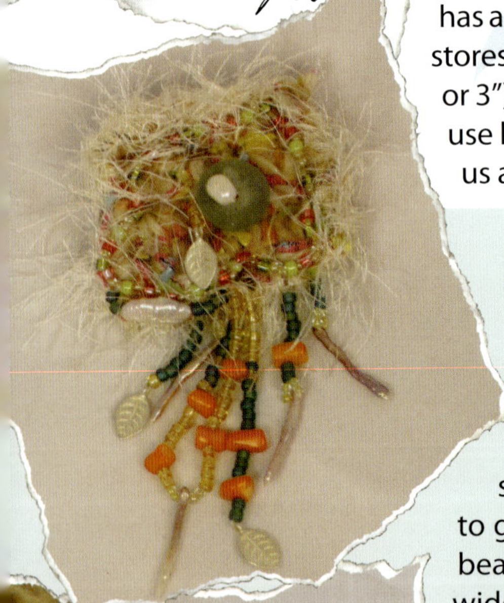

I chose to make my brooch around a beautiful large sea glass bead that I got from an artist friend in trade for some seed beads! (Ha! I'm certain I got the better of the deal!) I accentuated the soft blue-green color of the sea glass bead with snow white and sandy-yellow yarns, and a pink/multi-color confetti yarn. This combination of fibers crocheted into a thick luscious bed for my beads. In addition to the sea glass bead, I used an assortment of white/pink pearls, silver leaves, and a few bits of orange coral to give the piece some pop! (Yes, as always, there is a supporting cast of seed beads.) So as not to overwhelm the focal bead, I made my brooch five stitches wide and five stitches high.

Tools and Supplies: You will need a medium or large crochet hook; four to six yarns in different colors and textures (dare to make one of them an eyelash yarn!); a sewing needle (the size of which will depend on size of bead holes); thread (in a color that best blends with your yarn); orange coral, silver leaves, tendril-like

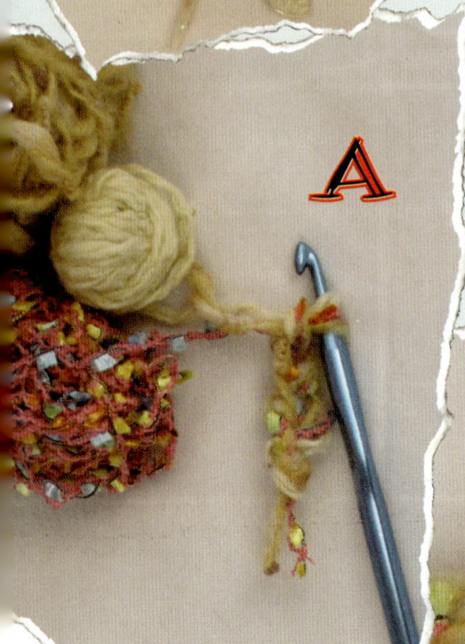

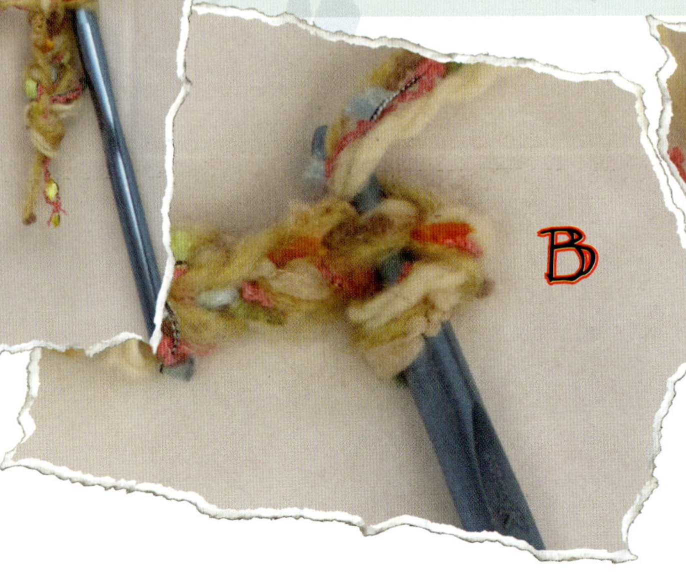

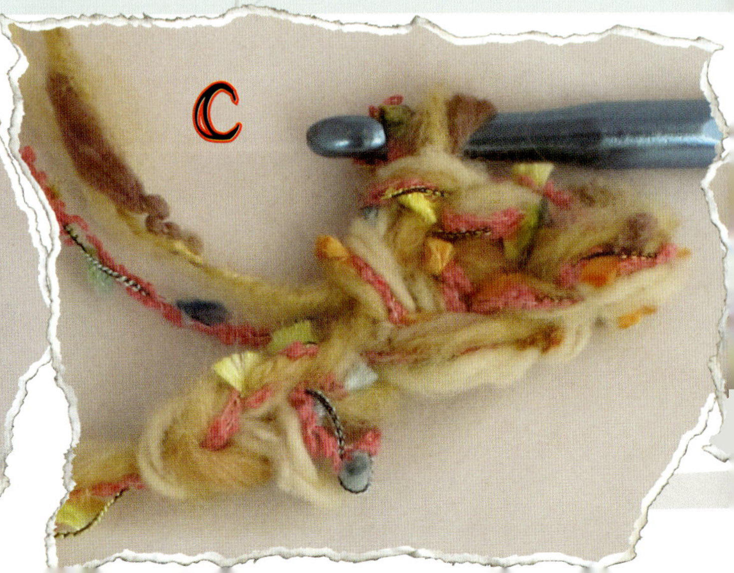

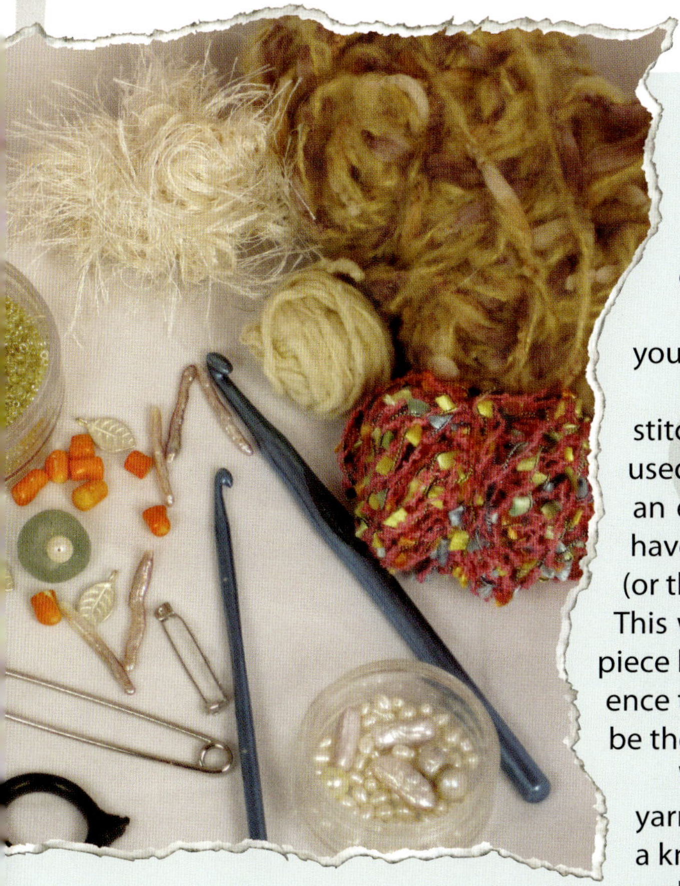

pearls, and a focal bead; size #8 or #9 seed beads, a sharp pair of scissors, and a kilt pin.

Let's begin. Using a large hook, crochet a foundation chain five chains long **{A.** (Don't forget to add the extra chain stitch before you turn around!)

Turning around with this project can feel clumsy because you are working with such a large amount of yarn. **{B & C**

Don't rush it when wiggling your hook between the stitches. It requires some finesse and can take a little getting used to. Then go back and do five single crochet stitches. Add an extra chain stitch and turn around. Repeat this until you have crocheted five rows high. Your piece should be square (or thereabouts!). Don't worry if your square is a little lopsided. This will just give your work character and individuality. (Each piece has a little life all its own!) For me, these "flaws" often influence the progress of the piece and spark my imagination. Let it be the same for you!

When you have completed your square, trim the excess yarn and finish the ends by using a needle and thread (with a knot on the end!) to make a series of small stitches through and over the ends until they are bound. **{D**

Then, using a small size hook and an eyelash yarn, crochet an edge around the square using a slip crochet stitch. (I used the off-white eyelash yarn.) Add an extra stitch at the corners by inserting your hook back into the corner of the square near where the yarn exits before continuing on. This will help keep your border from pulling the square into itself. **{E & F**

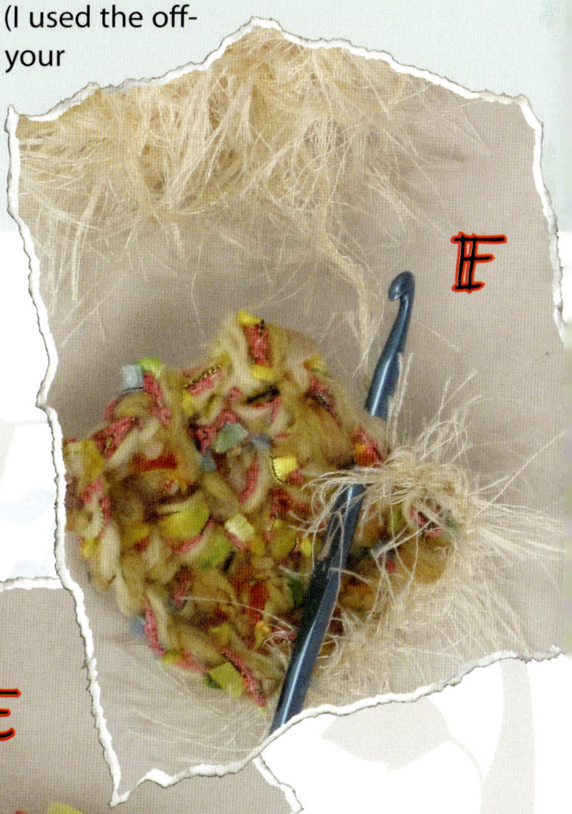

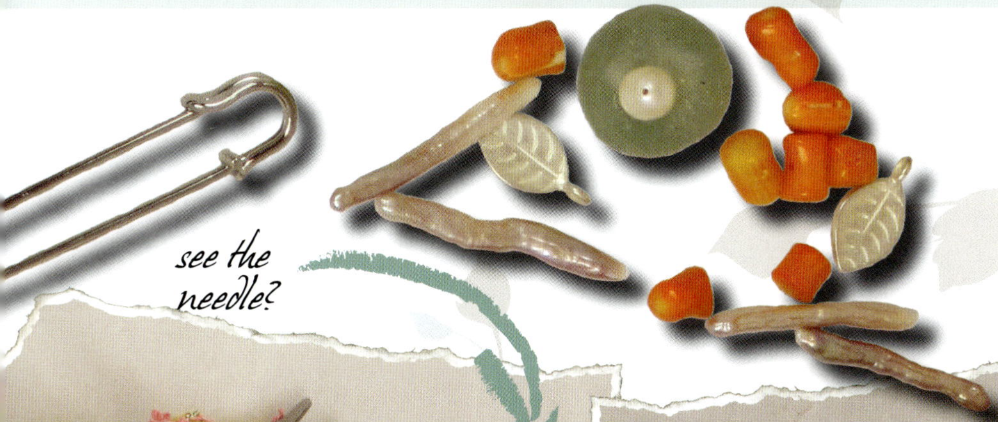

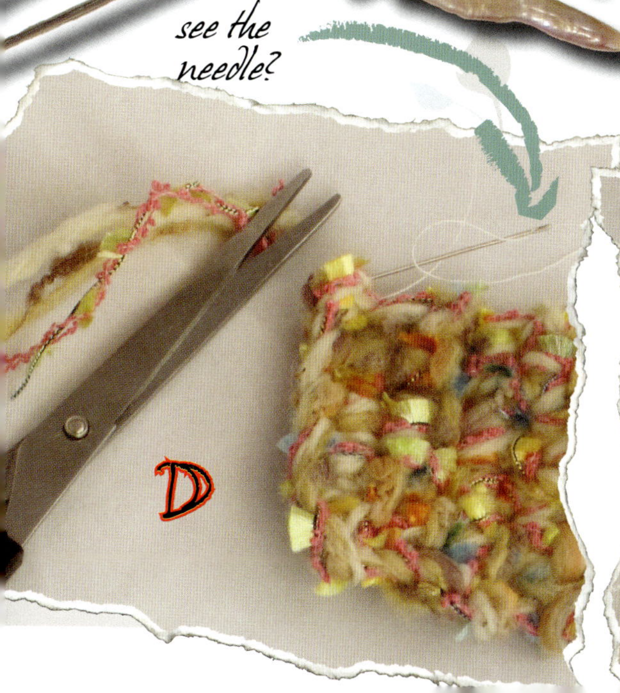

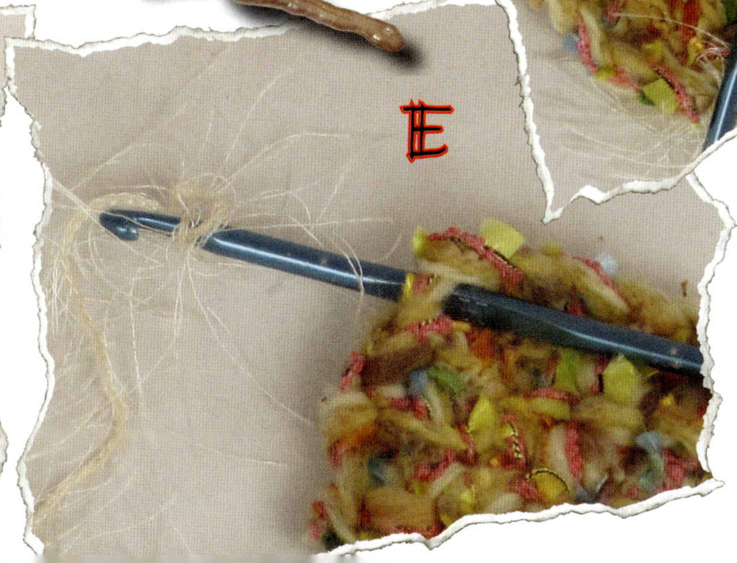

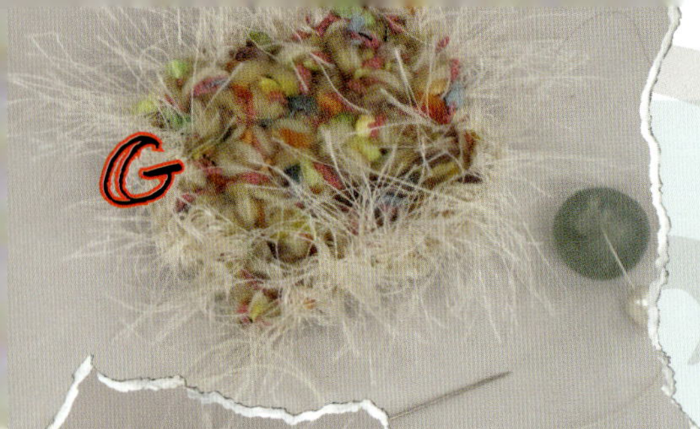

G

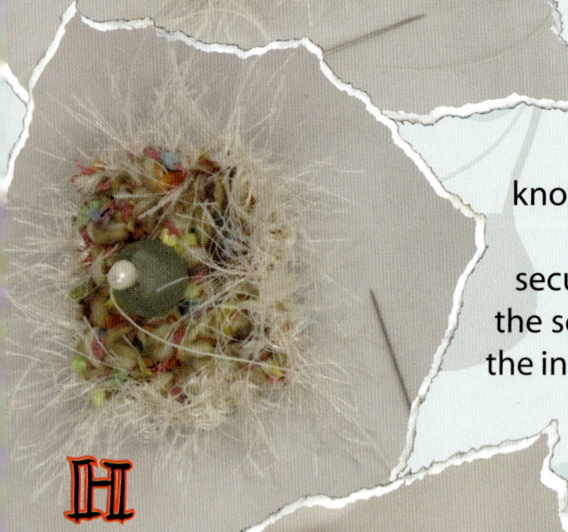

H

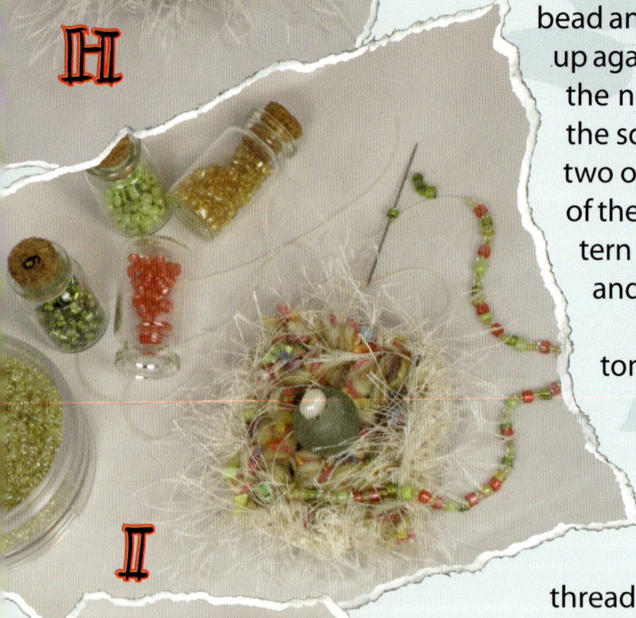

I

Time to add the sea glass bead! Using a needle and knotted thread, secure your thread to the center of the square. Make sure it's good and tight by giving it a tug. Then string your beads as follows: First, the sea glass bead. Second, a large round pearl. (Because the hole in the sea glass bead is so large, the pearl is needed as a stopper bead.) Then put the thread back through the sea glass bead and pull tight! You may have to fuss a little to get the stopper bead to sit just where you want it. If possible, go through the sea glass bead a second time before securely knotting the thread and cutting off the excess. {G & H

Next, add a squiggly line of beads just inside the edge of the border. First, secure your needle and thread (with a knot on the end!) near the border of the square. Then put enough beads onto the thread to go completely around the inside of the border. Sew the beads onto the inside of the border in a gently meandering pattern as follows: Pierce the needle back through the first bead and then down into the body of the square near the edge and back up again. Repeat that step using groups of two to three beads, i.e., pierce the needle through two or three beads, then down into the body of the square near the edge and back up again. You get the idea—every two or three beads, the strand of beads is being tacked onto the body of the square near the border. Continue in a squiggly and irregular pattern for the entire interior perimeter of the edge. Keep the feel organic and natural by not making a perfect square. {I, J & K

Now you must decide which side of your brooch will be the bottom so that it may be further embellished with some "tendrils." {L

First, decide approximately how many tendrils you want so that you can get an idea of the proper spacing. (Personally, I do not decide in advance; I just go until the piece "feels" complete. On my brooch I ended up with six tendrils.) Working from left to right (or right to left) securely attach approximately 18 inches of thread to the body of the square near the bottom at your chosen starting point. Then string the desired amount of #9 seed beads for your first tendril

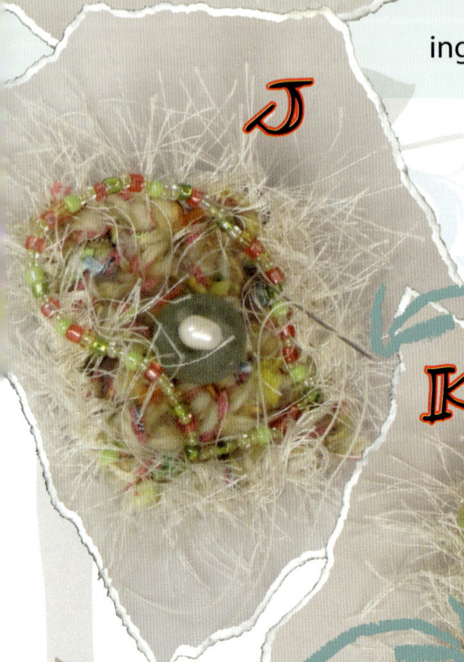

J

see the needle?

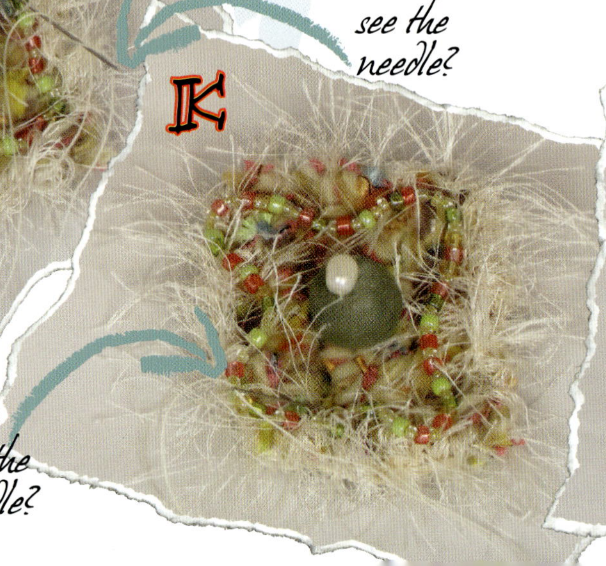

K

see the needle?

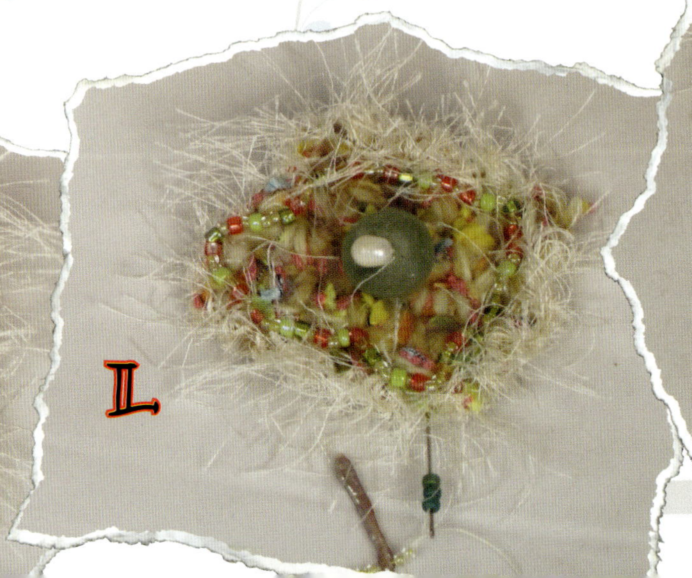

L

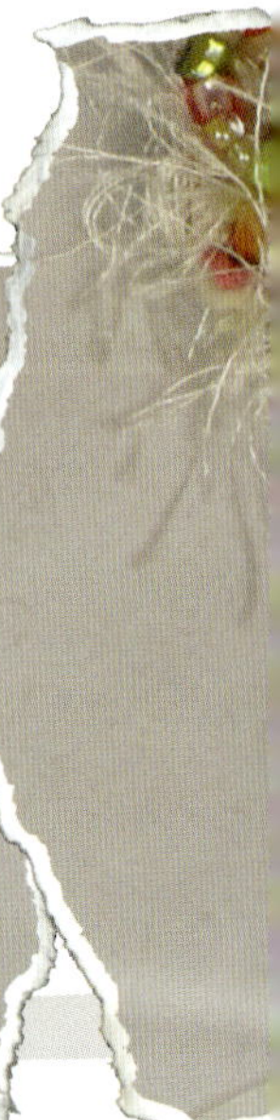

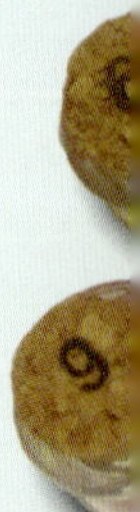

onto the thread. (I used three deep blue-green beads to accent the pale sea glass bead.)

Then string the end piece or stopper bead onto the thread. (I used either a fresh water pearl or a silver leaf. A little extra work is needed to hide the thread on a fresh water pearl because the hole is drilled horizontally and somewhat down the body of the pearl. I added two smaller seed beads on each side of the pearl to hide the thread. With the leaves, I just went through the hole.) **{M & N**

Once the end piece or stopper bead is strung, thread the needle back up through the seed beads and into the body of the square. Secure the thread to the body of the square, but do not cut! Rather, use the thread to complete your tendrils. Using the same technique, make different length tendrils across the bottom of the brooch.

Personally, I think it looks best when the tendrils are longer near the middle. This creates a "V" shape that is pleasing to the eye. Get inspired! Add accent beads (like the orange coral I used) or vary the end pieces! To nudge the symmetry and make my brooch feel a little more organic, I added some blue-green seed beads with a large flat pearl at one of the corners. **{O & P**

As a last, finishing touch I let three sand-colored seed beads with a dangling silver leaf peek out from behind the sea glass bead **{Q & R**

Finally, properly orient your square onto the pin back near the top of the piece (so that it hangs correctly) and stitch it securely in place. That's it! **{S**

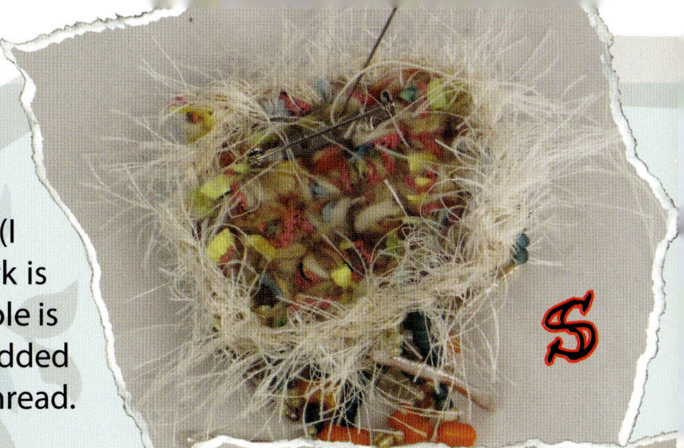

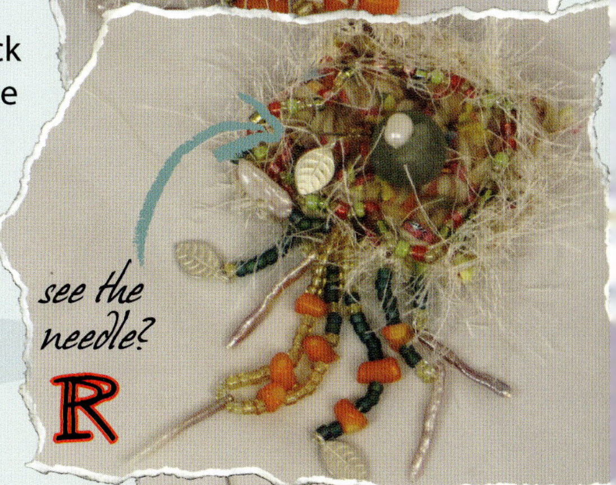

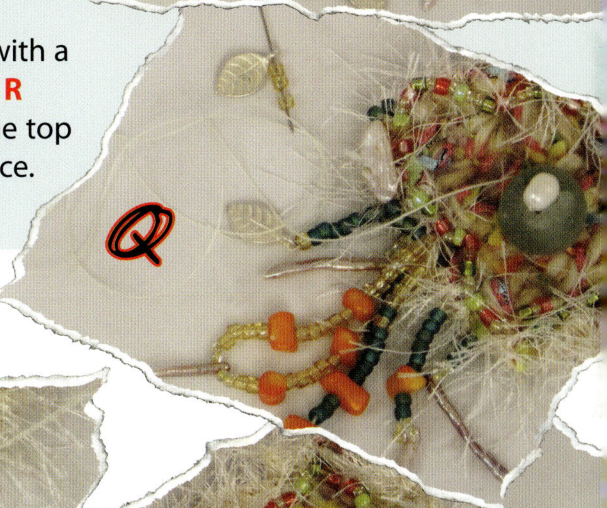

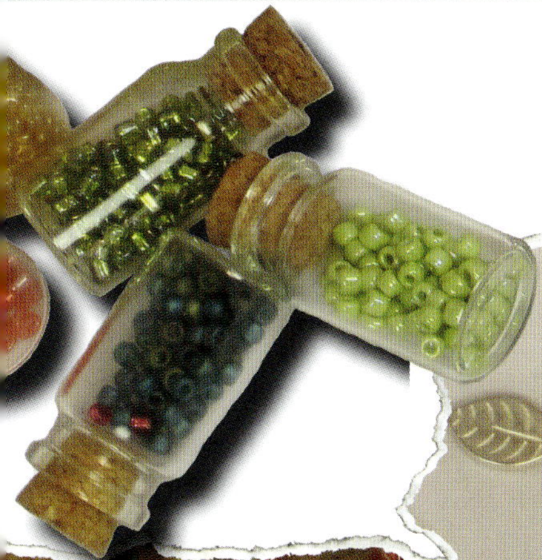

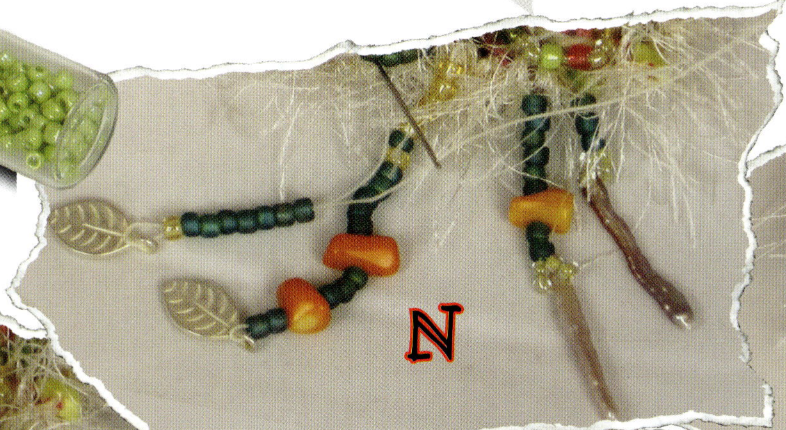

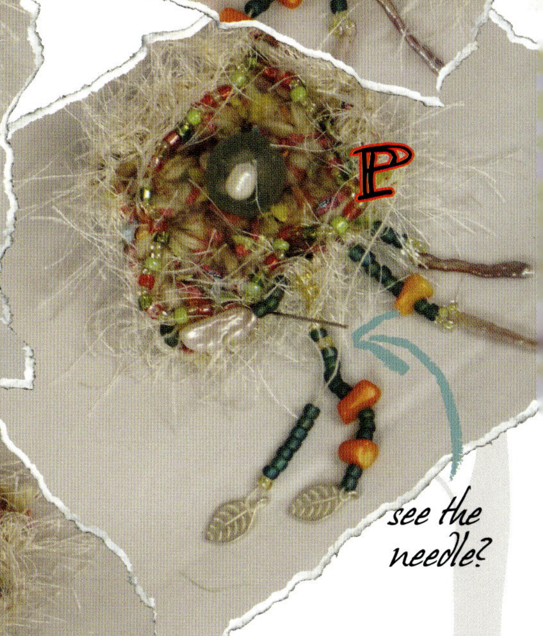

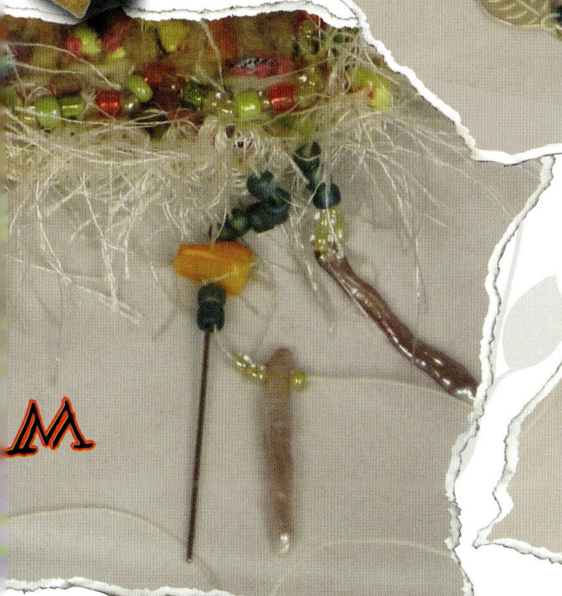

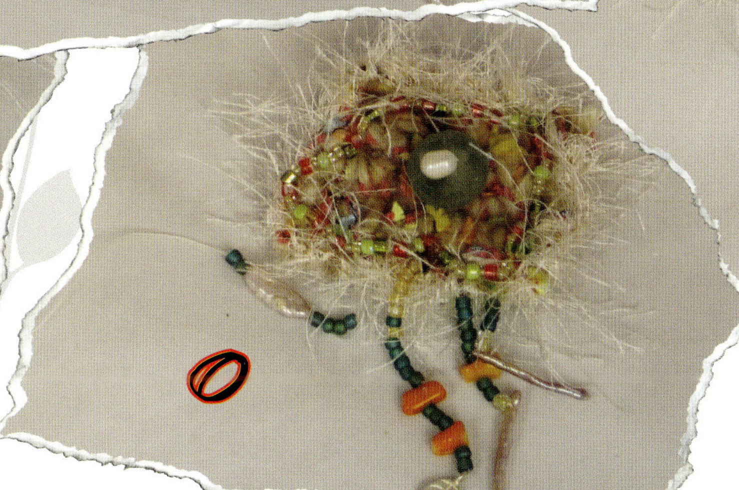

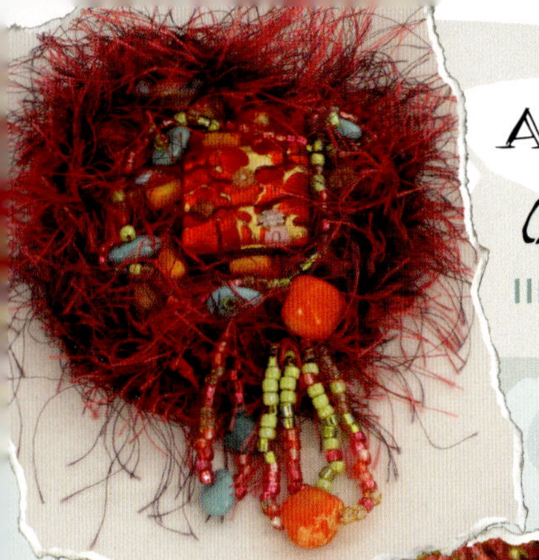

ANOTHER CLOAK PIN
(A Ten-Stitch Chunky Cloak Pin)

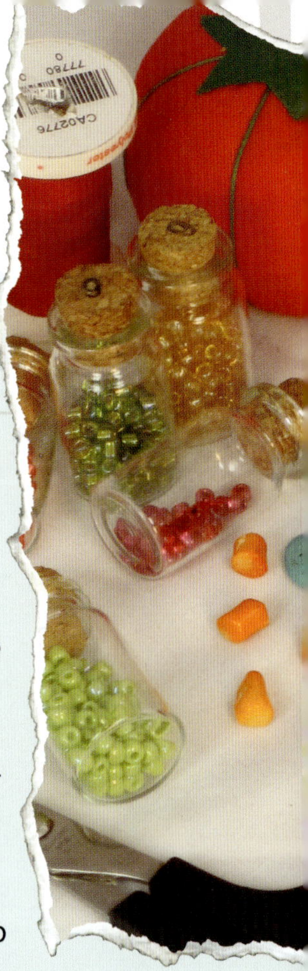

Tools and Supplies: I started by selecting my materials. For yarns, I chose a pink/multi colored confetti, a deep red faux angora, a sandy yellow faux angora, an eggplant faux angora, a hot pink eyelash and a deep purple eyelash. For beads, I chose a square red Murano glass chunk, #9 seed beads in hot pink, salmon, two greens and a sandy yellow. (The Murano glass was a special gift schlepped back from Italy by my friend Lesley.) I also chose some bright orange coral chunks and blue turquoise bits.

I crocheted a foundation chain ten stitches long using all of the yarns except the deep purple eyelash yarn. Then I crocheted ten rows of single crochet stitches to make a square. **{A & B**

Next, I crocheted an eyelash yarn border around the square. I doubled up the hot pink and the deep purple for a super fluffy look. **{C & D**

I securely stitched my Murano glass chunk onto the center of my square. (Yea, Lesley!) **{E**

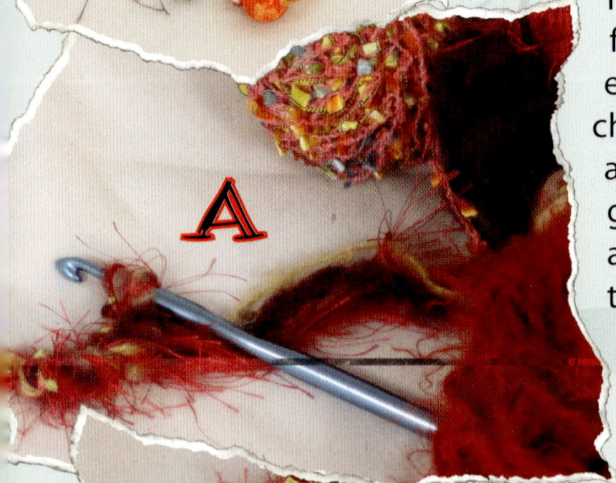

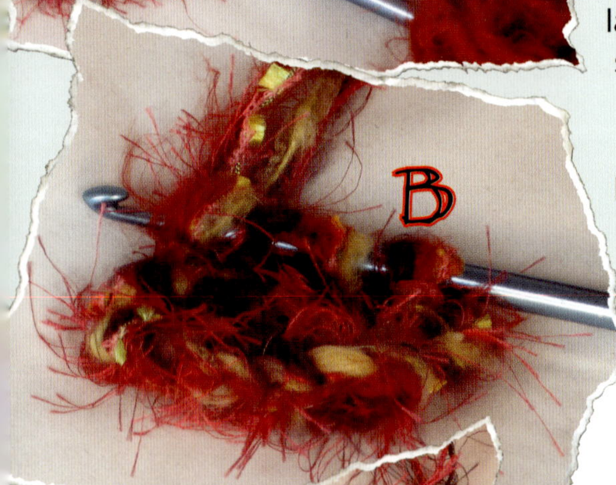

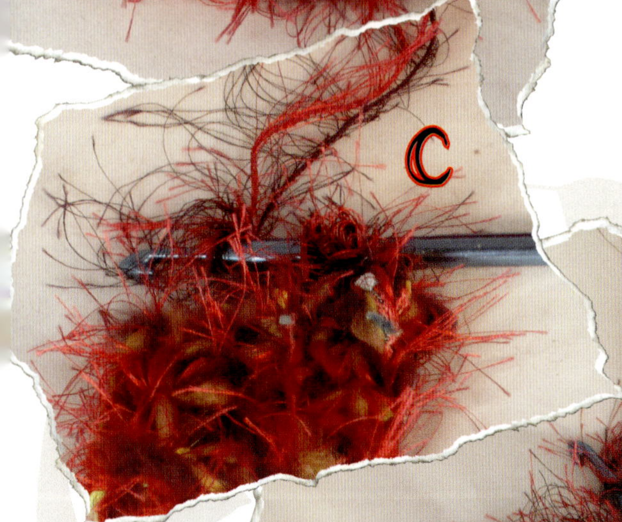

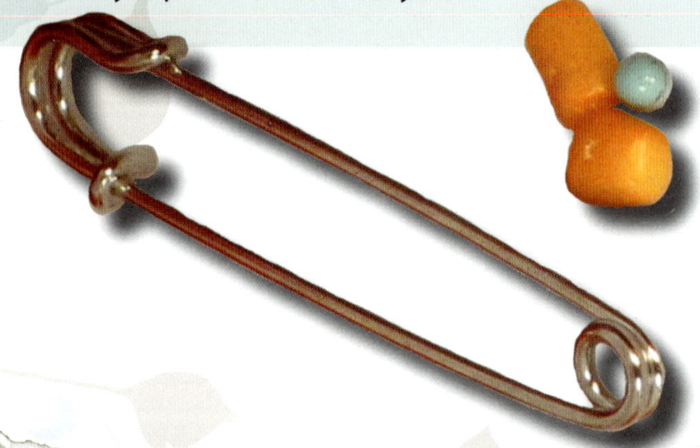

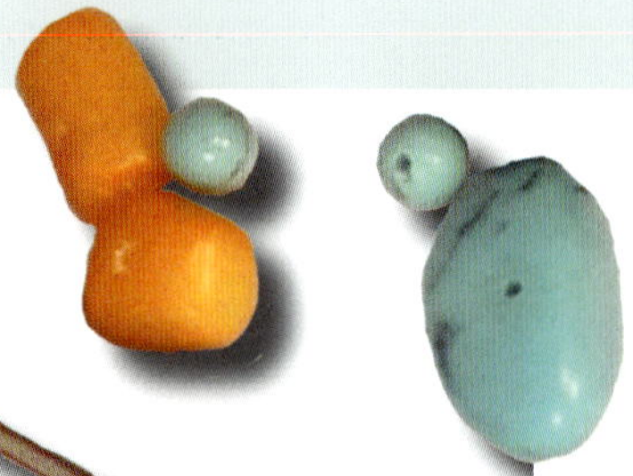

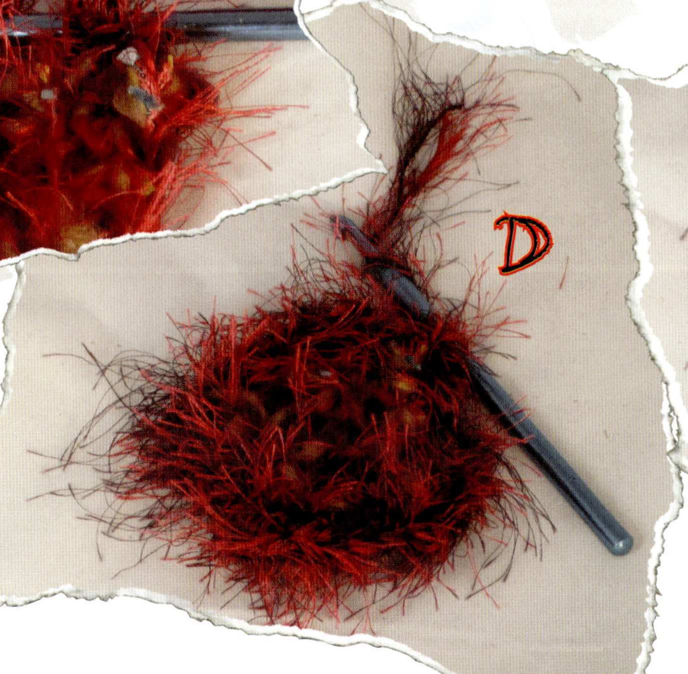

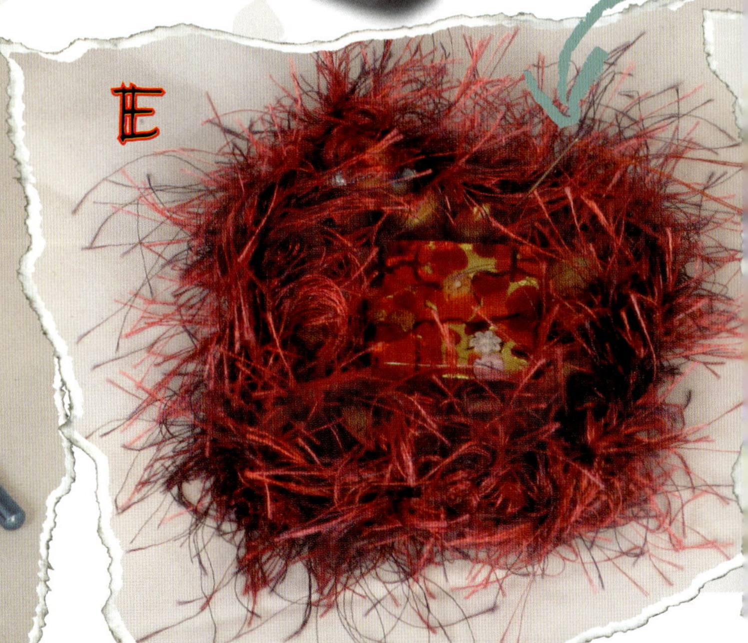

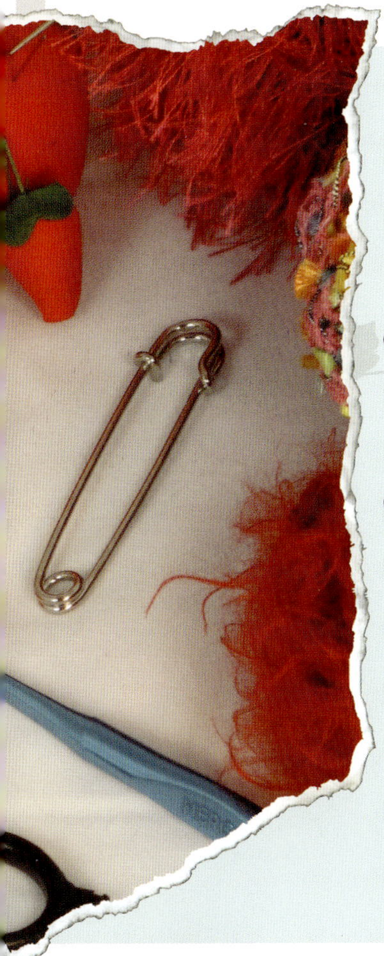

A meandering strand of seed beads was strung and stitched down around the glass square. I made sure that the strand was long enough for plenty of squiggles and twists! **{F, G, & H**

I then added accents by tucking chunks of turquoise and bits of coral among the squiggly lines, using seed beads as stoppers. **{I, J, & K**

A large chunk of coral was sewn onto one side of the square, off of which I dangled three swags of beads **{L**. (Hey Suzy, what is the difference between a tendril and swag? Good question! For a tendril, the thread goes back up the same line of beads it came down through after exiting the end piece or stopper bead, resulting in a single strand. For a swag, the thread does not go back up the beads. Rather, it is re-attached back to the square near where it starts, to form a dangly loop or "swag.")

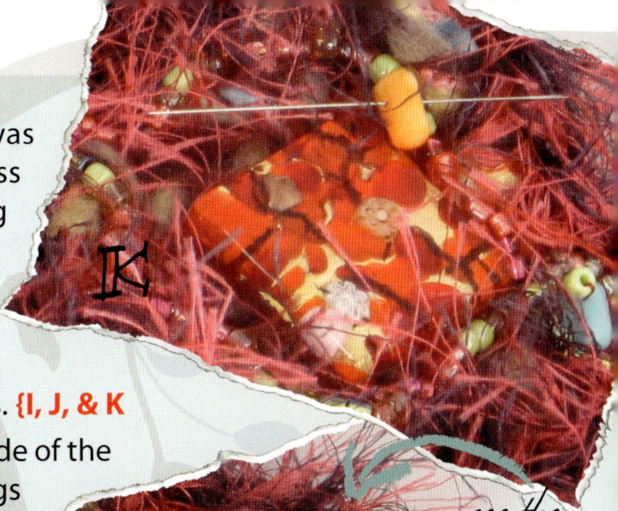

K

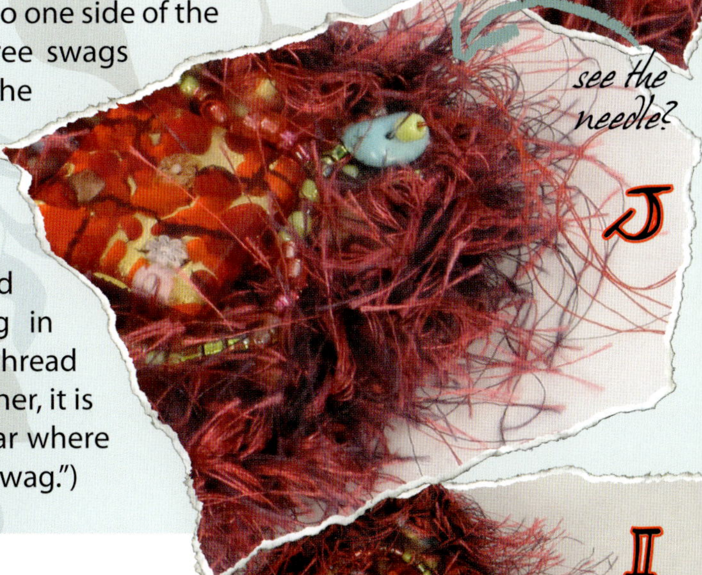

see the needle?

J

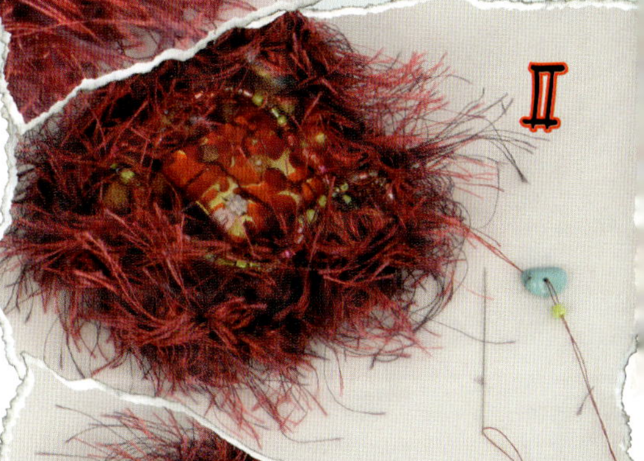

I

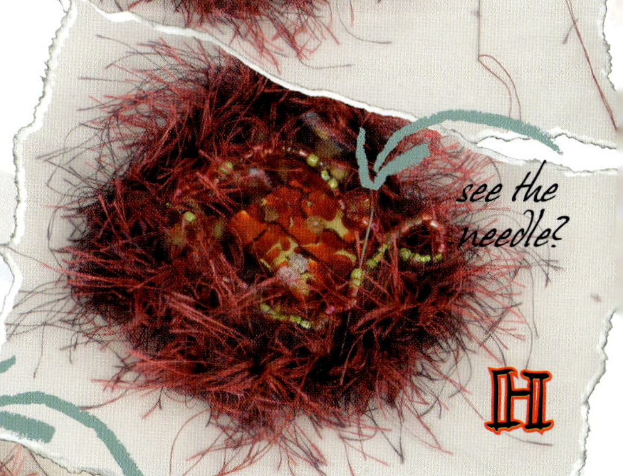

see the needle?

H

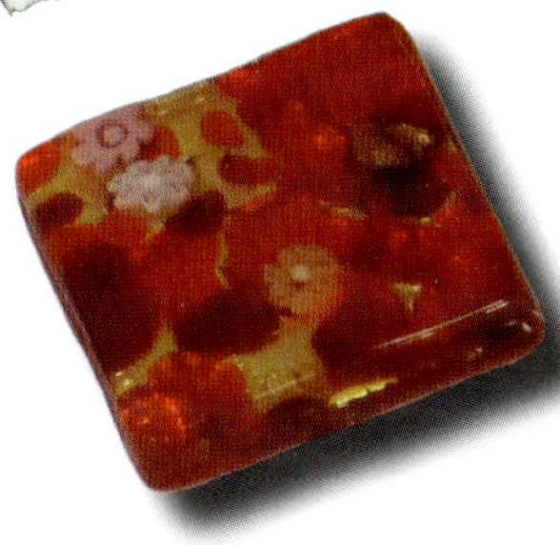

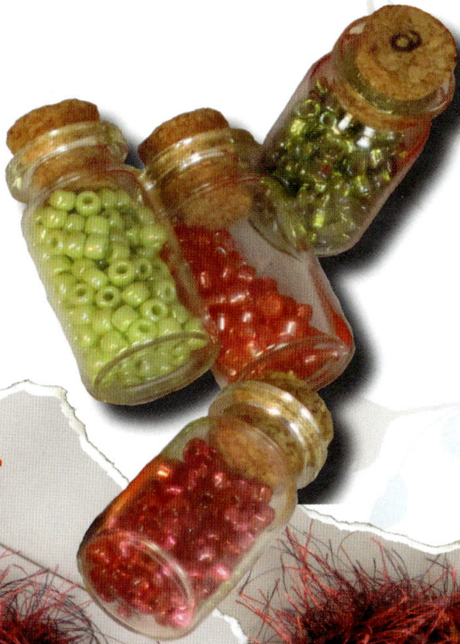

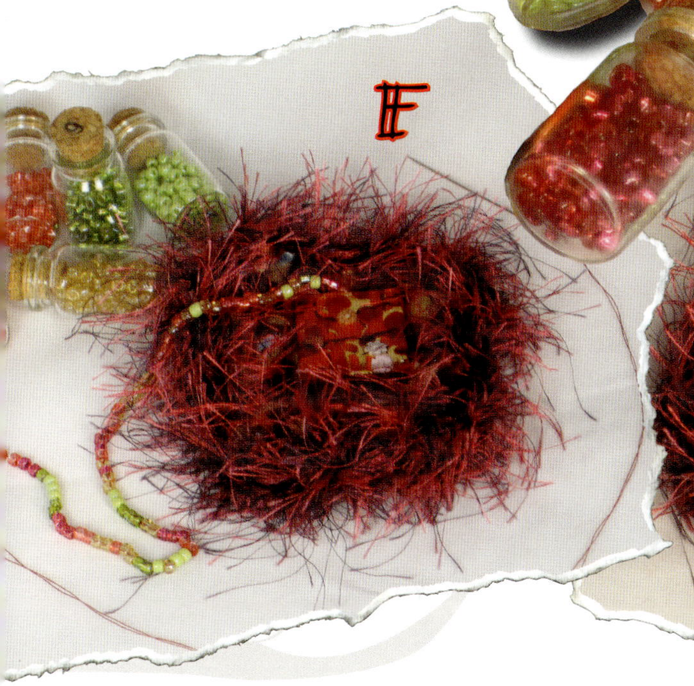

F

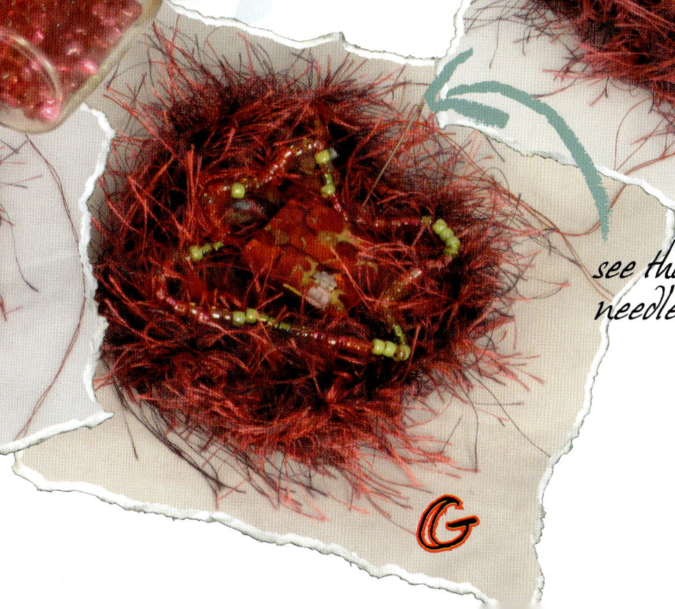

see the needle?

G

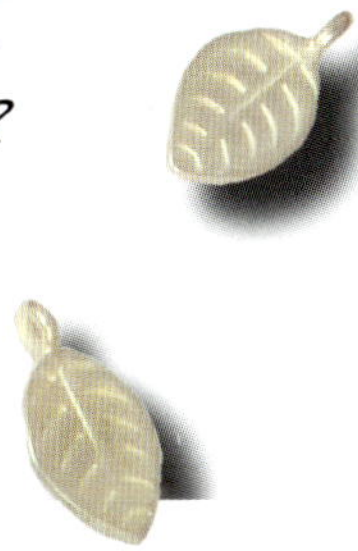

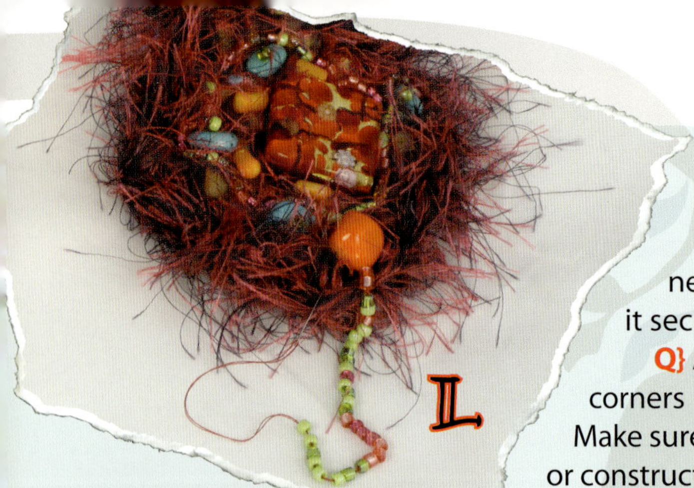

L

If you want, accent beads may be added along the strand for a little extra oomph! {M, N & O
Finally, I properly oriented the square onto the pin back near the top of the piece (so that it hangs correctly) and stitched it securely in place. DONE! {P
Q} Another variation is to add a foundation chain to the top two corners of your square and transform your brooch into a necklace! Make sure the foundation chain is long enough to slip over your head, or construct it so it has a toggle in back (as in the solo pendant project).

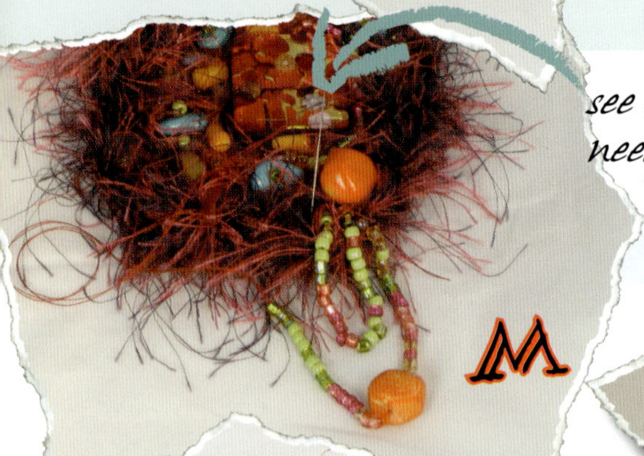

see the needle?

M

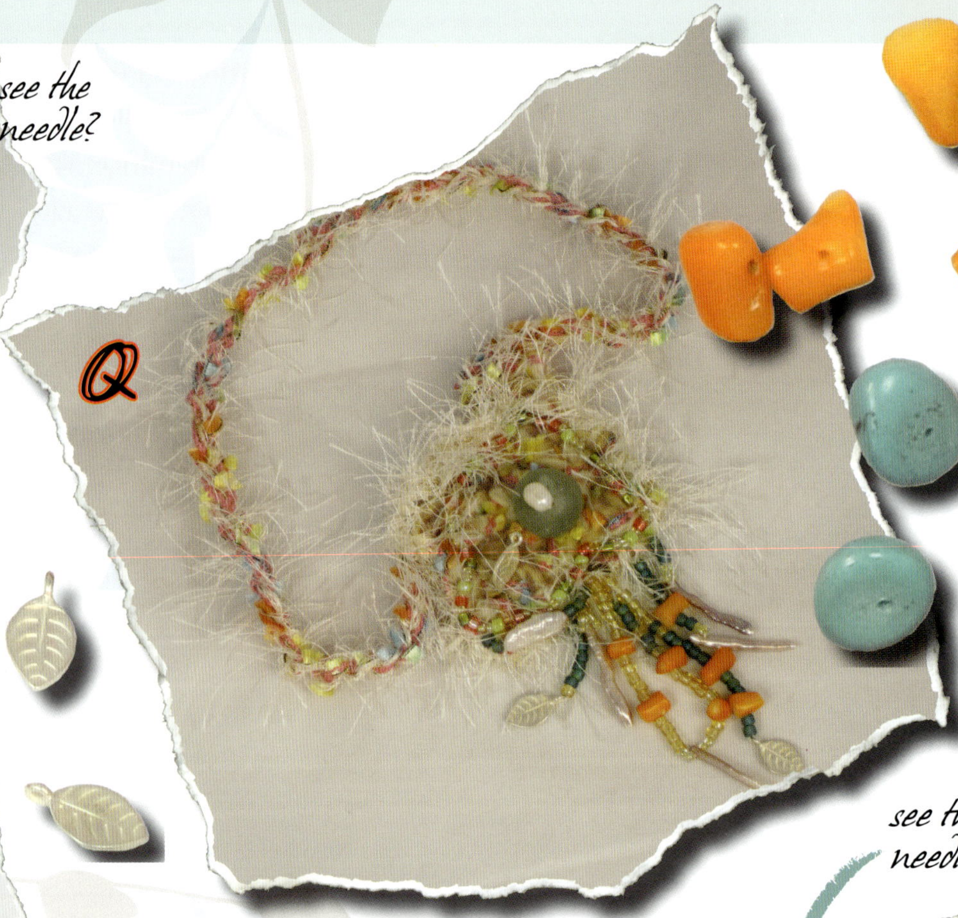

Q

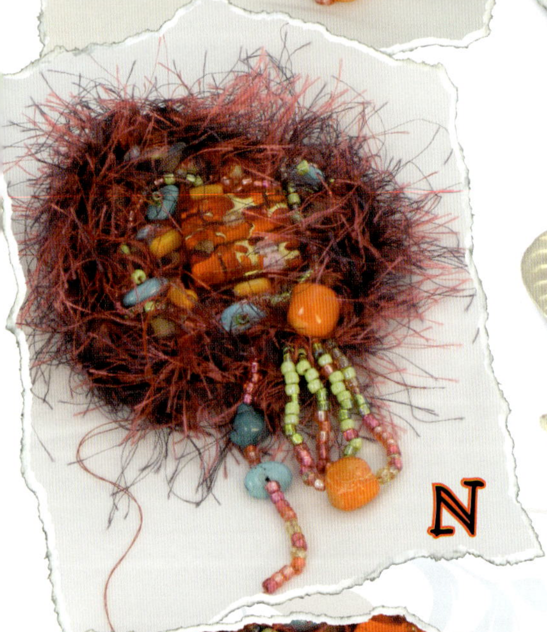

N

see the needle?

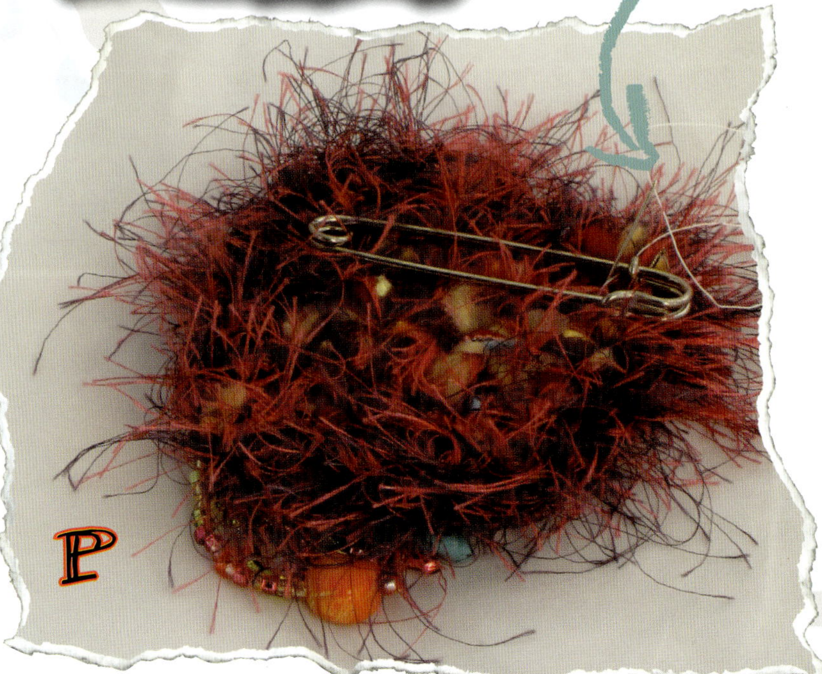

P

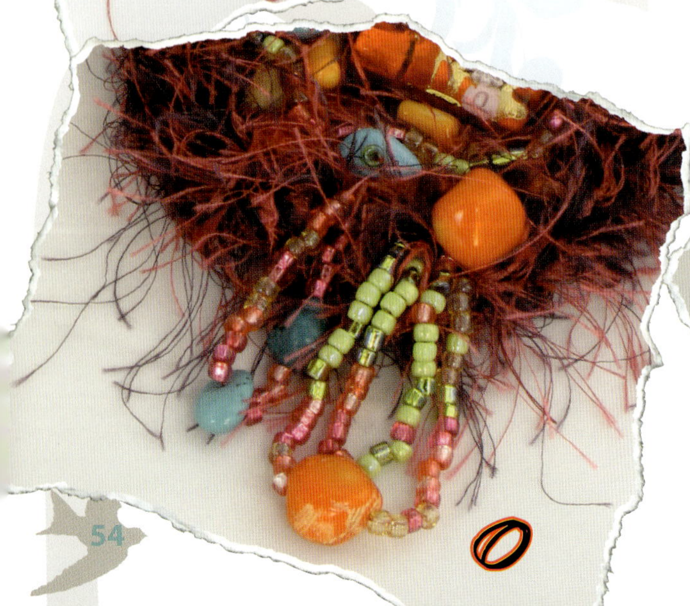

O

CHAPTER EIGHT

Grandma Terri's Necklace

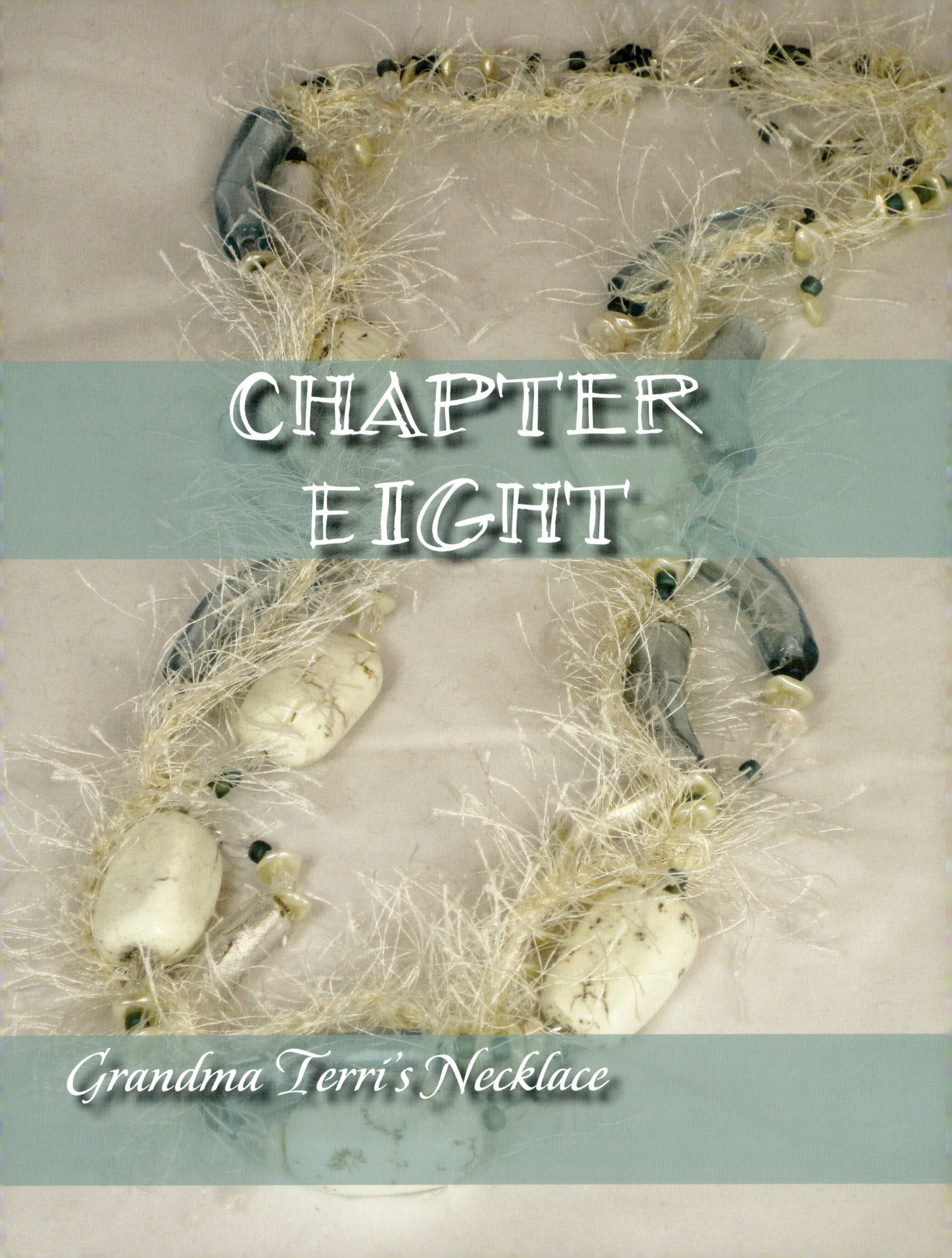

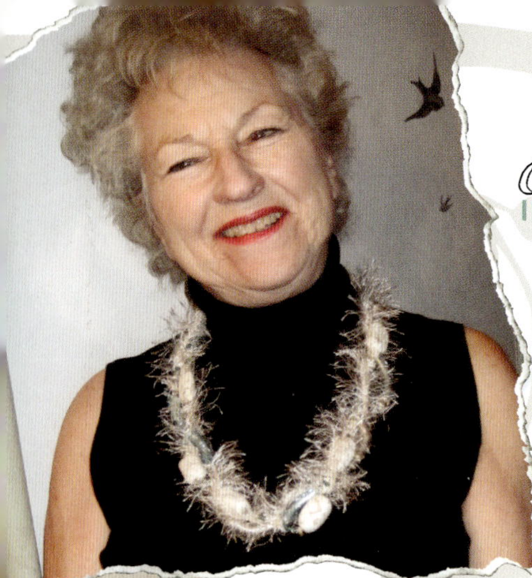

GRANDMA TERRI'S NECKLACE

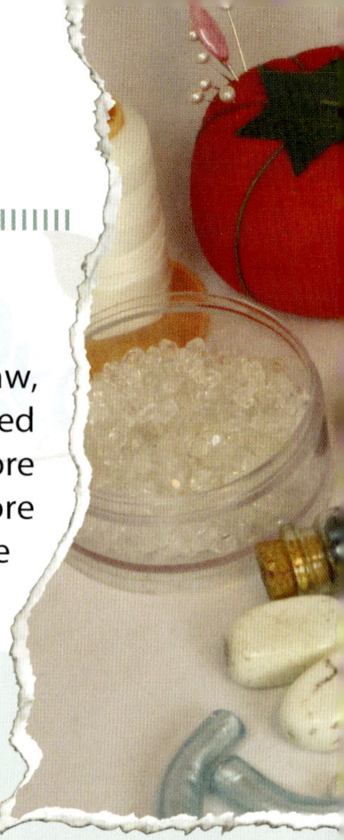

This necklace was designed for my mother-in-law, whose tastes run toward the classic (at least compared to mine!). Determined to tone down my usual more flamboyant approach and create something a little more wearable, I ended up with a half-beaded, half-fiber necklace that has become one of my most popular designs.

Supplies and tools: Wire cutters, pliers, scissors, beading wire, assorted beads, crimp beads, eyelash yarn, needle and thread, a toggle or clasp, and a large crochet hook.

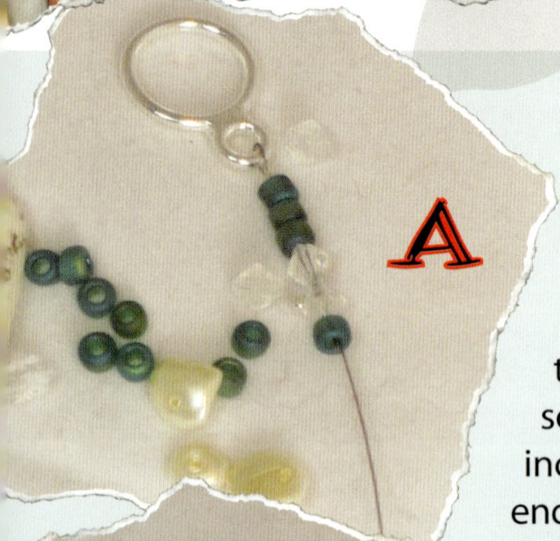

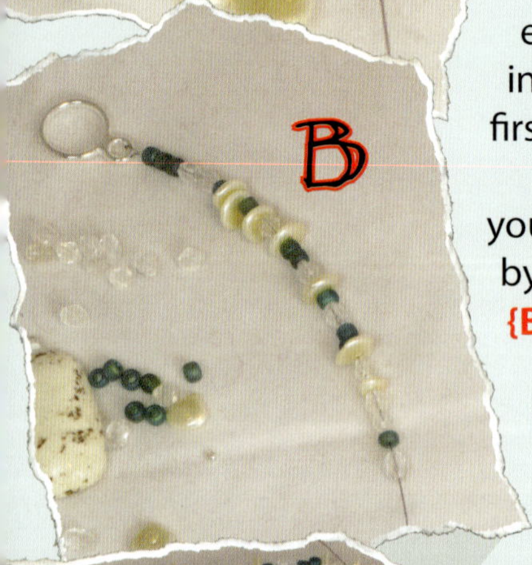

The first step is to make a traditional strung-bead necklace. You can make the necklace any length you want. I chose to make mine around 30 inches long, so that it would be nice and long and "drapey." Accordingly, I cut approximately 35 inches of wire to work with. Following the basic beading instructions, thread one end of the wire through a crimp bead, through one end of the toggle, and back down into the crimp bead. Leave enough extra wire so that it can be threaded through the first couple of beads (at least four). This will give your necklace strength. **{A**

Using your pliers, squish (crimp) the crimp bead. Now you can begin stringing your beads. I strung my beads in a random pattern. I maintained a balanced feeling by keeping my larger focal beads spaced approximately the same distance apart. **{B, C, & D**

When you are close to reaching your desired length, fold your necklace gently in half to make sure that the sides "match." (It doesn't have to be matchy-matchy. It can be a rough balance.) When done, finish off the necklace by threading the wire through another crimp bead, then through the (other!) end of the toggle, and back through the crimp bead, and down through the last few beads (at least four). Using your pliers, squish (crimp) the crimp bead. Finally, cut the excess wire as close as possible to the last of your final beads. **{E & F**

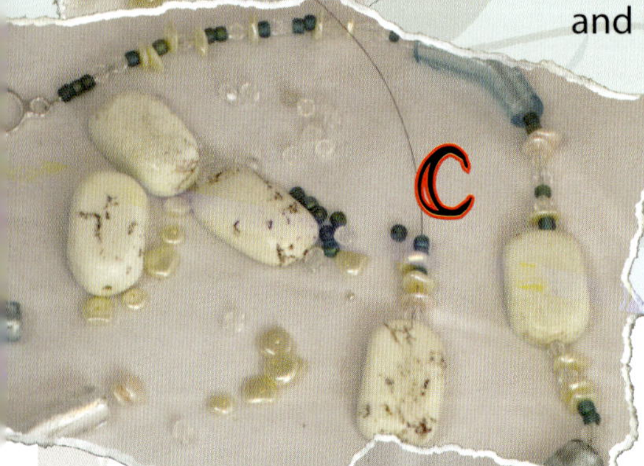

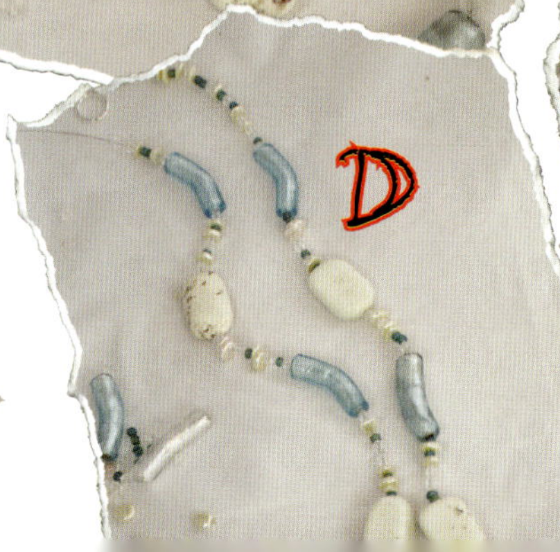

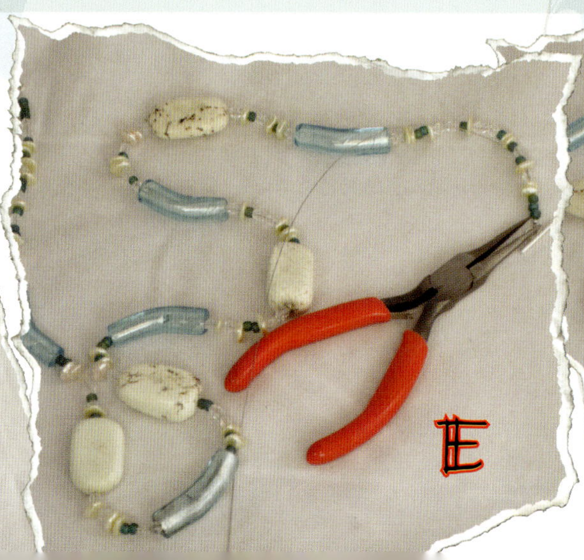

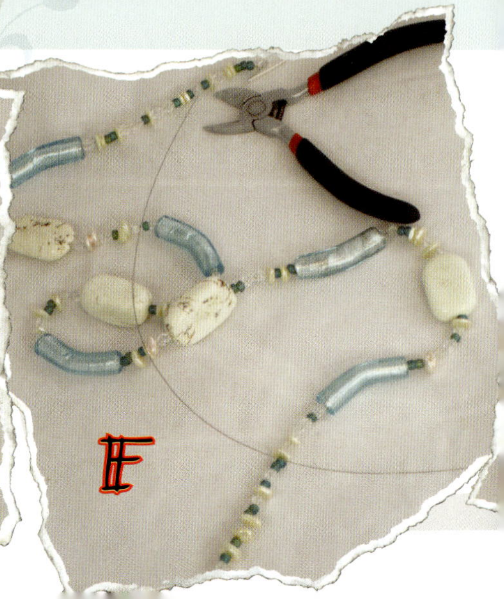

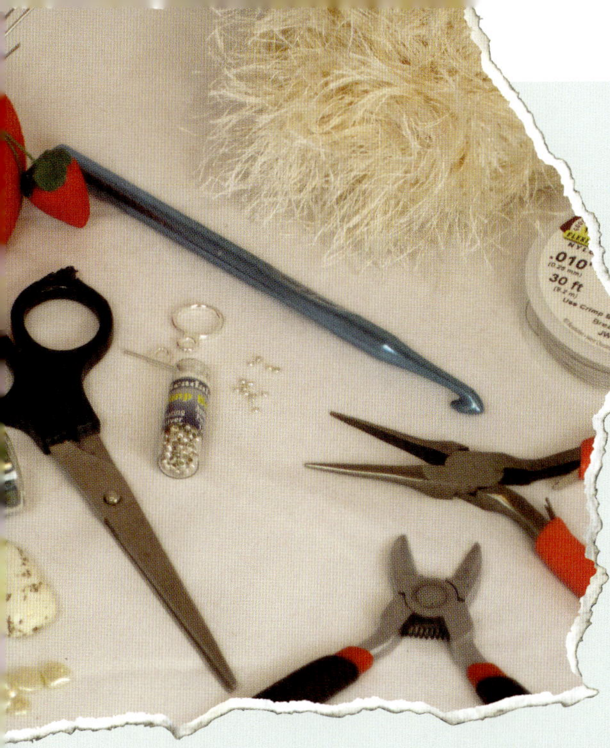

Now it's time to add the fiber! Knot a piece of eyelash yarn onto one end of your toggle. Then, putting your hook behind your beads, hook a loop of yarn and pull it around and through to make your first foundation chain stitch. Then make approximately 4 inches of foundation chain stitch. **{G & H**

When done, repeat the first crochet step; that is, put the hook behind the beads, hook a loop of yarn and pull it around. This will result in the fiber being attached to the beads every 4 inches of so by a single foundation chain stitch. Repeat until you finish the entire length of the necklace. Finish by tying the yarn to the other end of the toggle and cutting off the excess. **{I, J, & K**

With a needle and a thread (with a knot on the end!) stitch the knot of the fiber down on each end to prevent it from coming undone or fraying **{L**. And, again, violà! You're done!

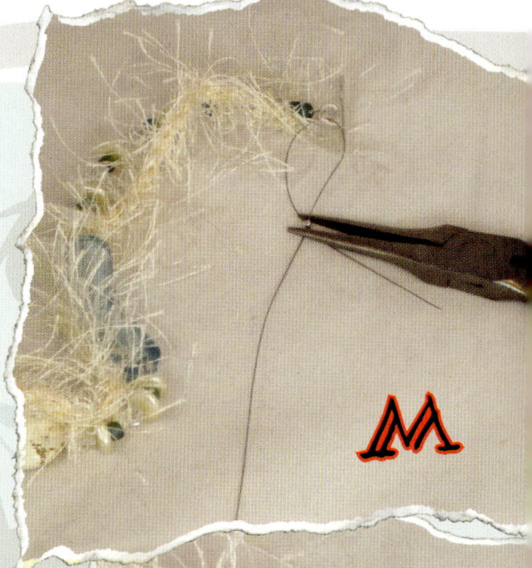

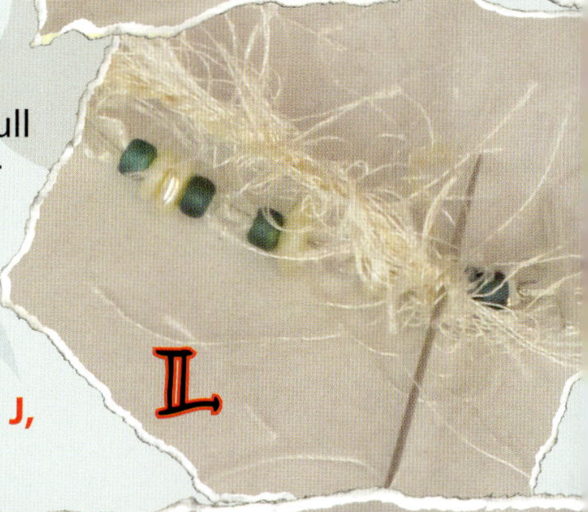

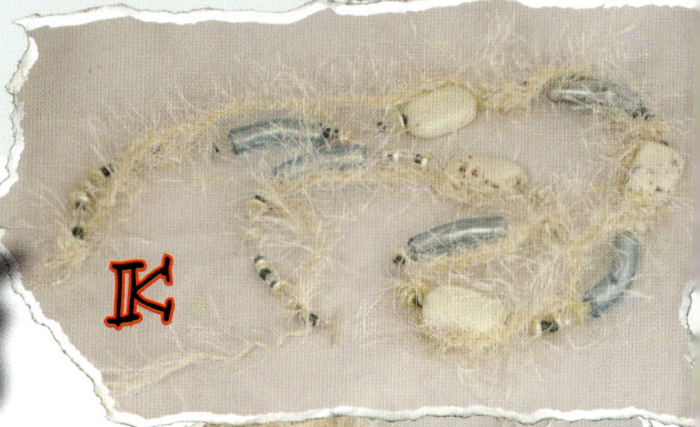

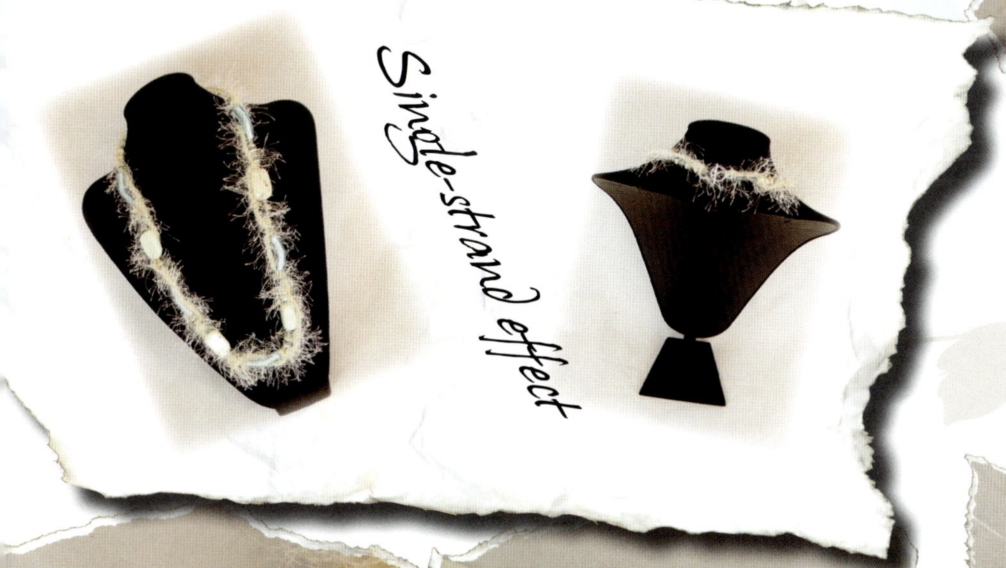

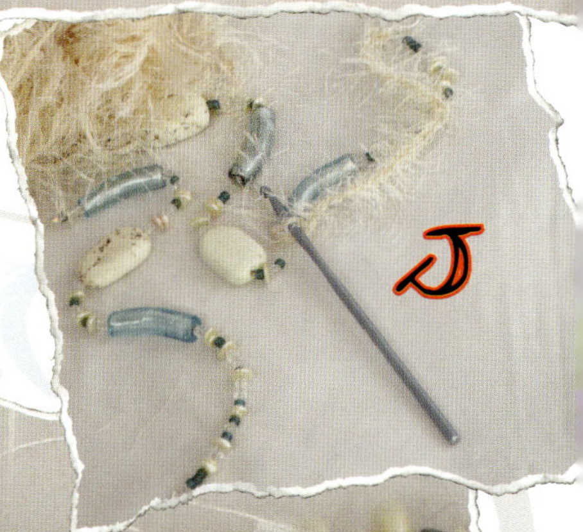

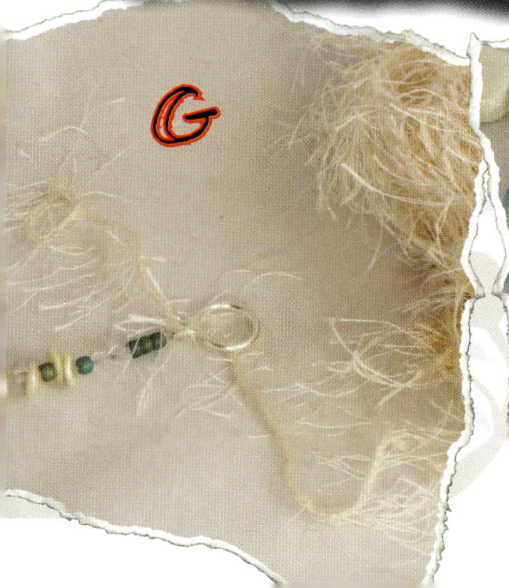

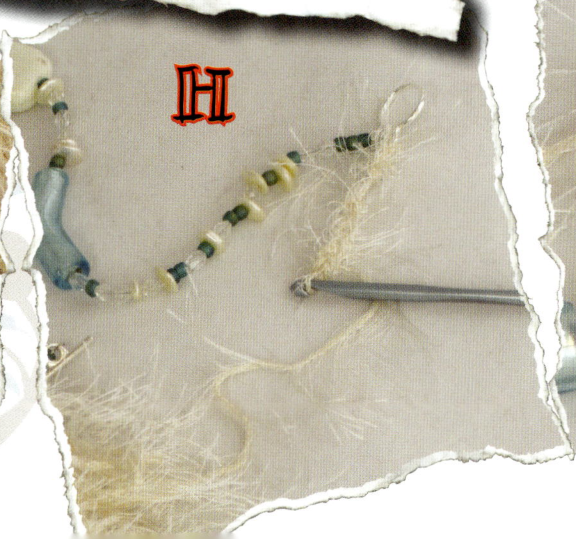

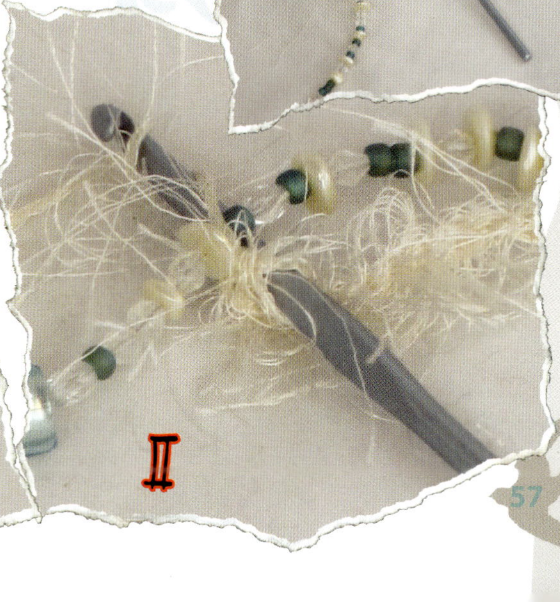

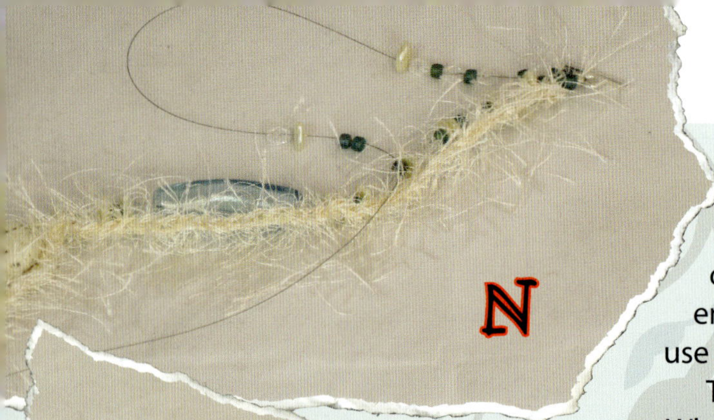

However, if you want to add a little extra bling, you can add another string of beads as follows: thread the end of a new wire through a crimp bead, through one end of toggle, and back down through the crimp bead. Leaving enough extra wire to thread through the first couple of beads, use your pliers to squish (crimp) the crimp bead. {M Then thread approximately 4 inches of beads onto the wire. When done, thread the wire through a bead on the already finished string of beads at approximately the same place as the fiber is attached. Pull the wire snug and bead another 4 inches or so of wire. You get the idea, you are mimicking the fiber "loops" with bead "loops." (Sorta like a DNA double helix!) Remember to pull each interval snug before proceeding, otherwise you'll end up with a droopy mess! When you reach the other end, repeat the process above—thread the end of a new wire through a crimp bead, through one end of toggle, and back down through the crimp bead and the last few beads (for strength). Using your wire cutters, trim the wire {N – R. Now it is fab-u-lous!

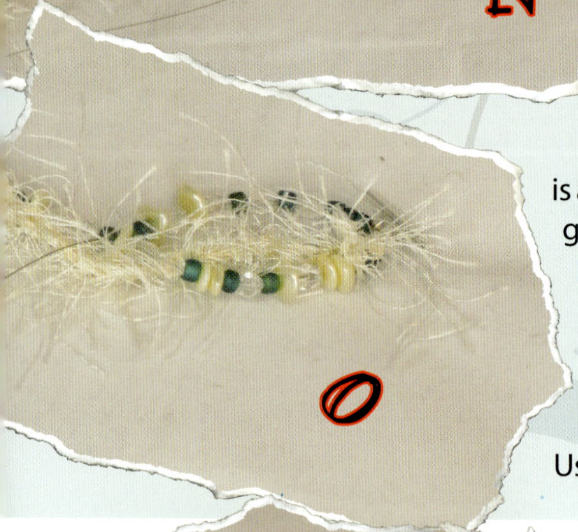

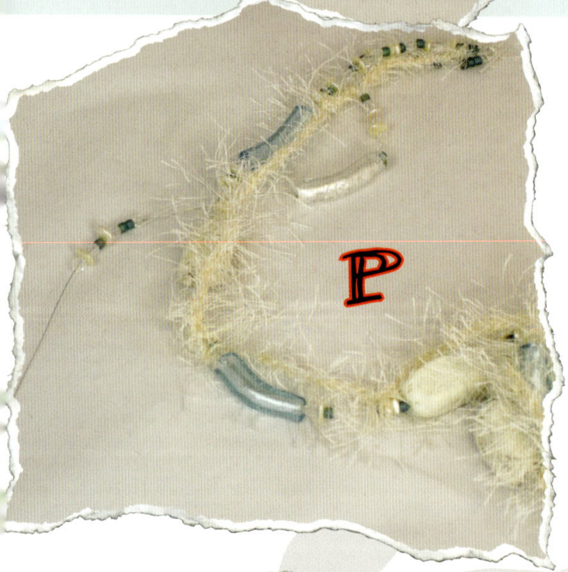

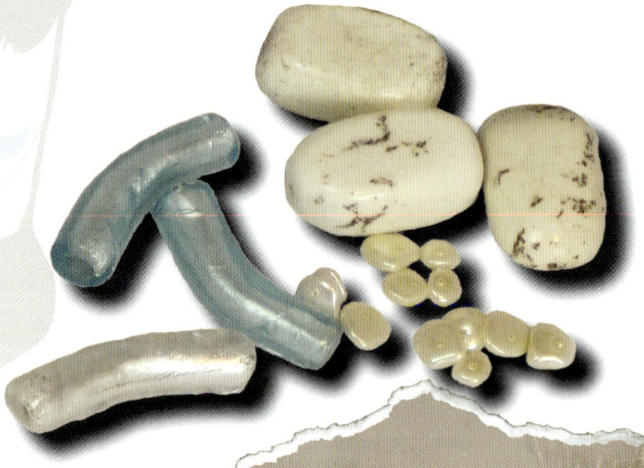

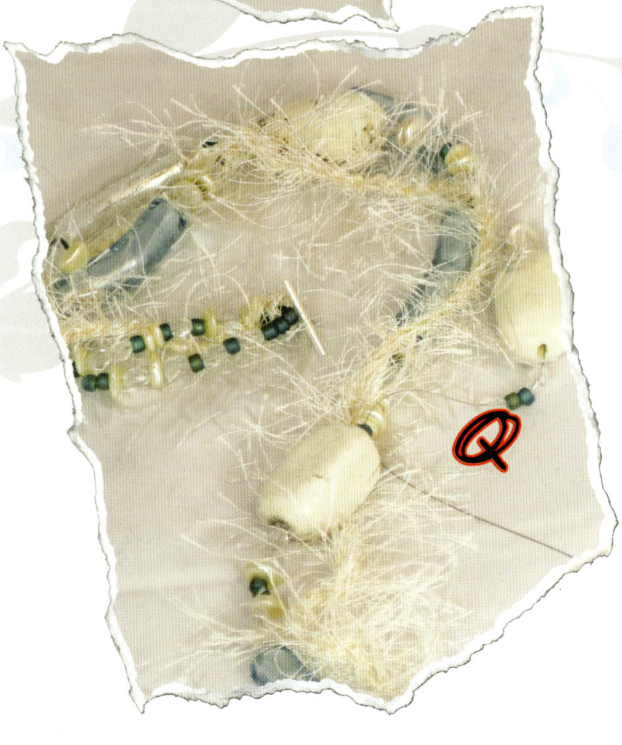

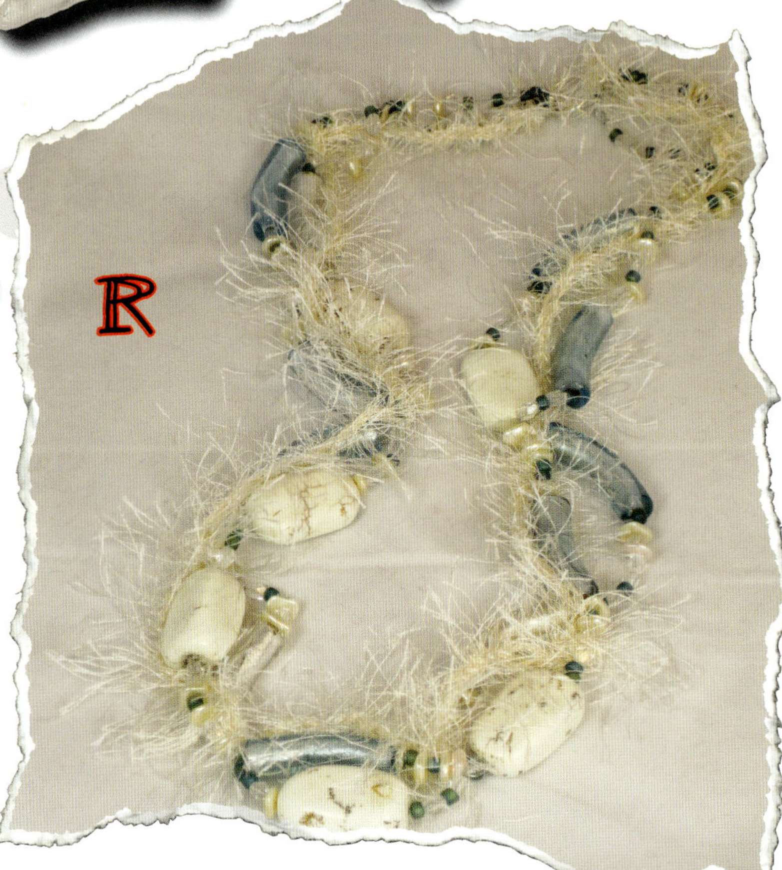

CHAPTER NINE

The Cuff Bracelet

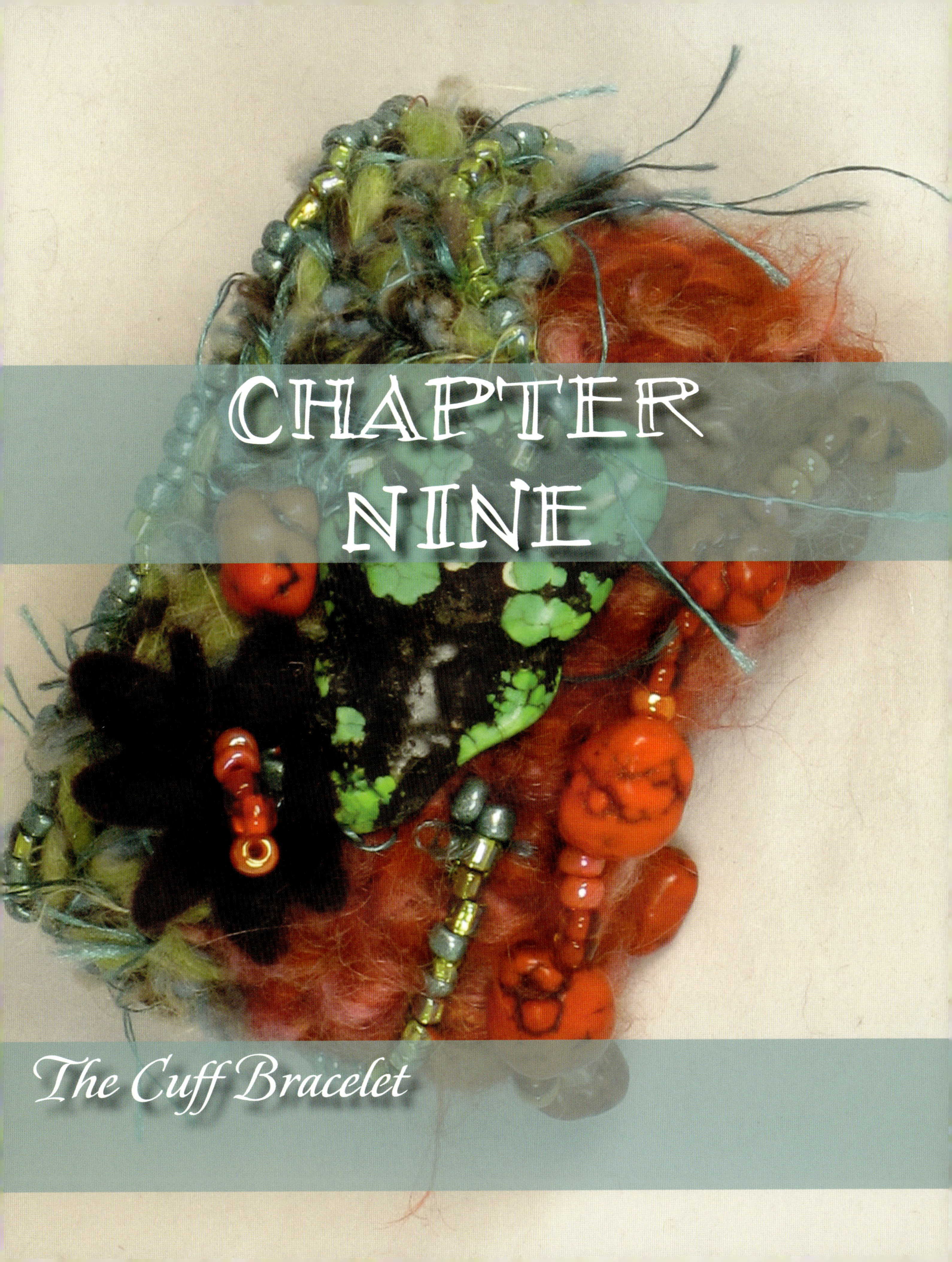

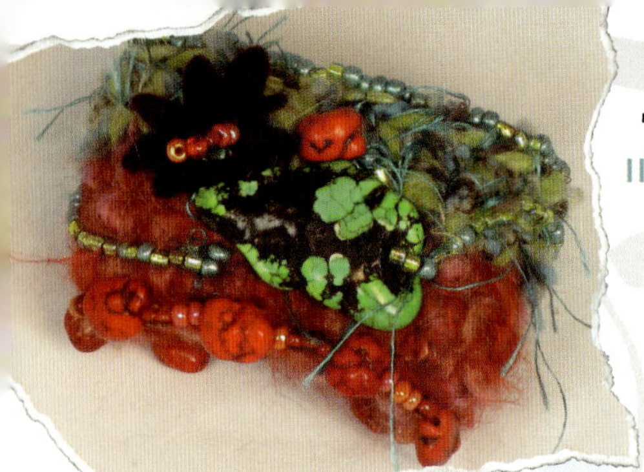

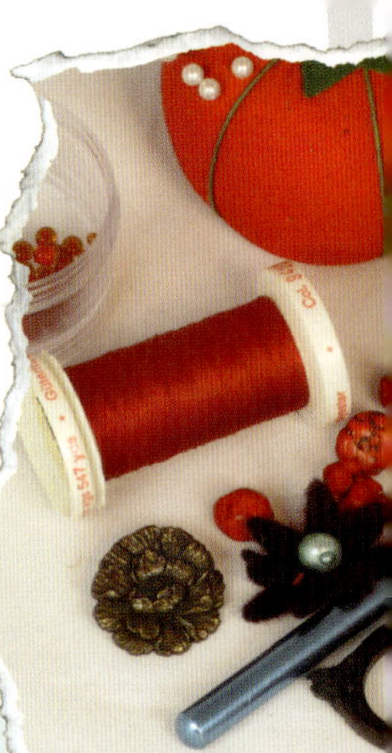

THE CUFF BRACELET

The project in this chapter is my take on a Native American bracelet. I love the bold statement that a wide cuff of silver and turquoise makes on a wrist (I wear one often when I go out!). The great thing about this design is that you can embellish the body of the cuff to whatever level you desire. You can keep it simple with just fiber or a single large stone, or you can go wild and throw in the kitchen sink!

In my example, I got a little carried away. The cuff just kept crying out for more stones and seed beads! The result is pretty terrific and I decided to make it a Christmas gift for my pal Reagan (who shares my passion for turquoise and Native American jewelry). I can't wait to give it too her!

Tools and Supplies: I used five yarns for this project—a red angora (synthetic), pink angora (synthetic), a teal and a brown bouclé, a light green angora (synthetic), and a deep teal eyelash yarn. The focal bead is a chunk of green turquoise with a fantastic black vein running right through the middle. I also used 10 to 20 small pieces of red coral for the outer trim, red, pink, green and turquoise-blue #9 seed beads, a burgundy/brown felt flower, and a brass button. Also needed are a fine sewing needle and strong thread, sharp scissors, and a medium to large crochet hook.

I have a friend w suffers from aches and pains in her wri bones; she says that her cuff keeps her wrist toasty warm!

Let's begin! First, crochet a foundation chain with your red and pink angora yarns sufficient to wrap around the circumference of your wrist leaving a 1" to 1-1/2" gap (for the closure). {A

A

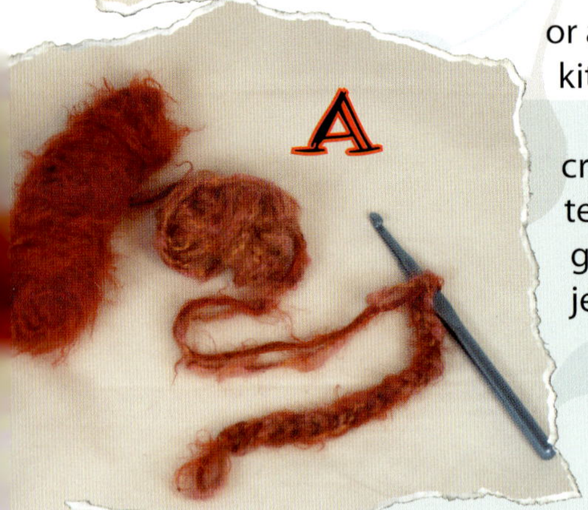

B

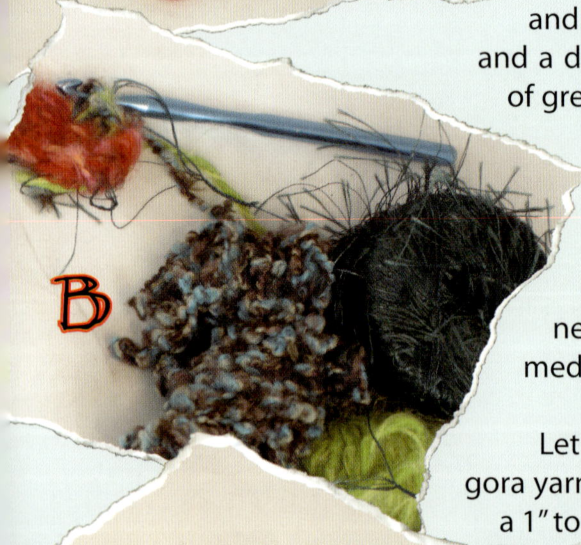

C

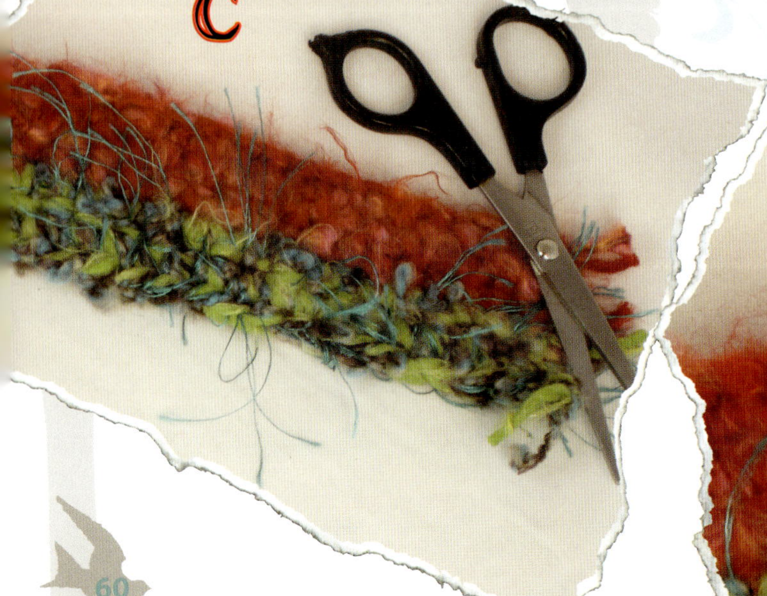

D

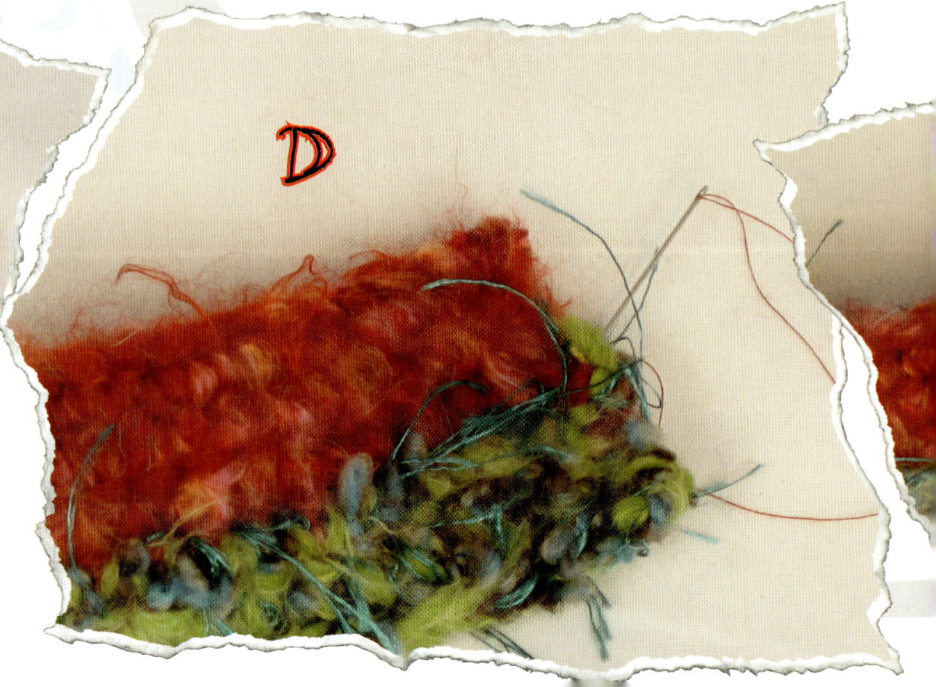

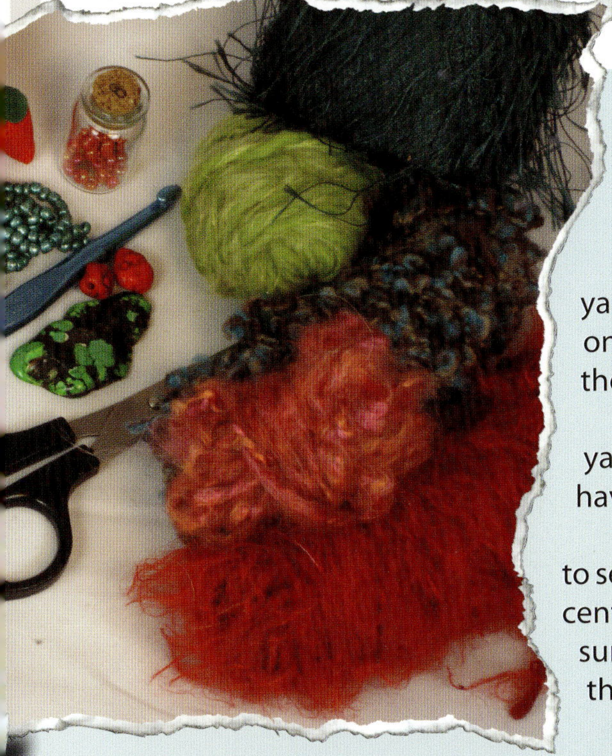

Turn around and crochet three rows of a single crochet stitch. Now change the colors by cutting your red and pink yarns and tying on your blue/brown bouclé, green angora and teal eyelash yarns. **{B**

Crochet three more rows. Cut yarns and pull them through the loop on the hook to make a knot. Now trim the ends. **{C**

Sew down the ends of the trimmed yarns with a needle and thread as you have done in previous chapters. **{D**

Don't cut the thread yet! Rather, use it to sew on your button. The button should be centered and slightly in from the edge. Make sure to use at least four or five stitches so that the button is very secure. **{E & F**

Now you can cut the thread! With a fresh needle and either upholstery thread or double strong regular thread, make an embellishment for the edges. (I didn't have red upholstery thread, so I doubled my regular red thread). Start by securing your thread to the edge of your bracelet at either end (I started at the end with the button). Then string beads sufficient to run the length of the bracelet. My pattern was 4 red and pink seed beads followed by a piece of coral. When you reach the other end of the bracelet, secure the embellishment strand with a stitch or two. Then go back and secure the strand to the entire length of the bracelet by putting the needle back through the beads every half-inch or so and tacking the strand down to the bracelet. When you reach the end of the bracelet knot the thread well and cut. **{G, H, & I**

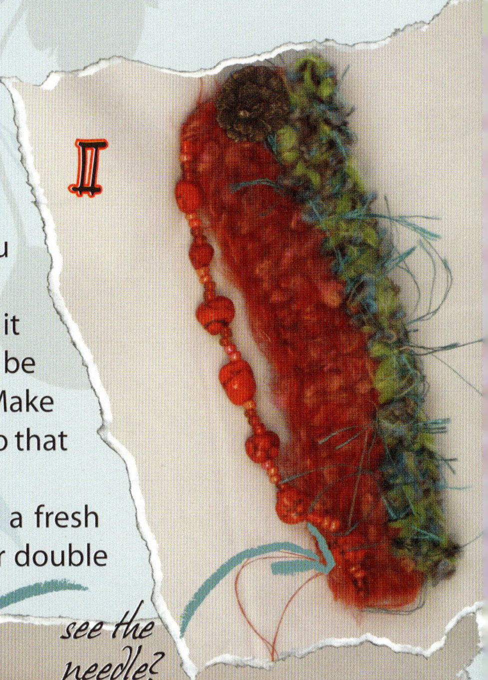

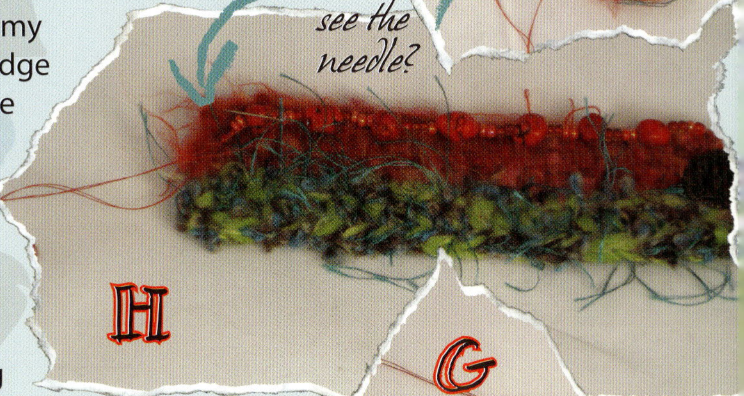

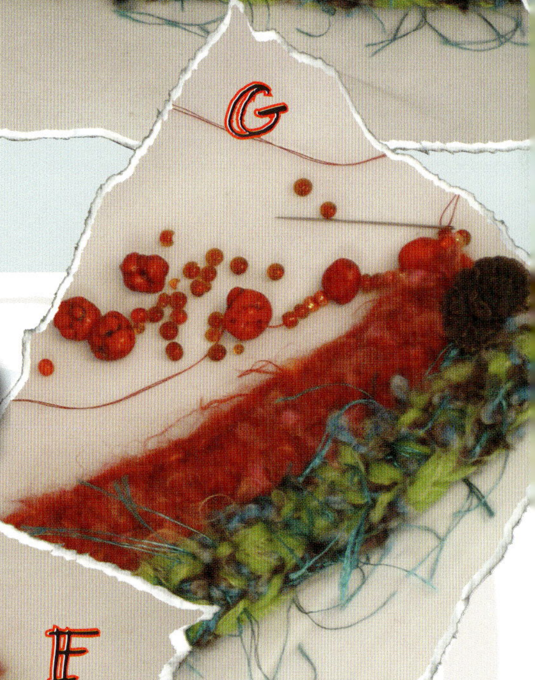

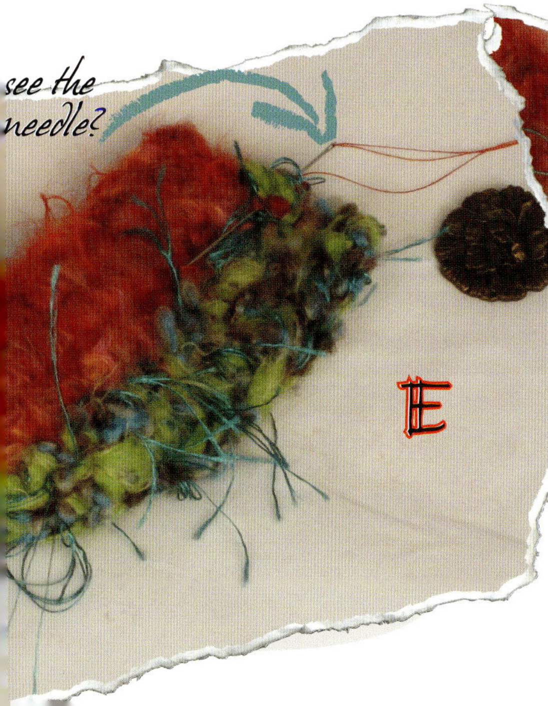

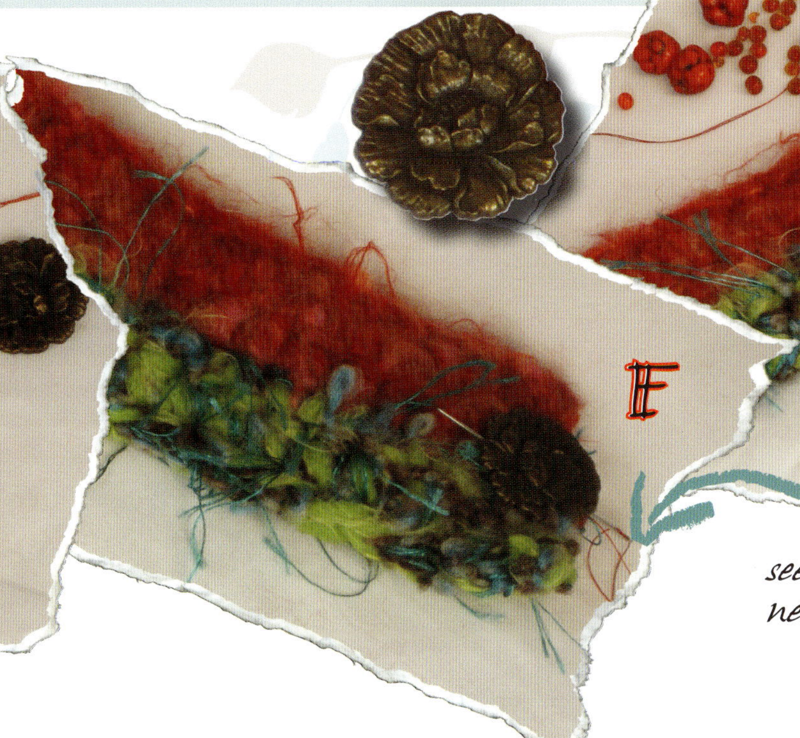

Now repeat the same process for the other edge of the bracelet! I used blue and green seed beads in a random pattern. **{J, K, L & M**

Now make a loop closure for your button. For this, you should choose a yarn with some heft! Make a foundation chain 1-1/2 to 2 inches long (just enough to go around button when the loop is sewn onto the body of the bracelet). Stitch the loop securely to the body of the cuff, centered on the end opposite the button end. (Use a lot of stitches to make sure it's secure!) **{N, O & P**

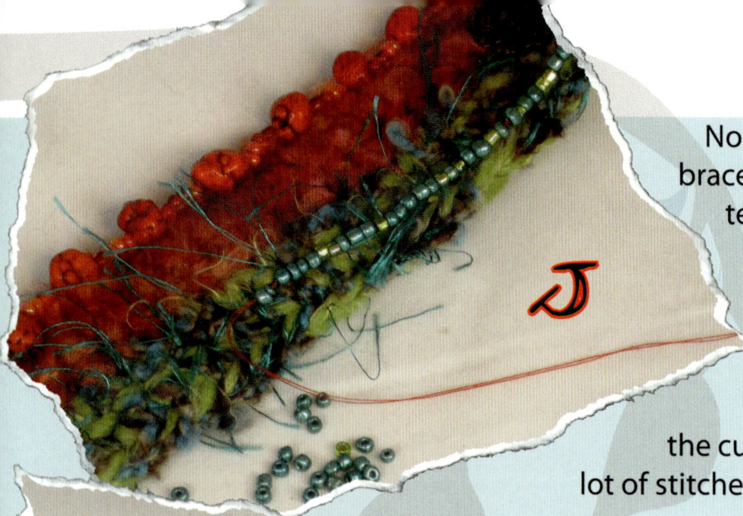

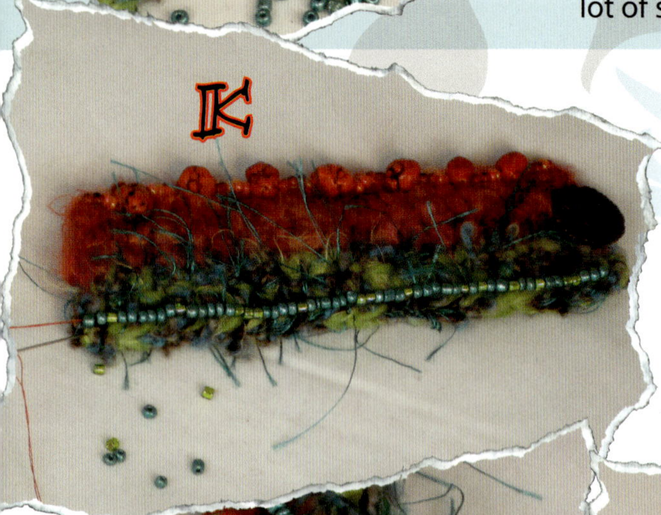

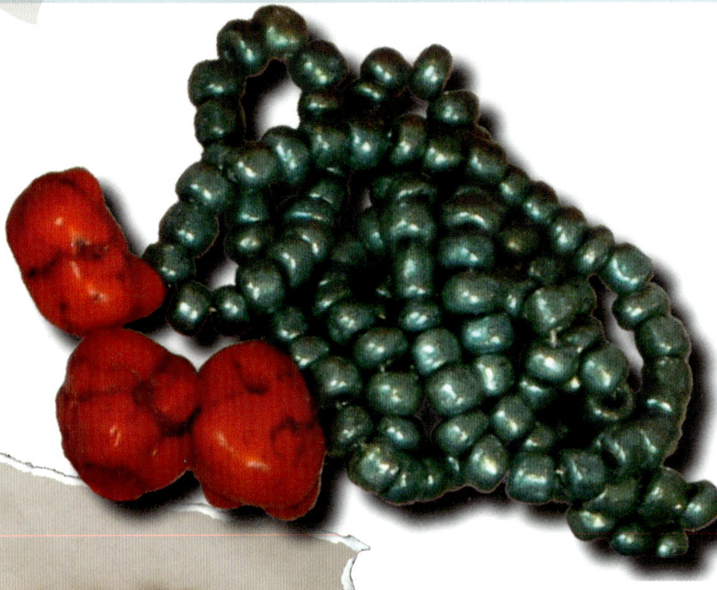

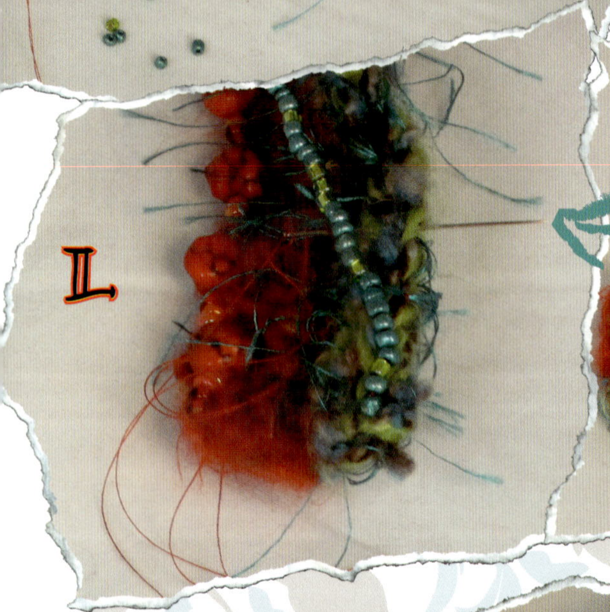

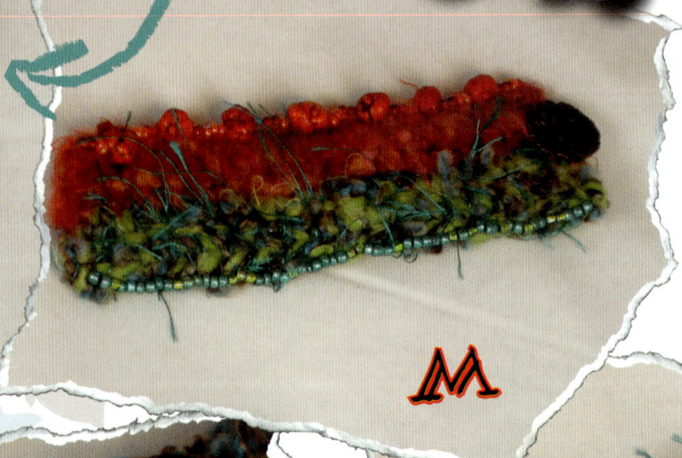

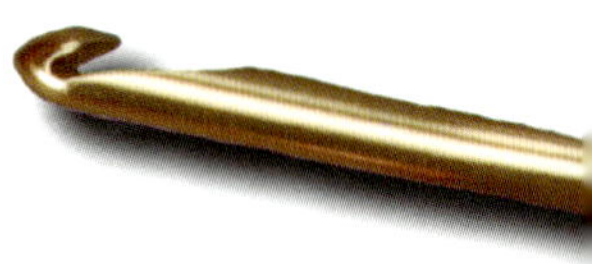

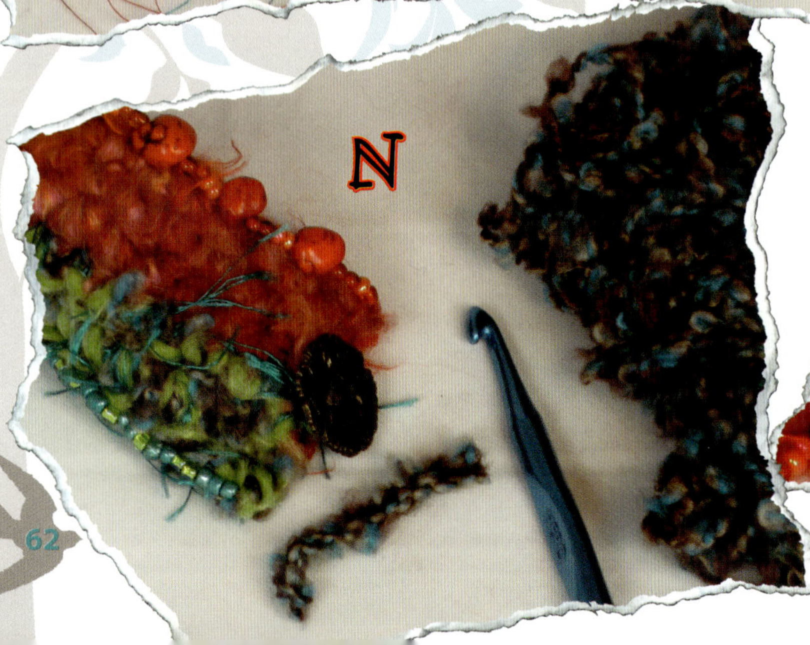

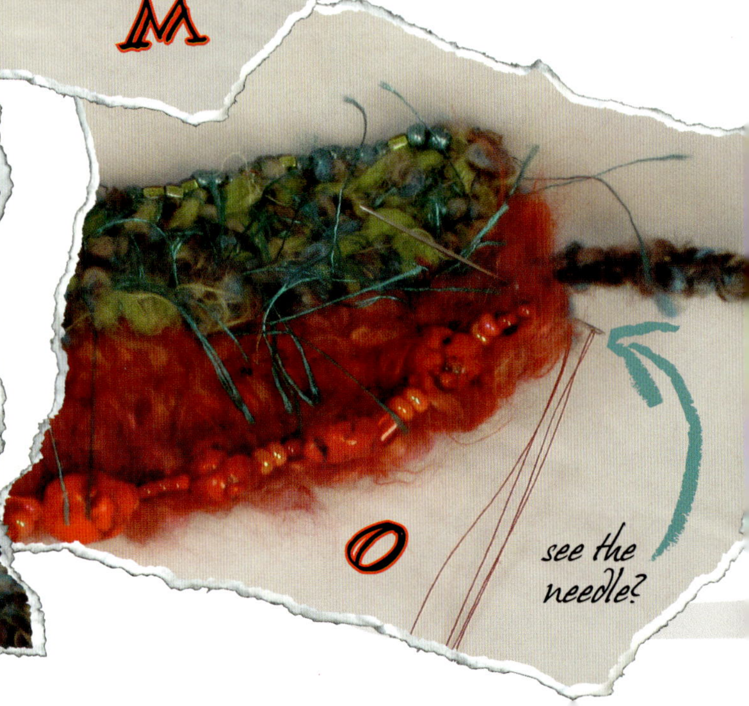

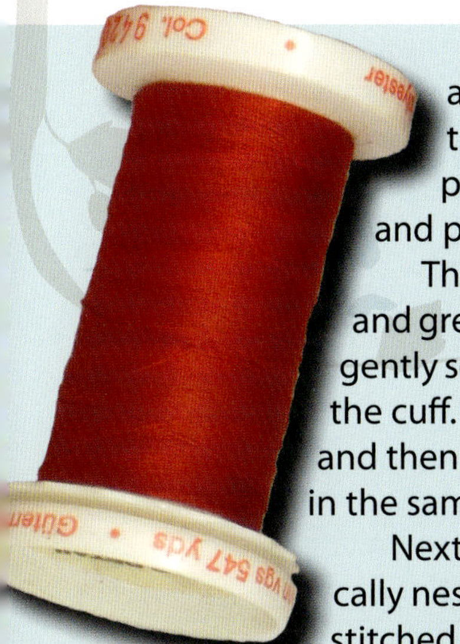

Now attach your stone by closing the cuff and locating the center. Using a needle and thread, stitch the stone down to the center, passing through the stone twice (if possible) and pulling it tight. {Q

Then string enough randomly selected blue and green seed beads onto the thread to make a gently squiggling line to the corner of one end of the cuff. Lay out the squiggly line out as desired and then tack it down to the body of the bracelet in the same way as described previously. {R

Next, securely stitch on your daisy flower so that it is asymmetrically nestled against the turquoise stone. Once the daisy is stitched down, you can make a loop (stamen!) as follows—bring the needle and thread up through the center of the daisy and string it with 5 to 7 red seed beads before piercing the needle back into the daisy near where it exits. For a little extra pop, I brought the needle back up and added a blue and green bead next to the loop. {S & T

I also added a piece of red coral (the same as used in the trim) and a few random blue and green seed beads around the daisy. {U

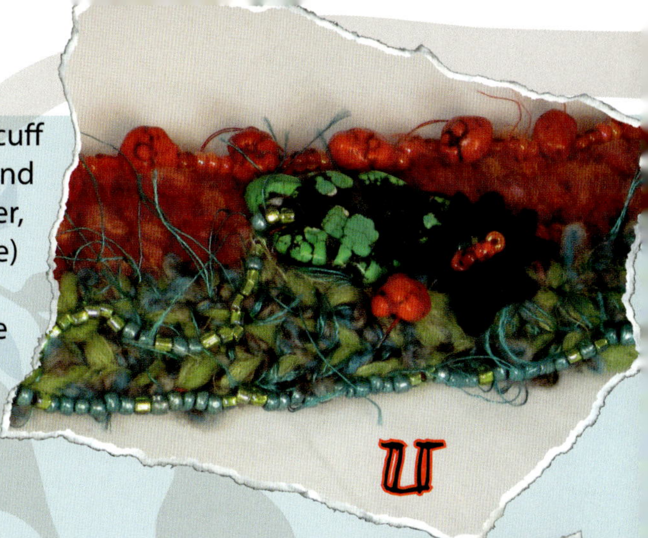

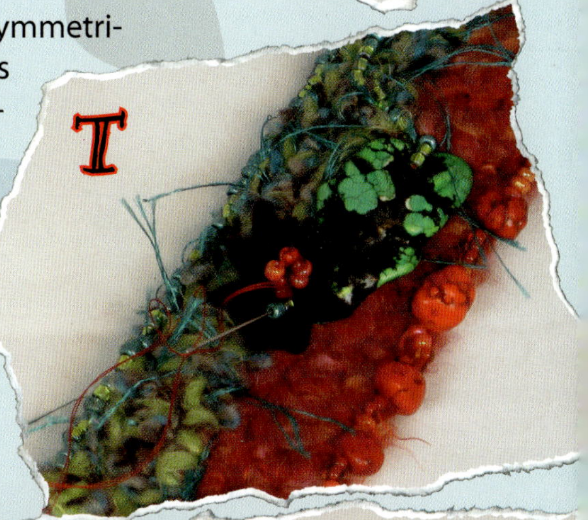

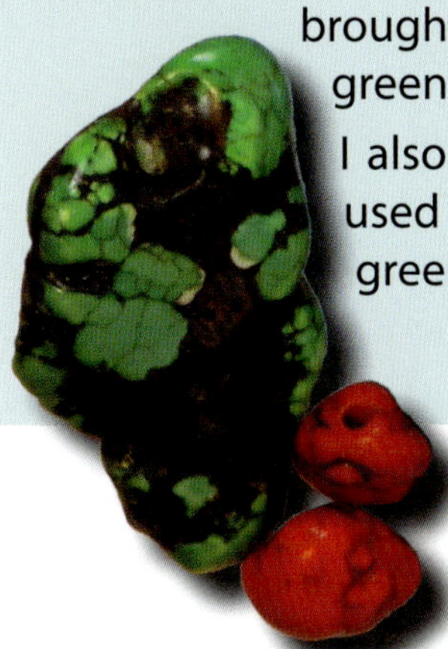

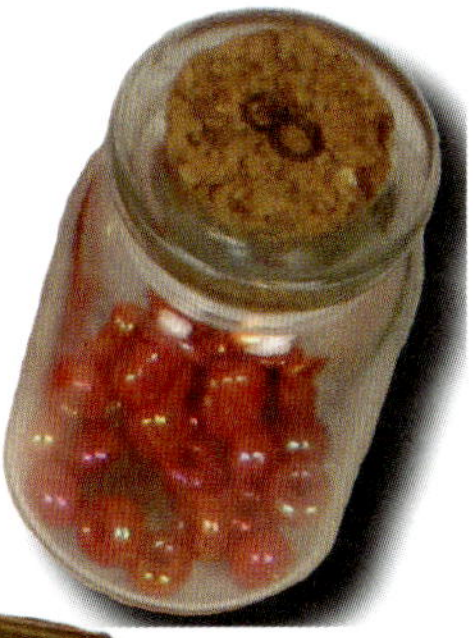

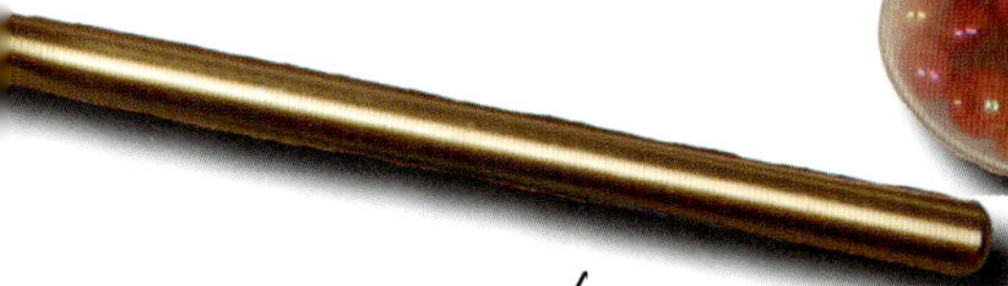

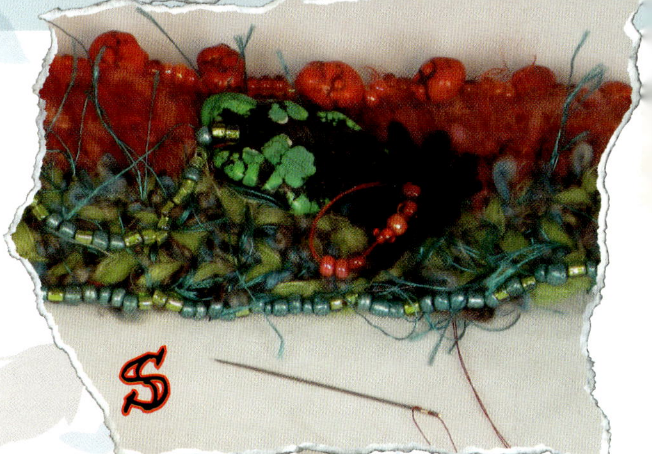

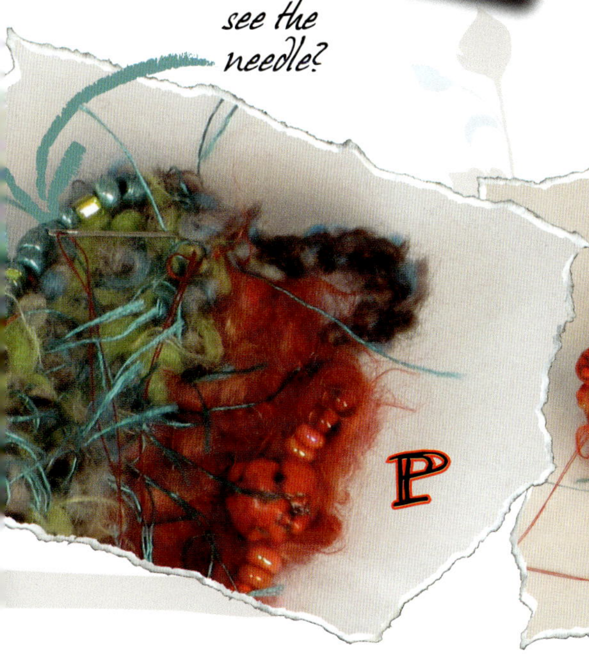

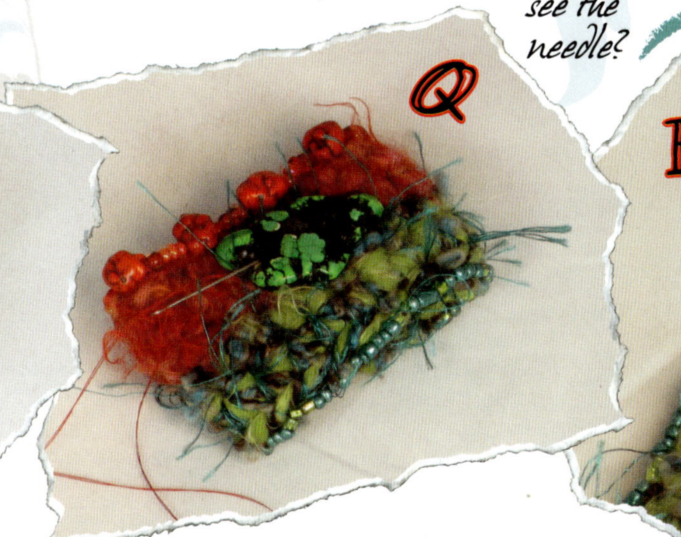

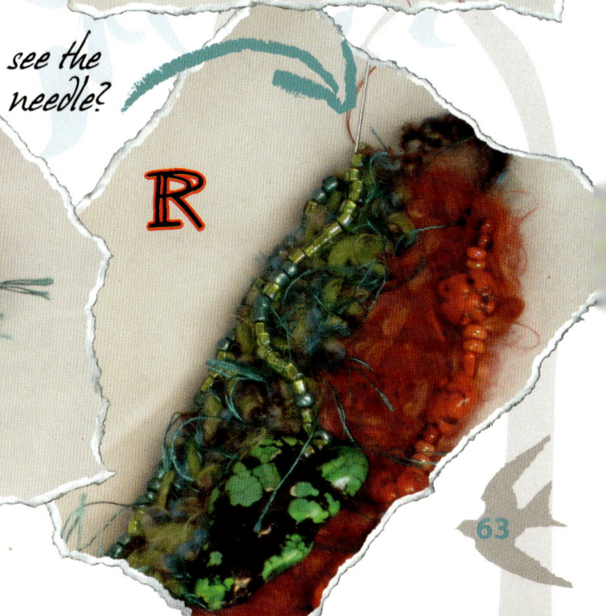

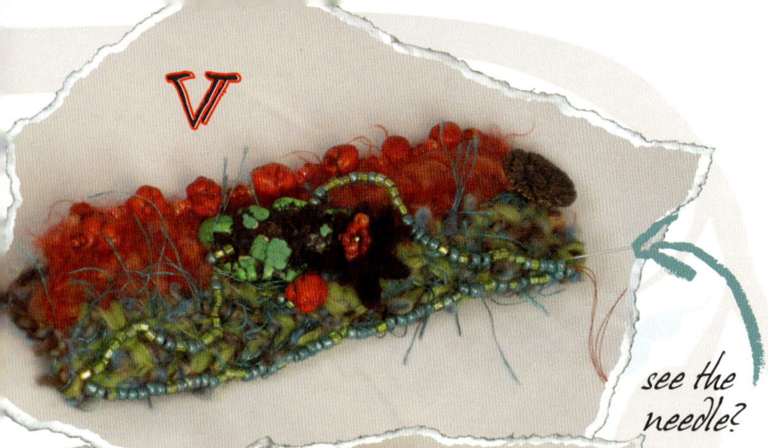

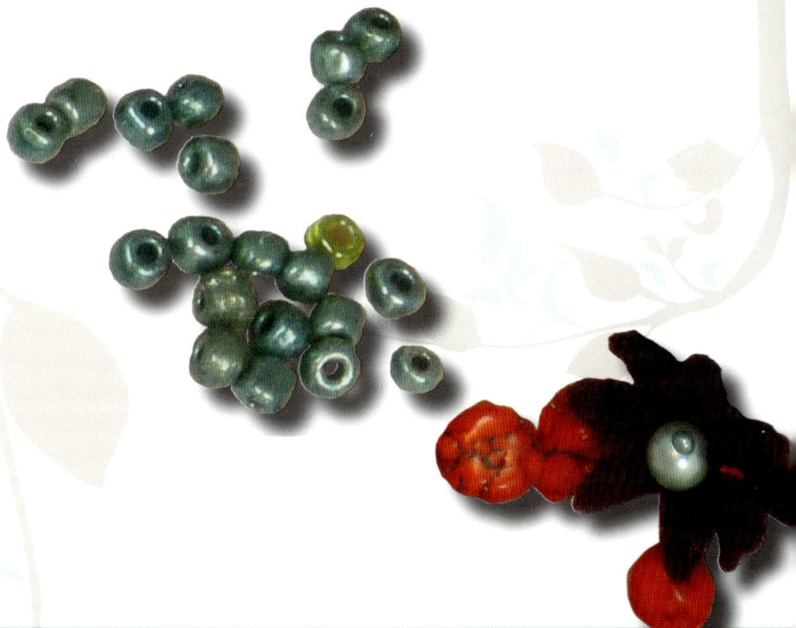

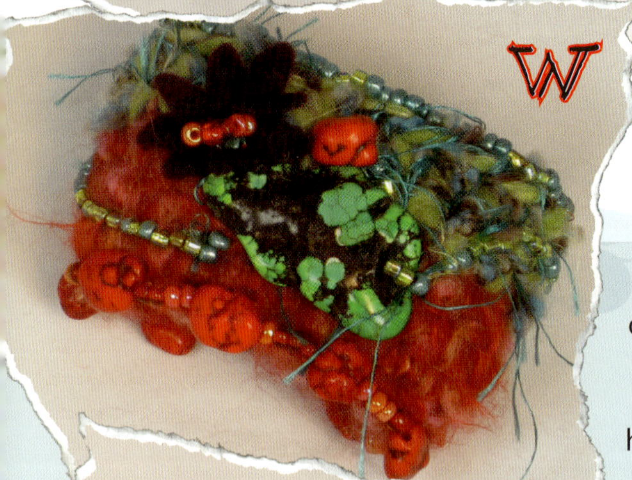

I then went back and made a squiggling line for the other side of the bracelet. **{V**

This is where I intended for my project to end. **{W**

However, I just couldn't stop **{X, Y & Z**! (I ran out of letters, so I had to finish there!)

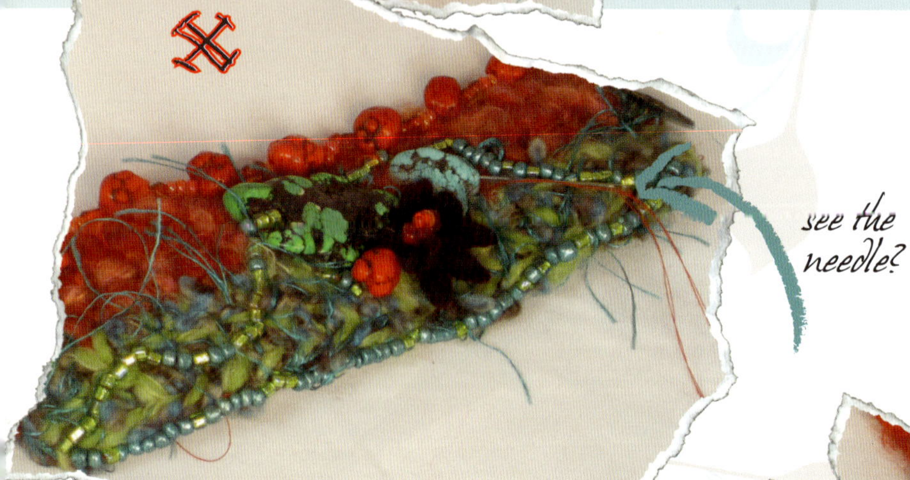

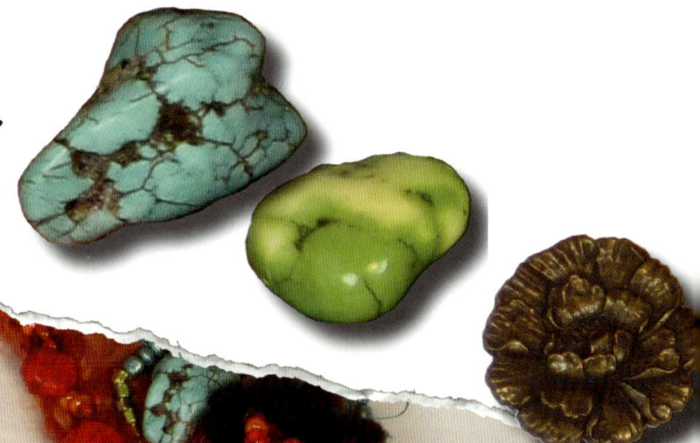

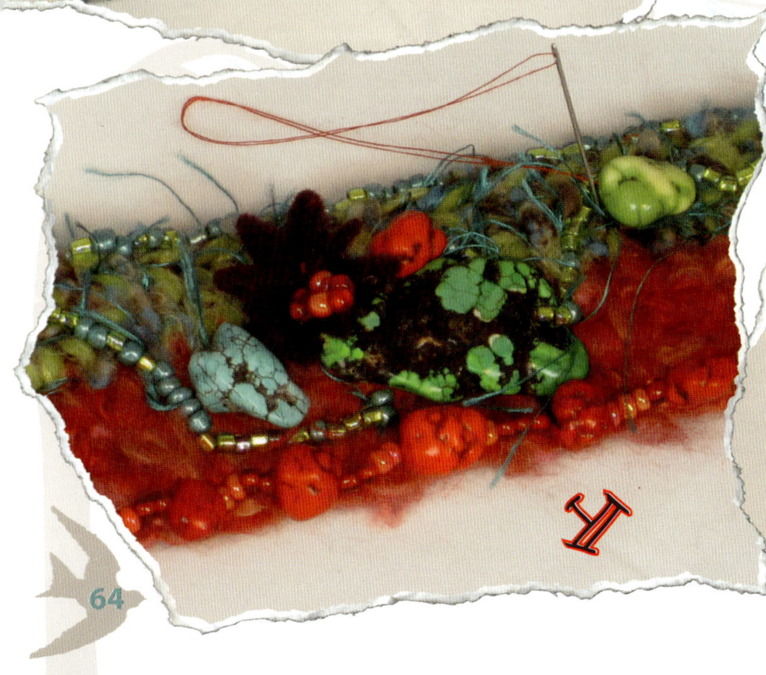

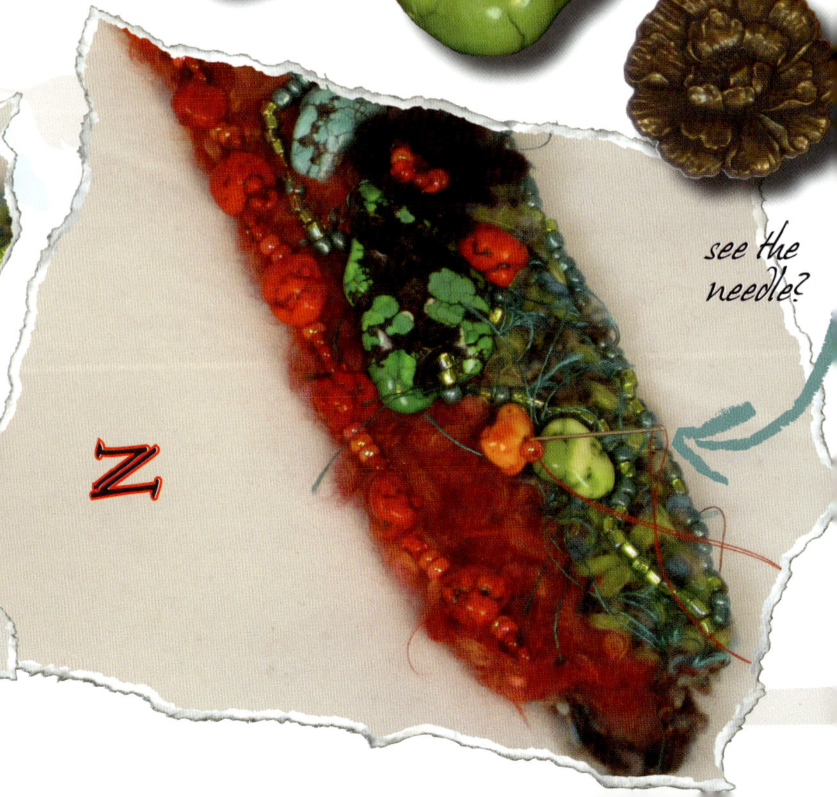

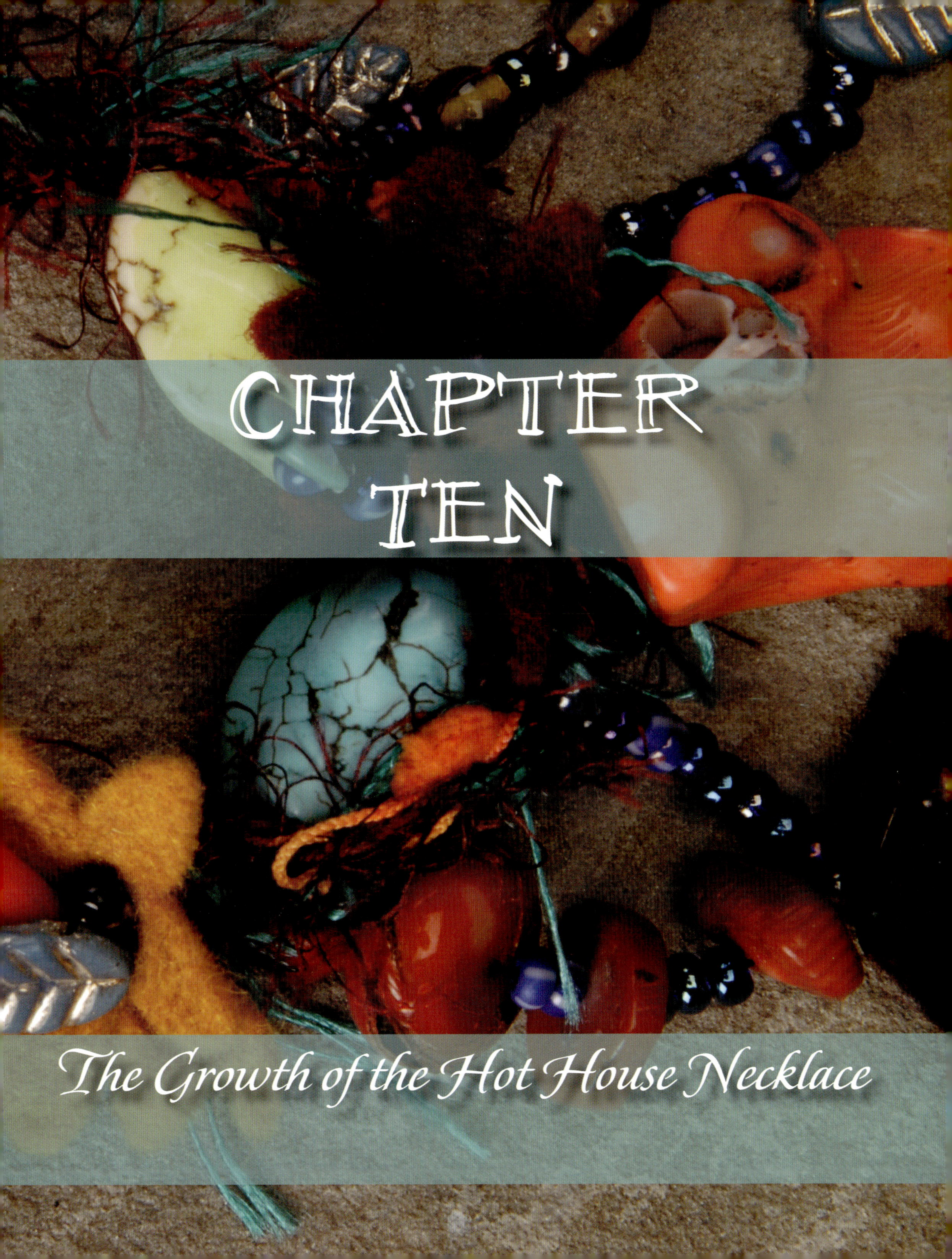

CHAPTER TEN

The Growth of the Hot House Necklace

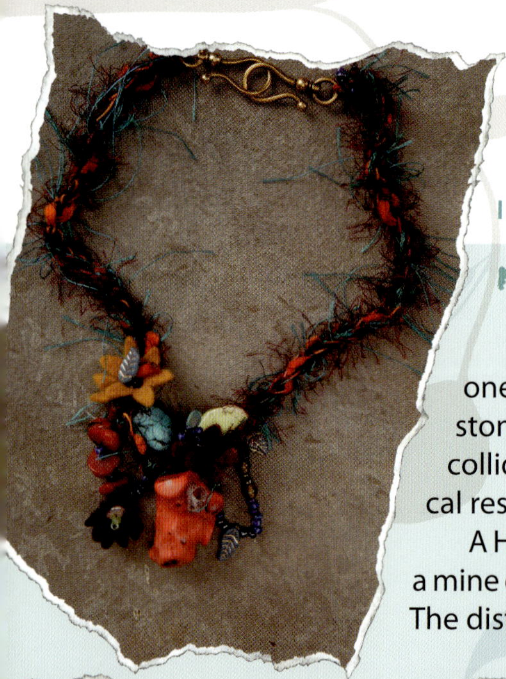

THE GROWTH OF A HOT HOUSE NECKLACE

This project started as a basic solo pendant and grew from there.

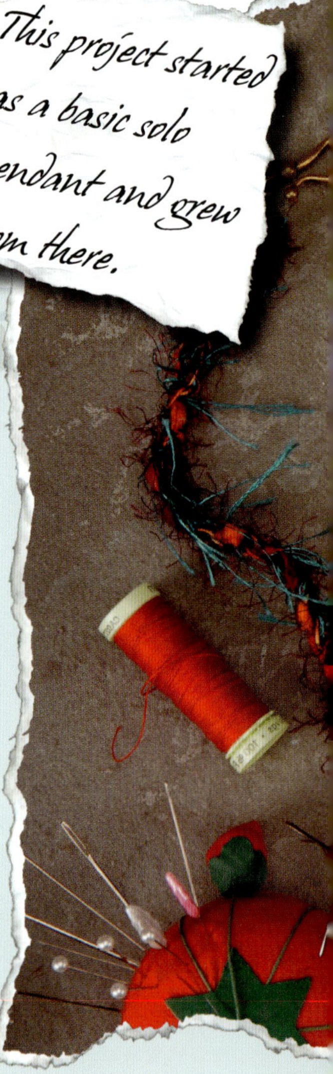

The Hot House collection is probably my favorite. It's my signature style and my personal choice when I go out on the town. It all came together one day while I was playing around with some beautiful stones and pretty felt flowers and the Victorian side of me collided with my love of all things Native American. The magical result—the Hot House collection.

A Hot House necklace should feel like a vine of wisteria with a mine of turquoise and a sea of pearls draped around your neck. The distinctive look comes from the combination of the dangly felt flowers and the shells and stones. It's a little tricky to get used to draping, swagging or just plain sewing the strands together, but once you get it down, you'll add more each time!

This final project chapter, folks, is presented in a mostly pictorial format. The skills and techniques needed are those you've learned throughout the book. Now that you've got them under your belt, I know you're ready to have some fun! Think vines of fiber with tendrils and swags of flowers, super great chunks of stone and coral, and glass beads. Have a peek! I hope it won't be long before you're improvising on your own!

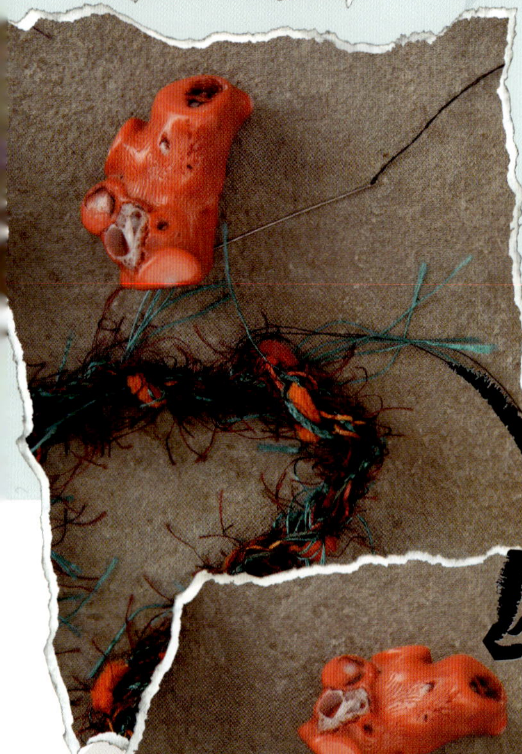

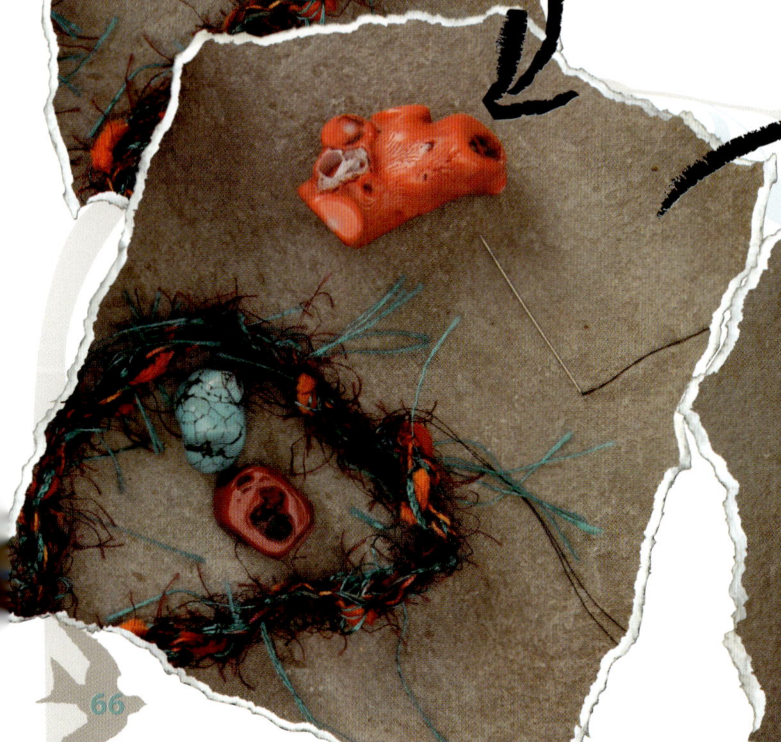

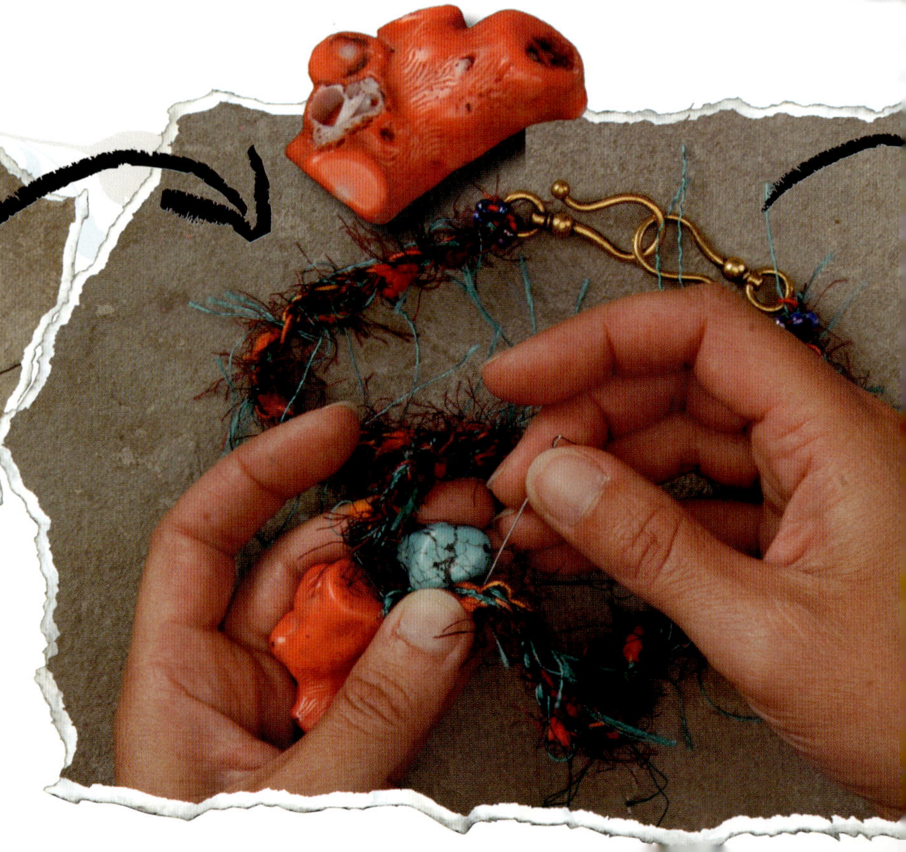

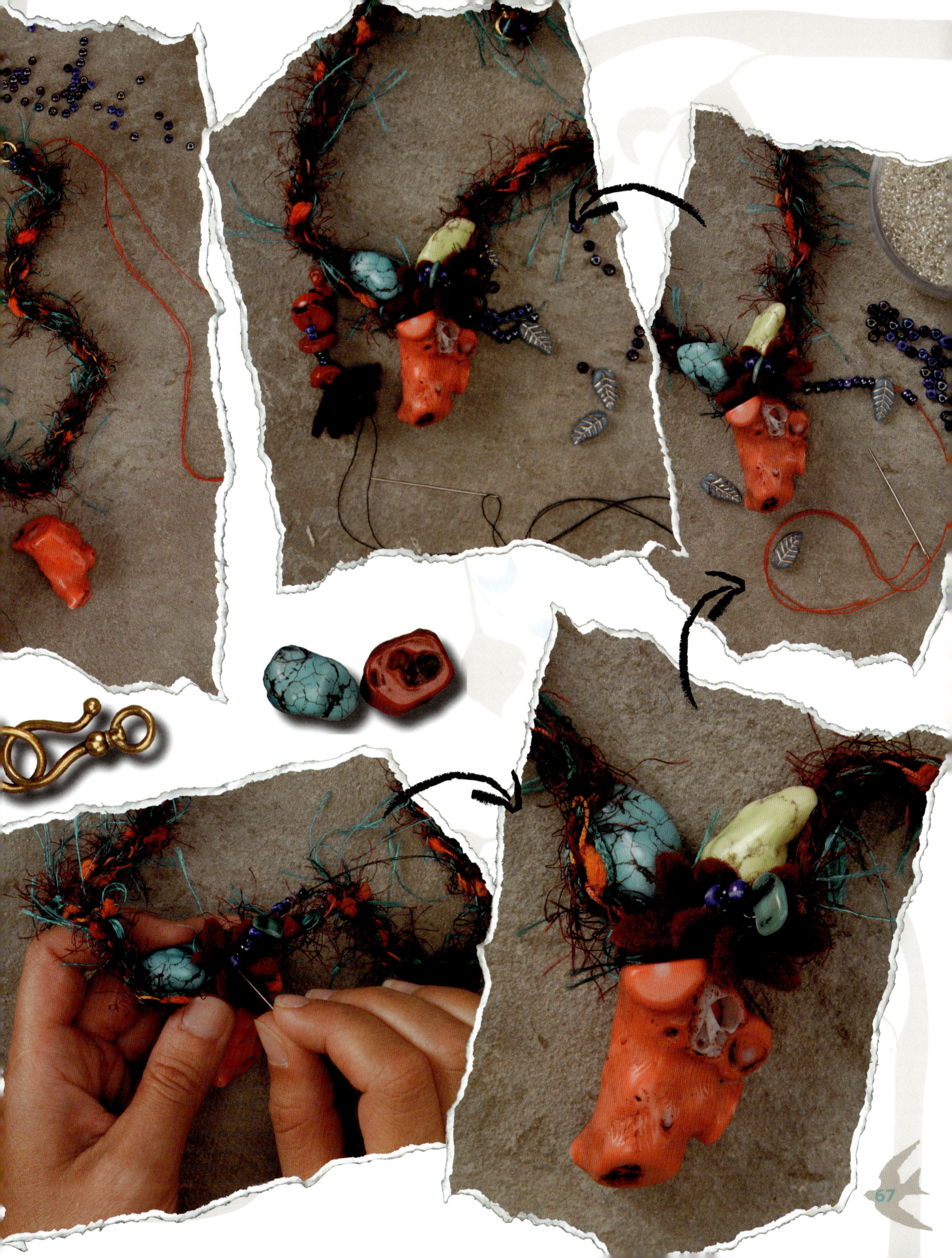

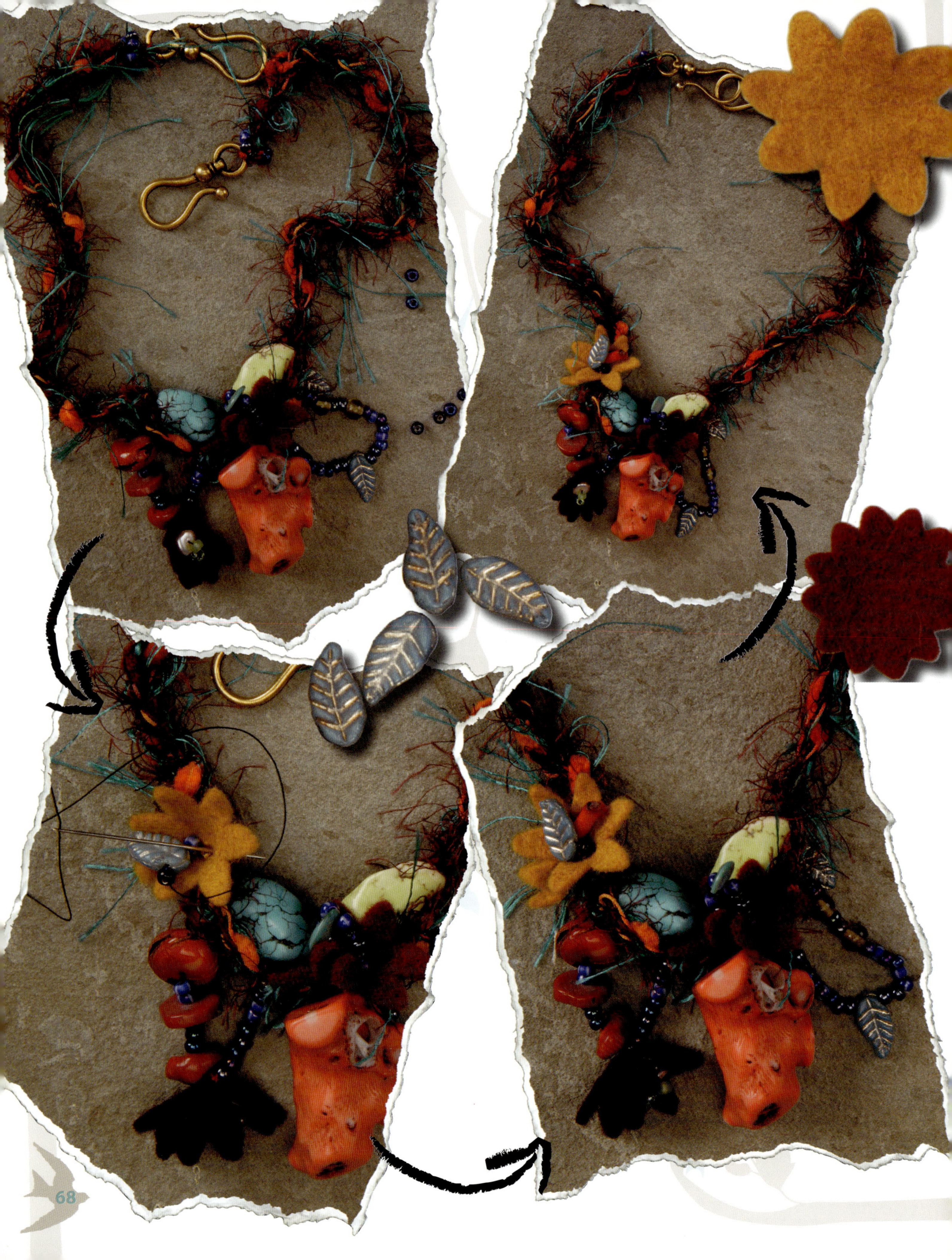

GALLERY

Inspiration Beyond this Book

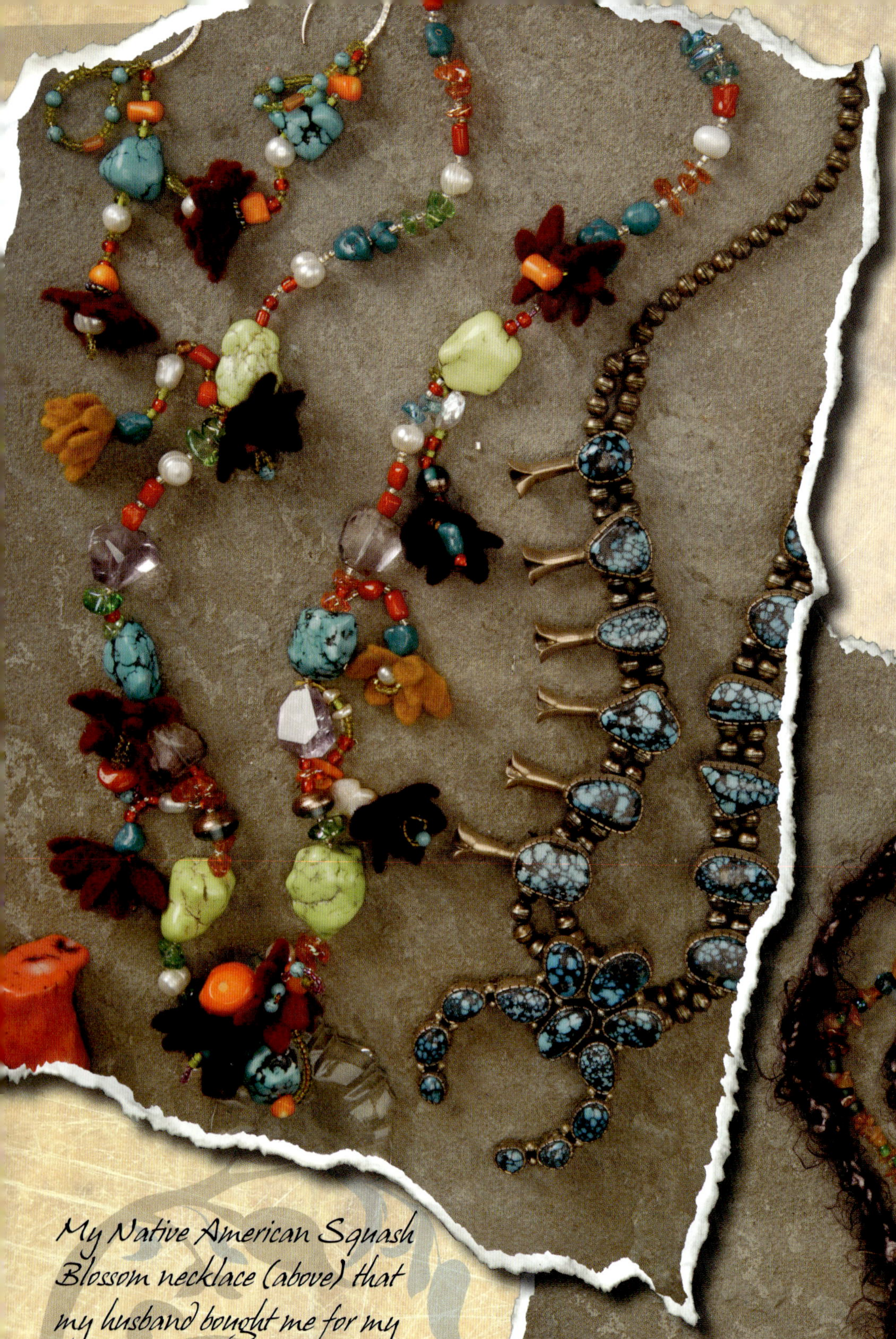

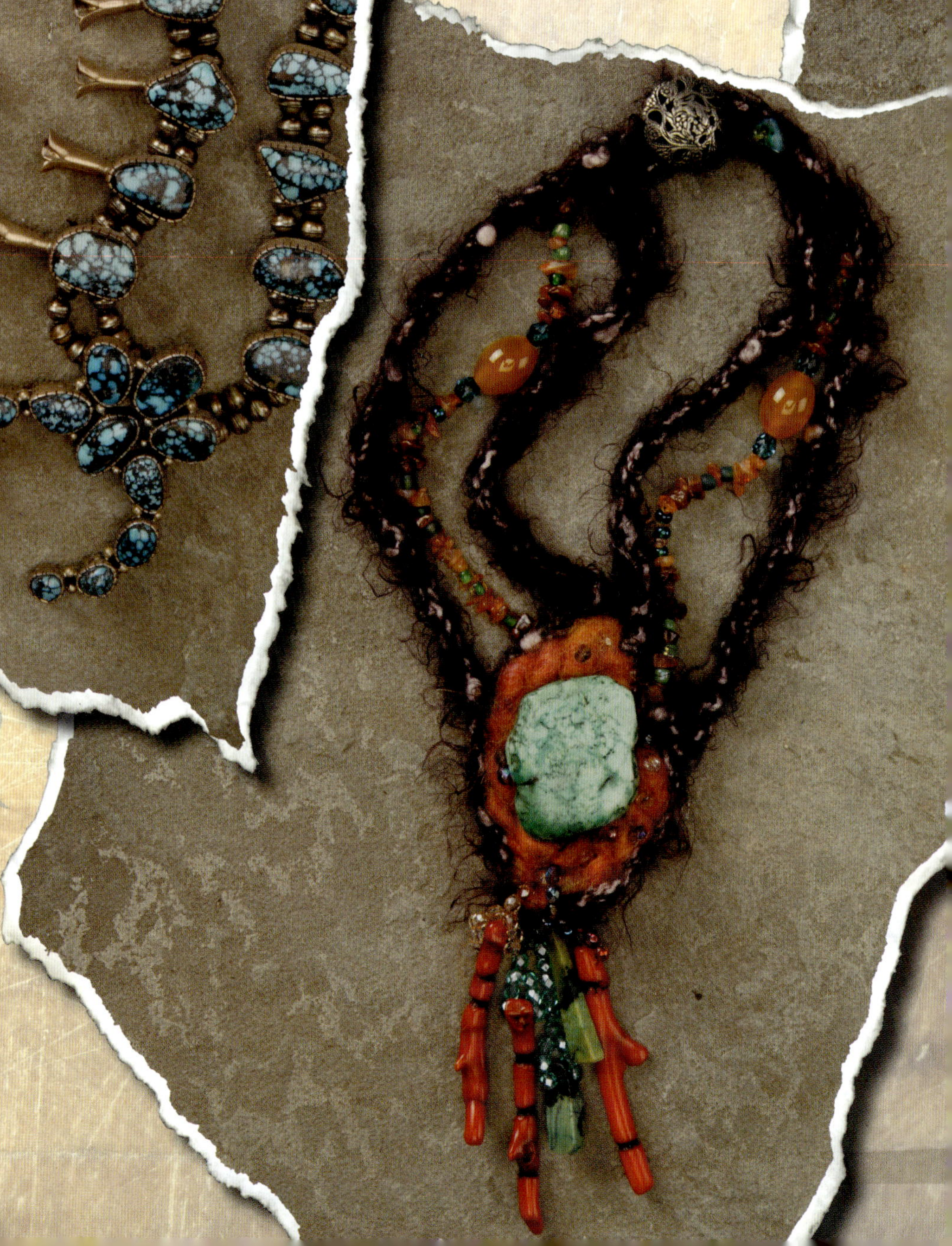

My Native American Squash Blossom necklace (above) that my husband bought me for my 40th birthday was the inspiration for this bead-strung necklace with vintage chandelier crystal and dangly felt flowers (with matching earrings)

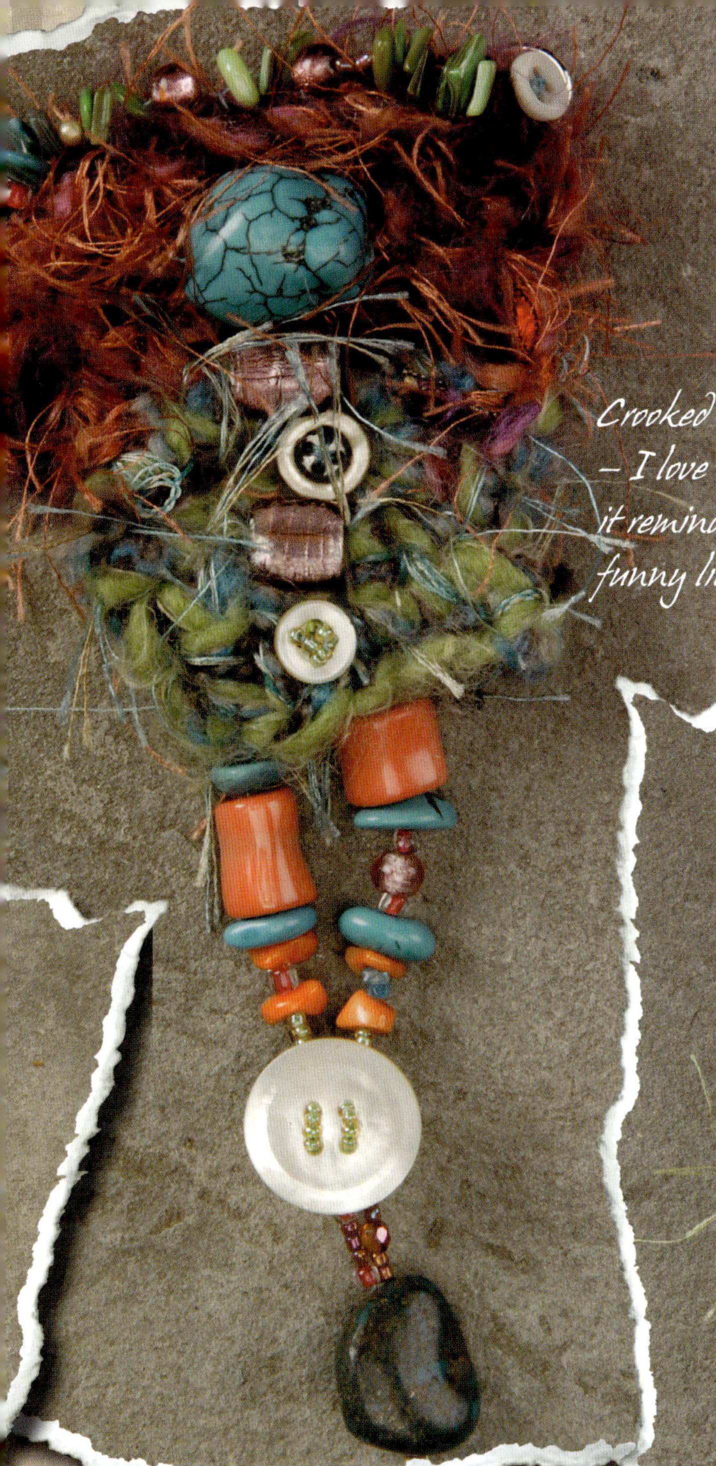

Crooked Cloak Pin – I love this piece it reminds me of a funny little person

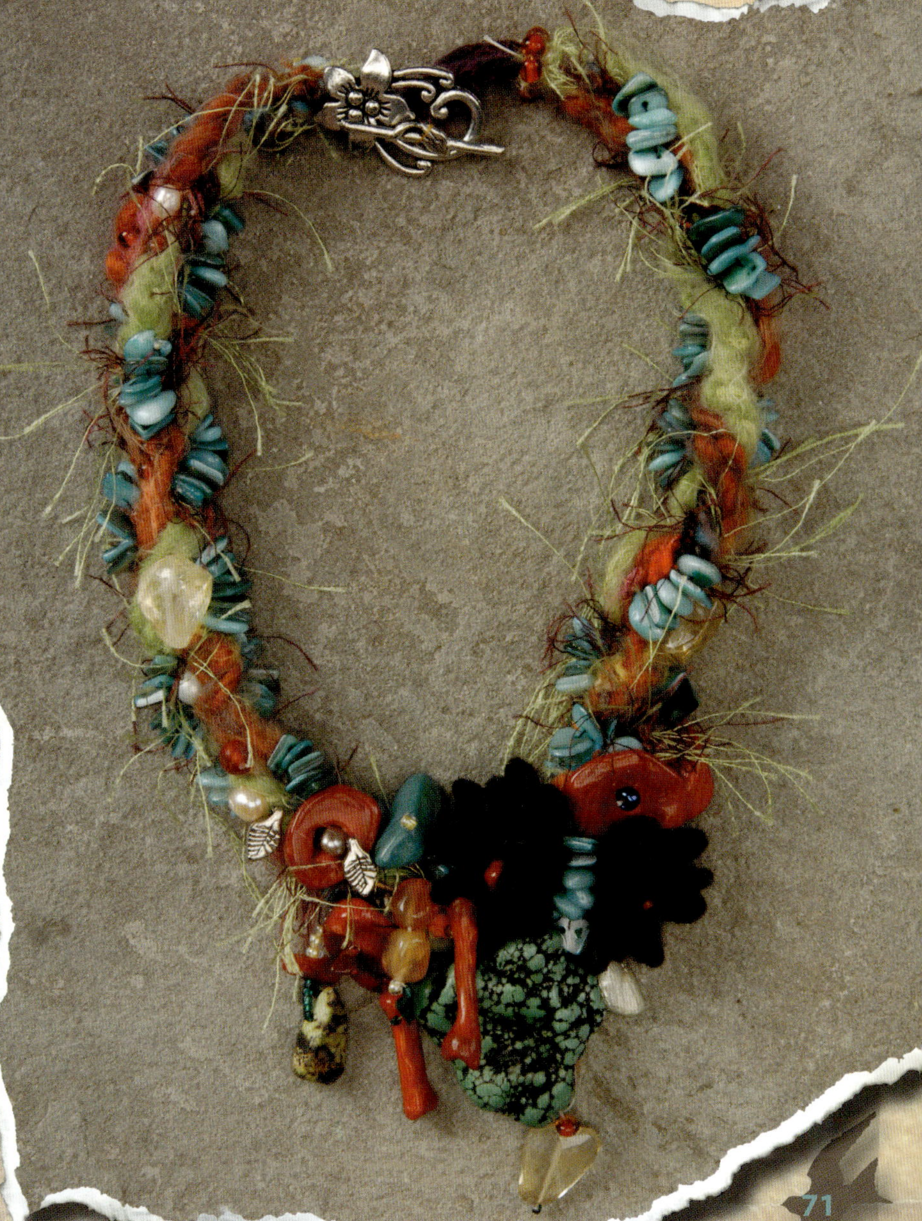

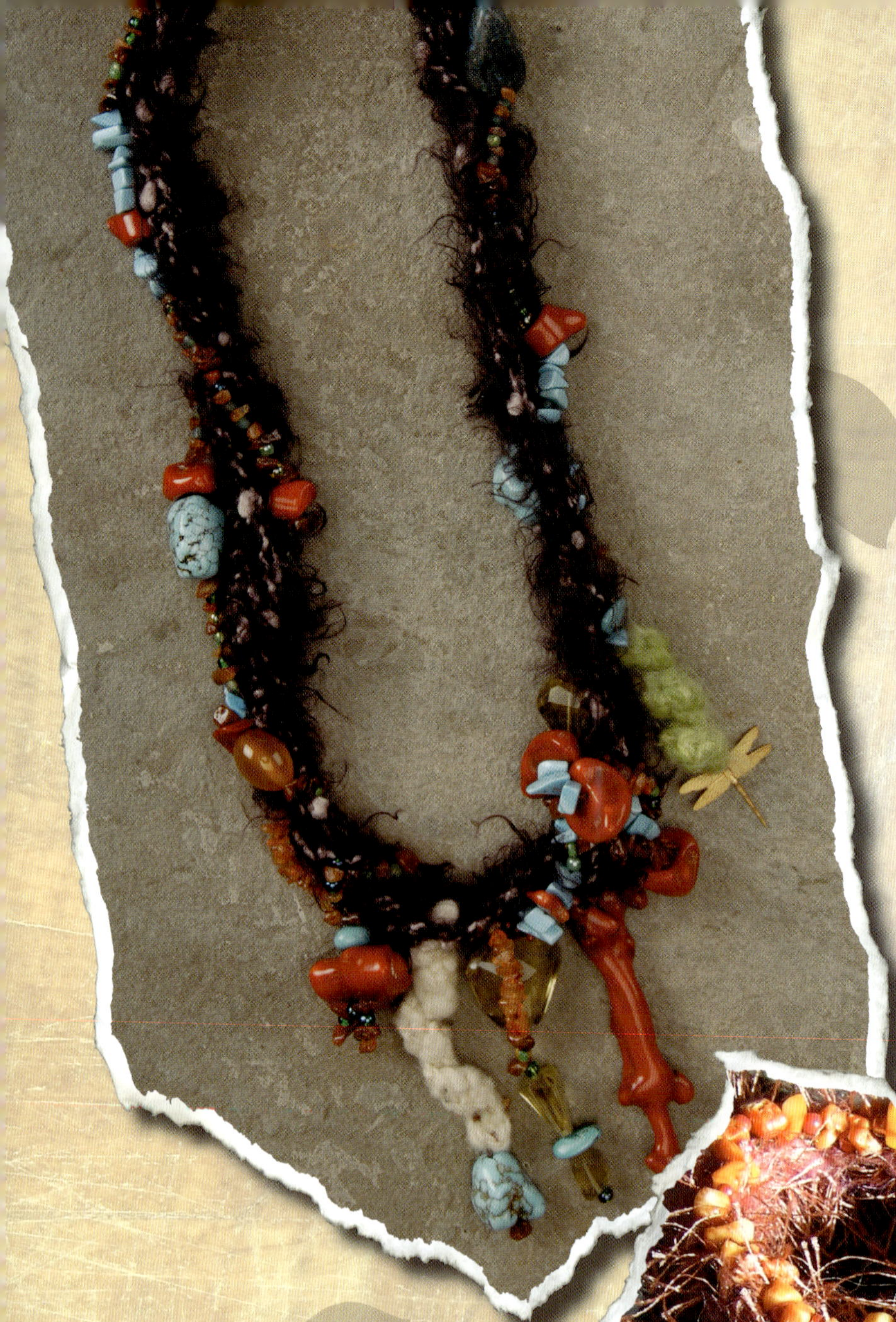

Interesting yarn combination to work with the turquoise and the pearls

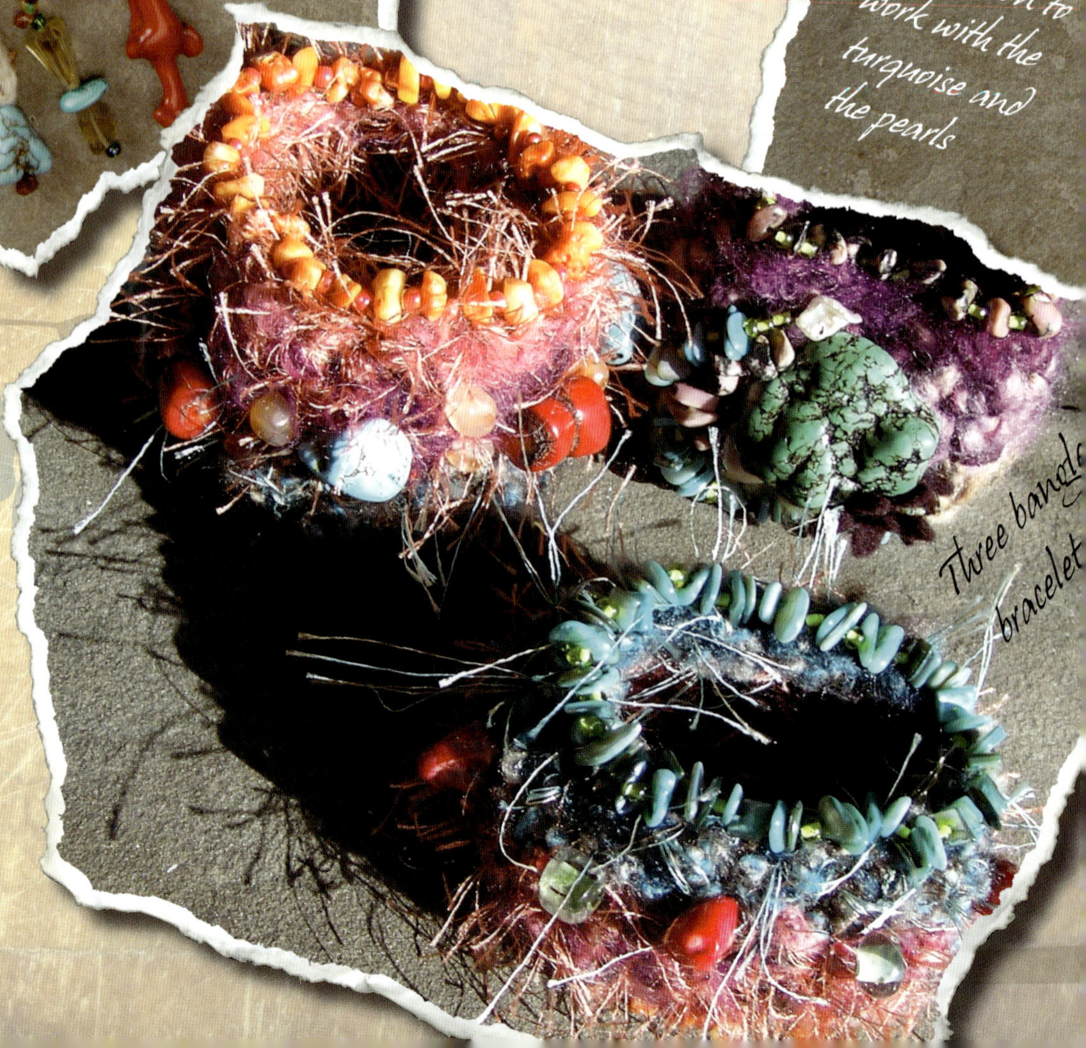

Three bangle bracelet

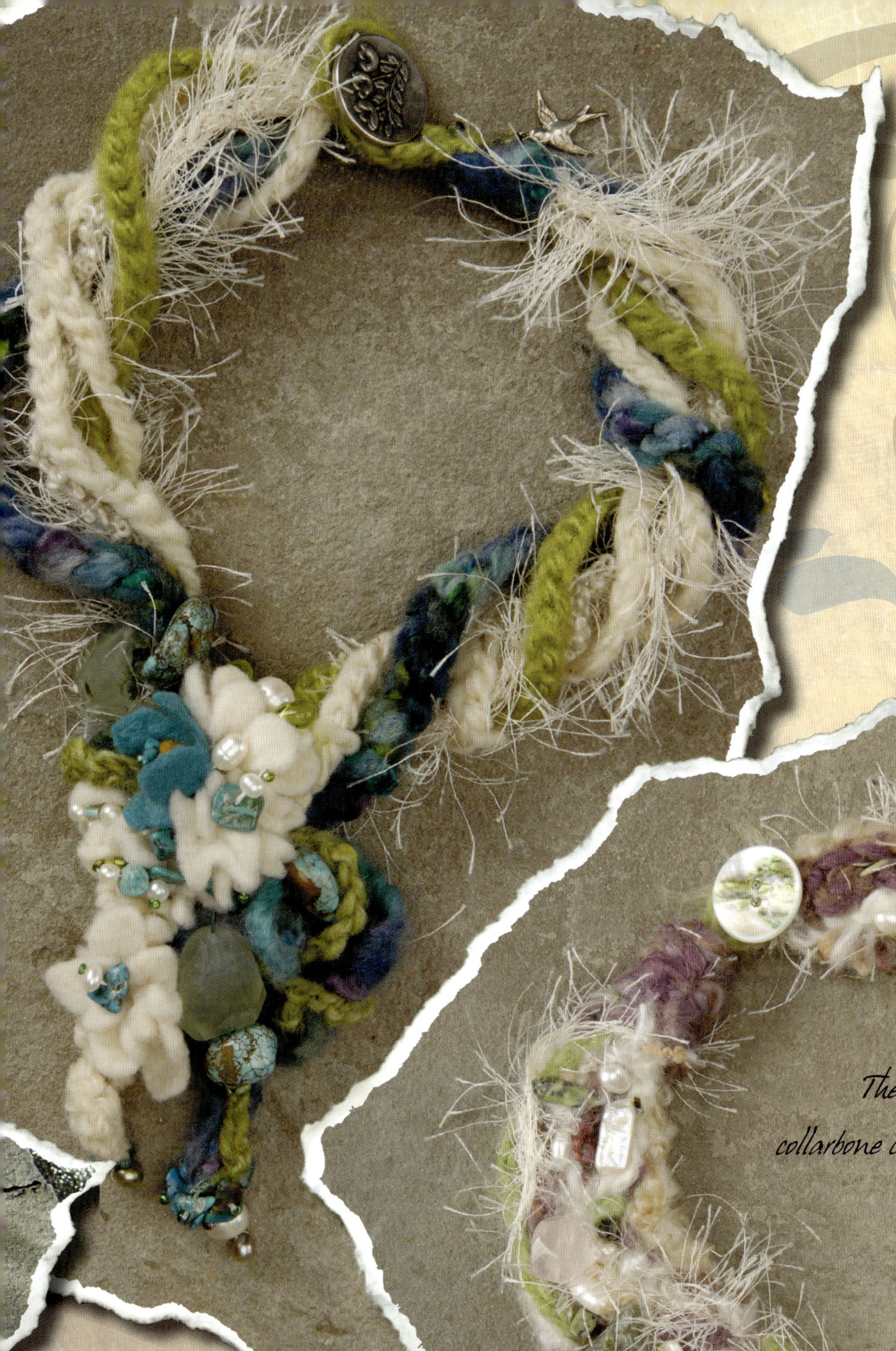

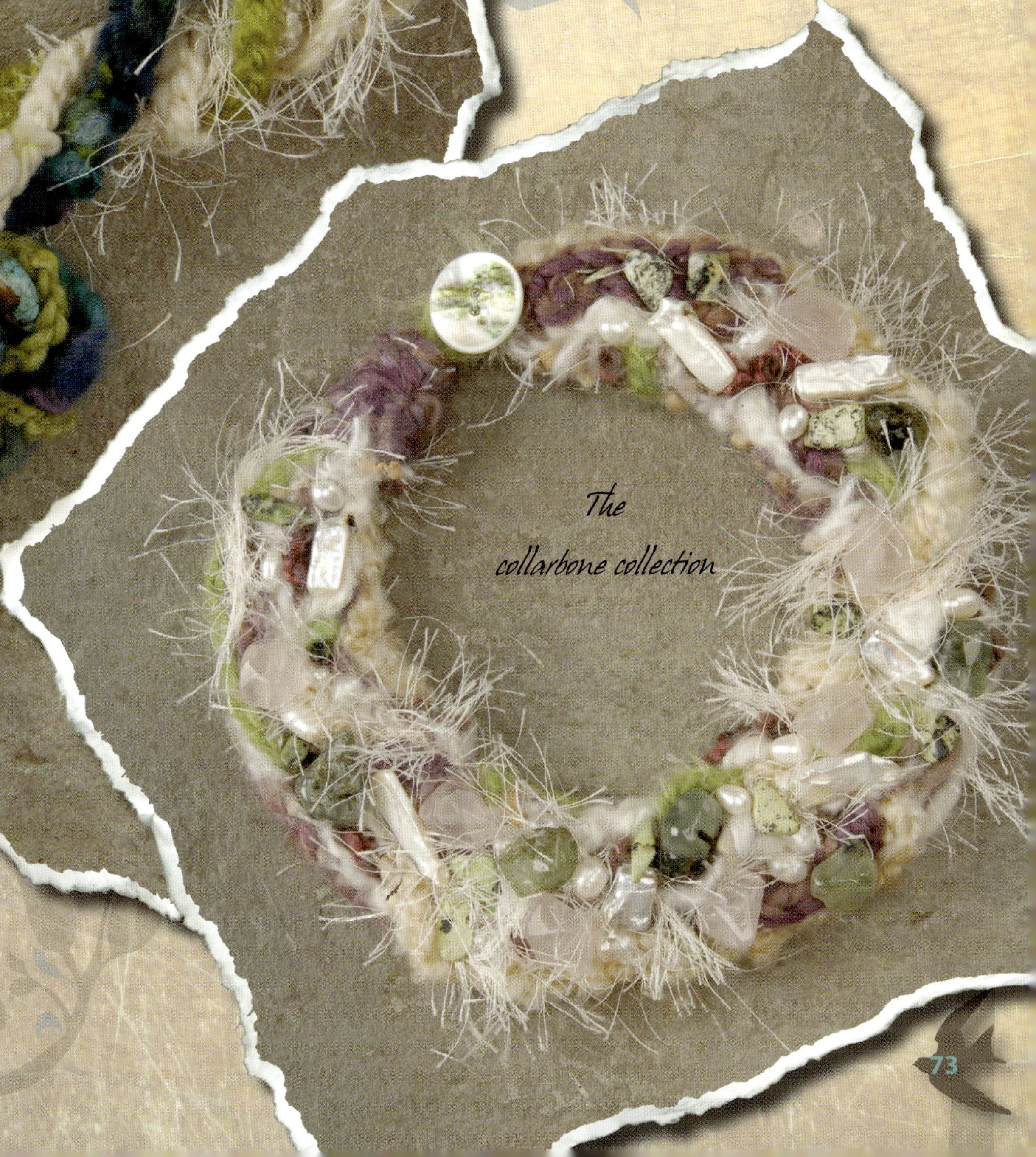

The collarbone collection

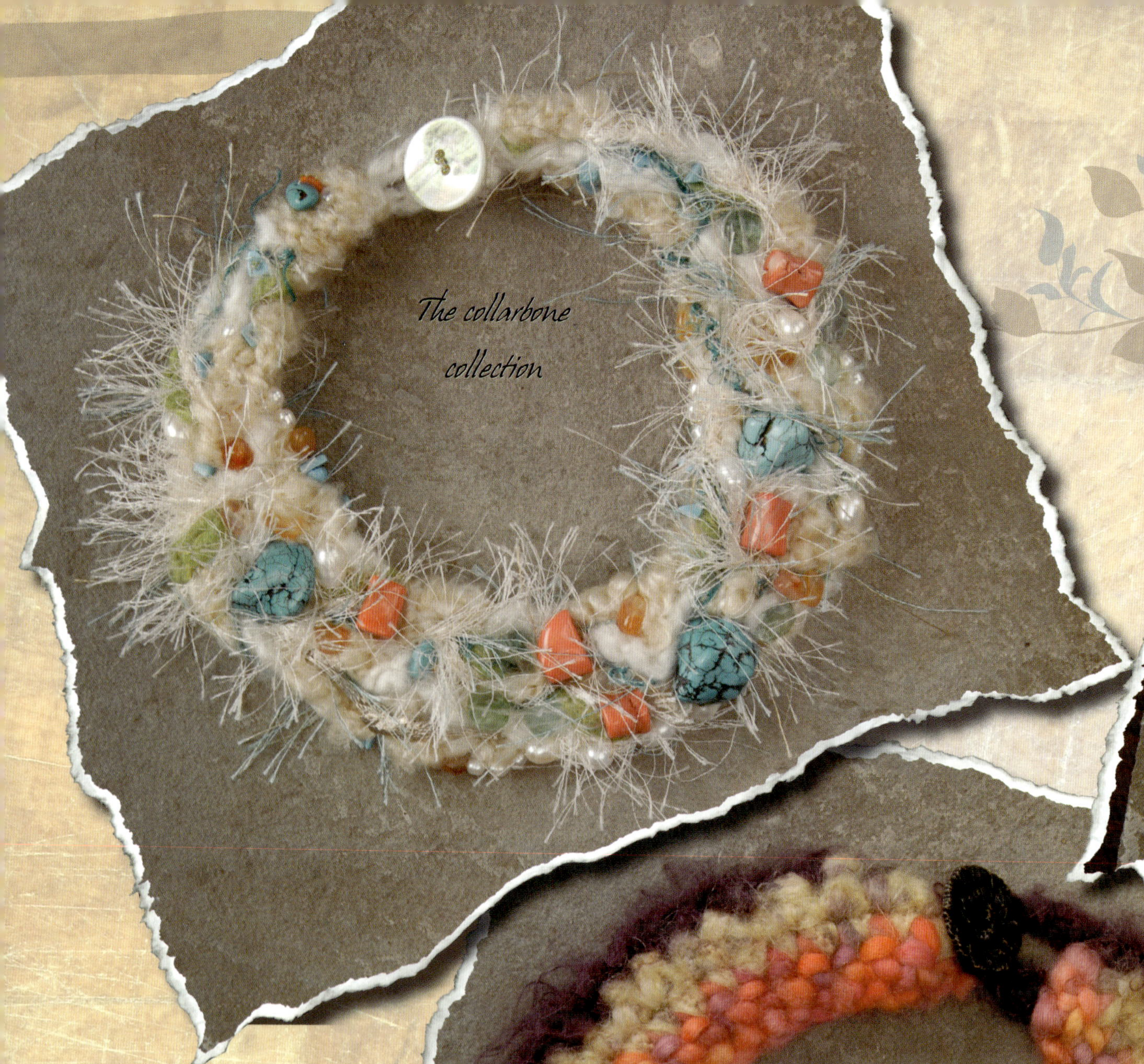

The collarbone collection

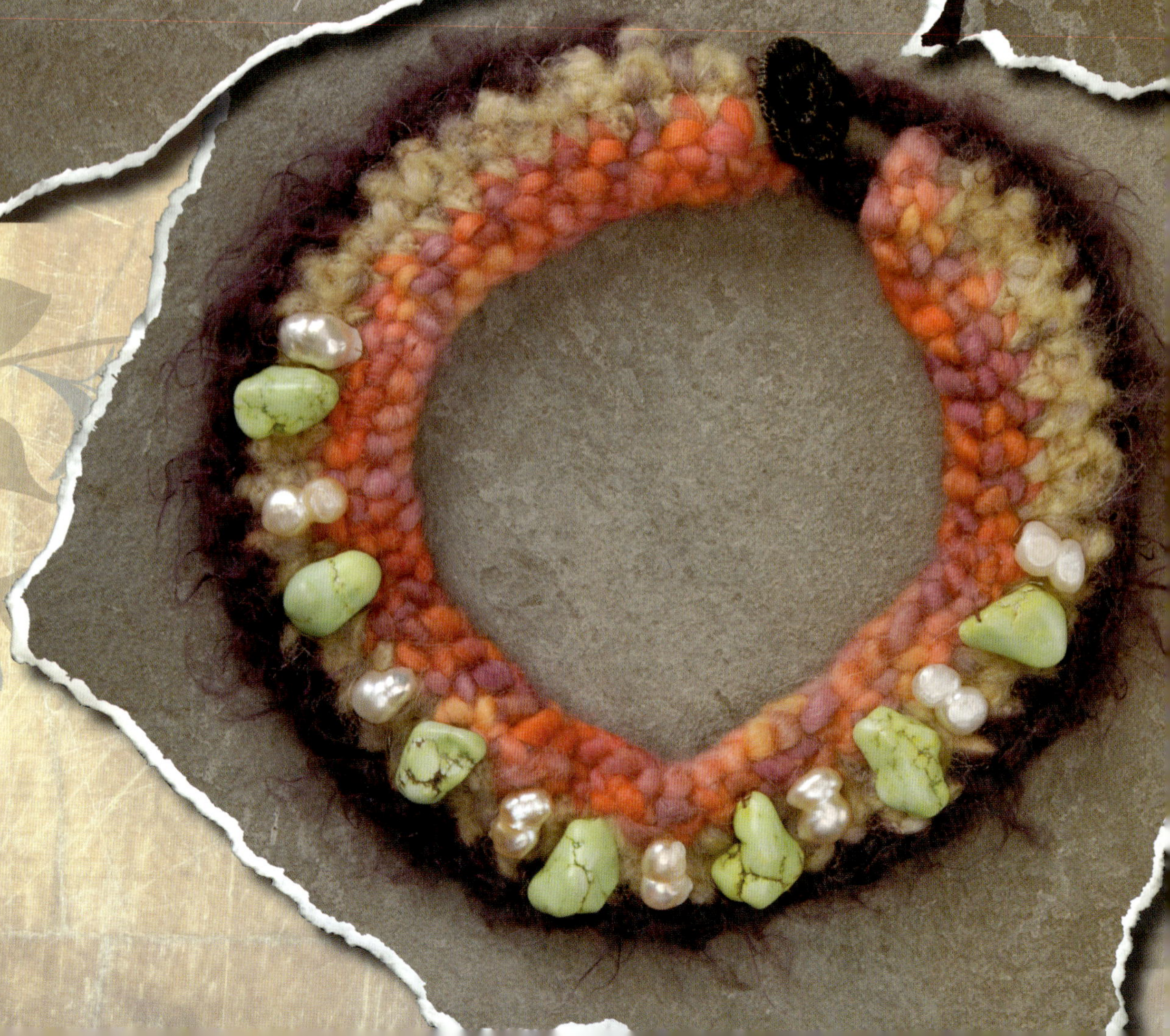

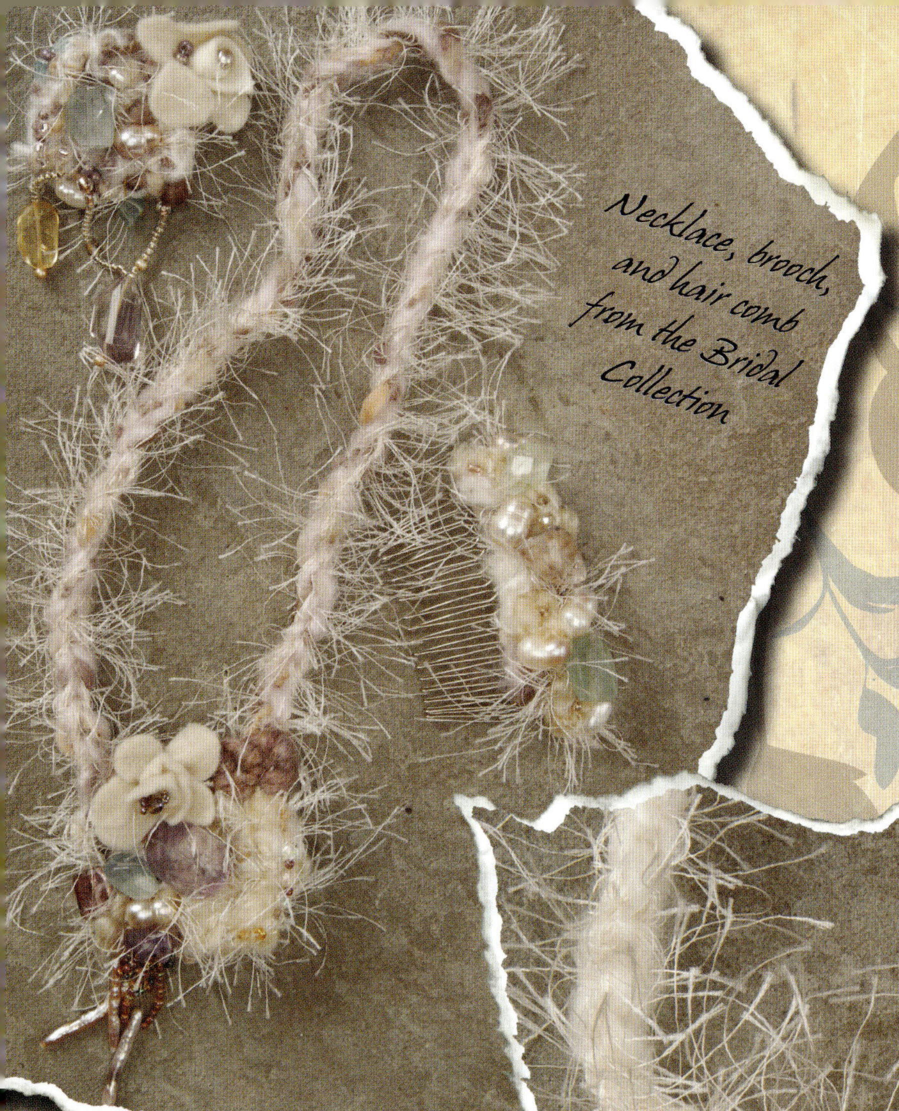

Necklace, brooch, and hair comb from the Bridal Collection

Cleopatra's Collar

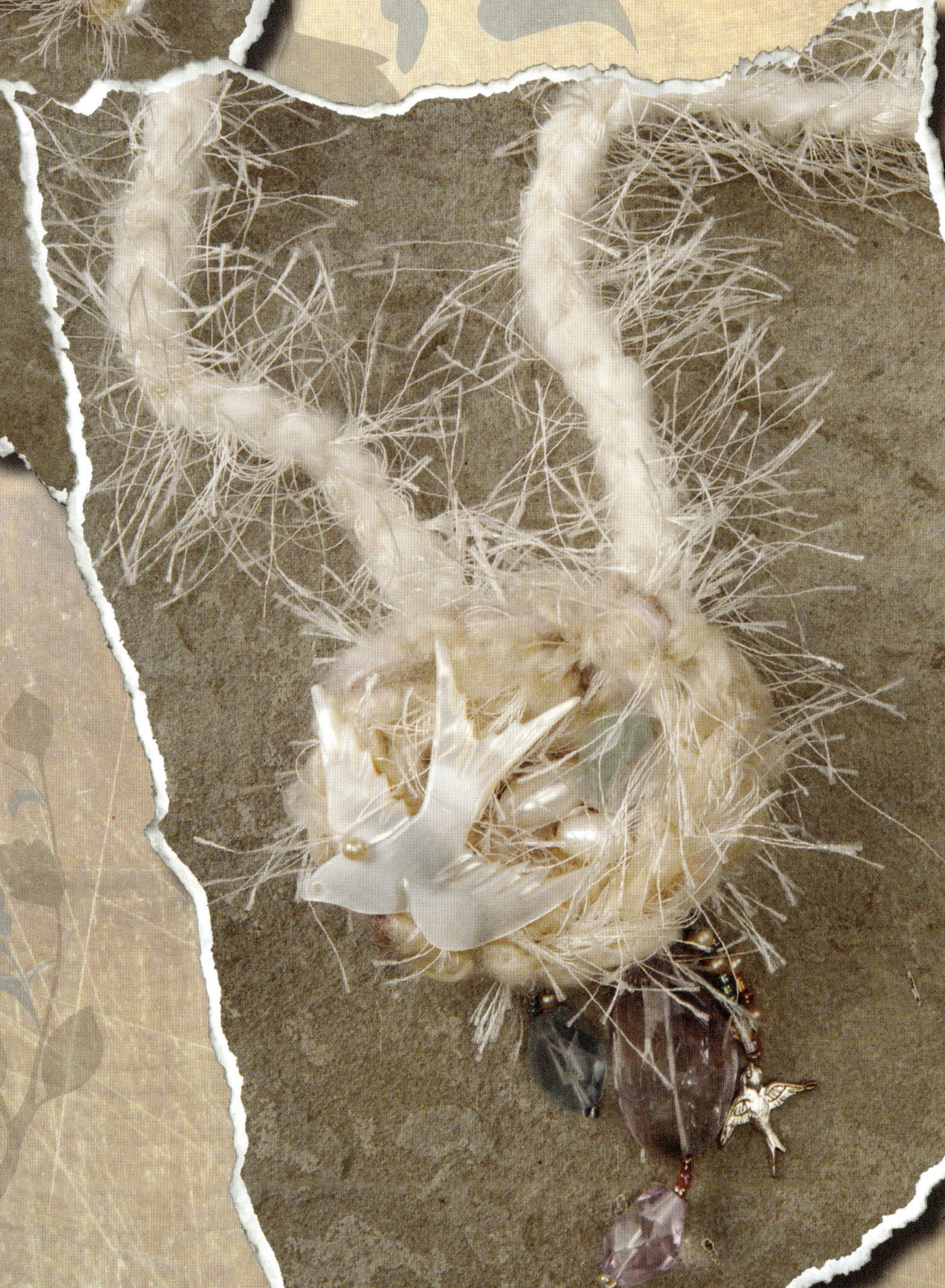

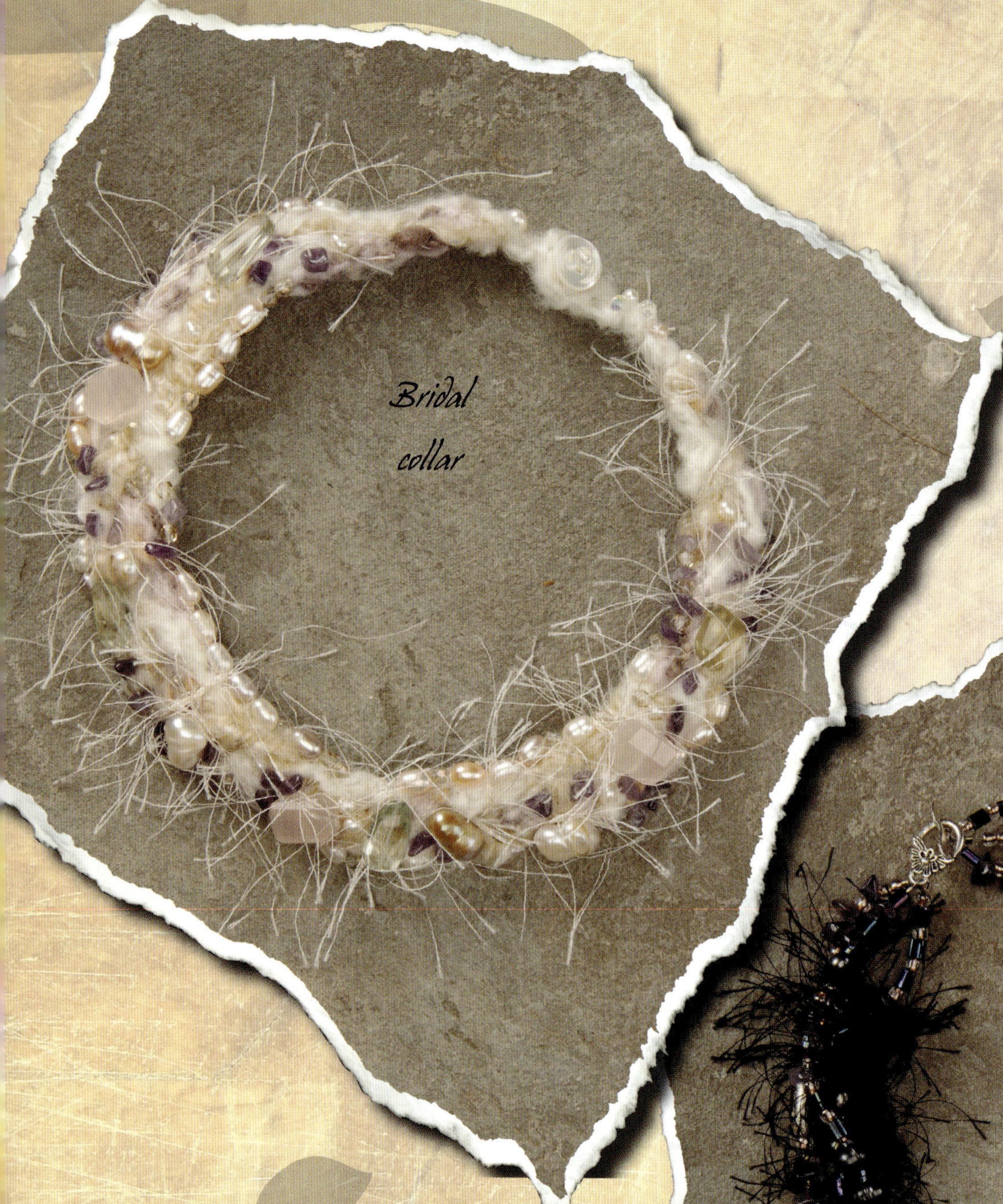

Bridal collar

Three variations of the Grandma Terri's necklace from Chapter 8

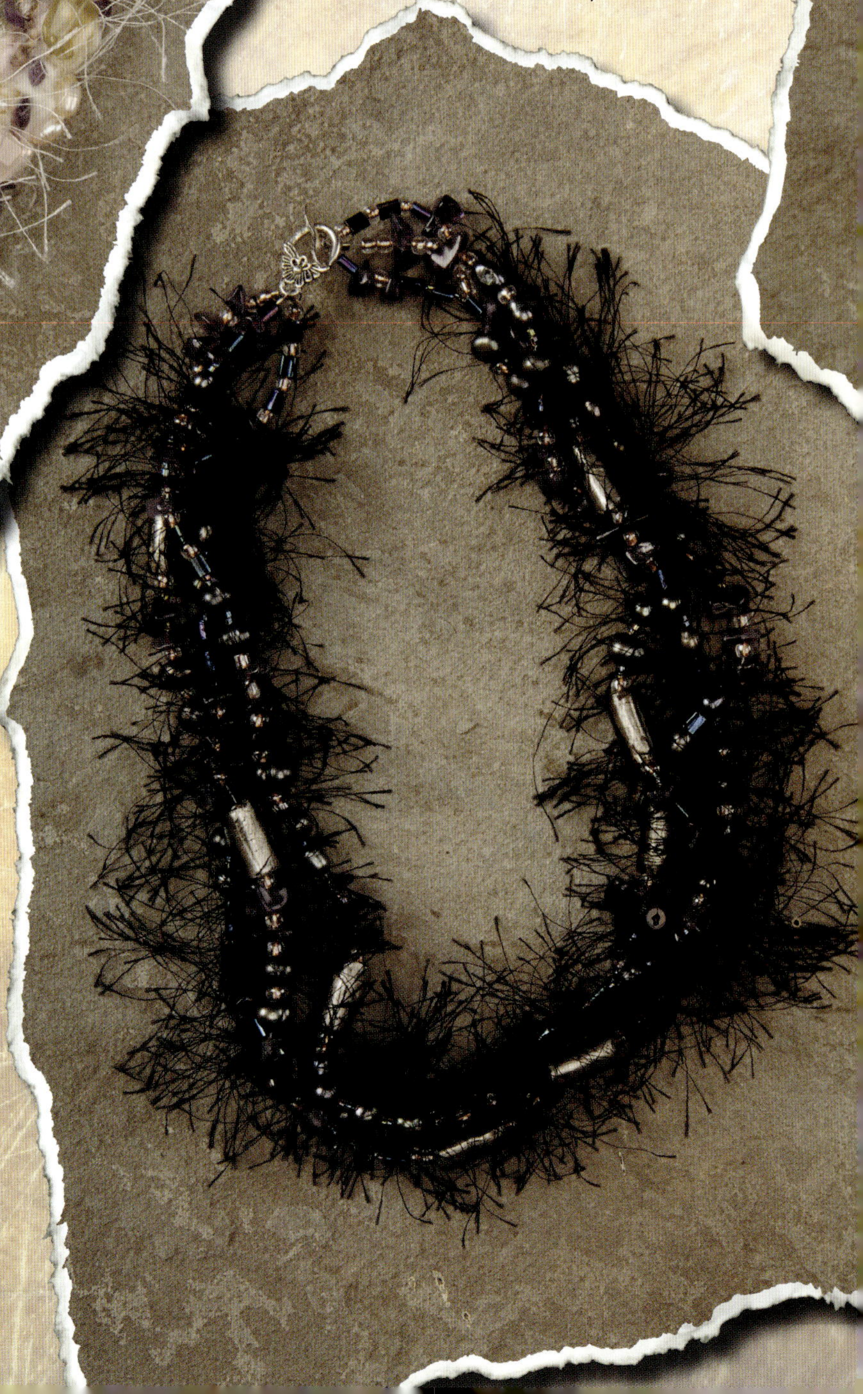

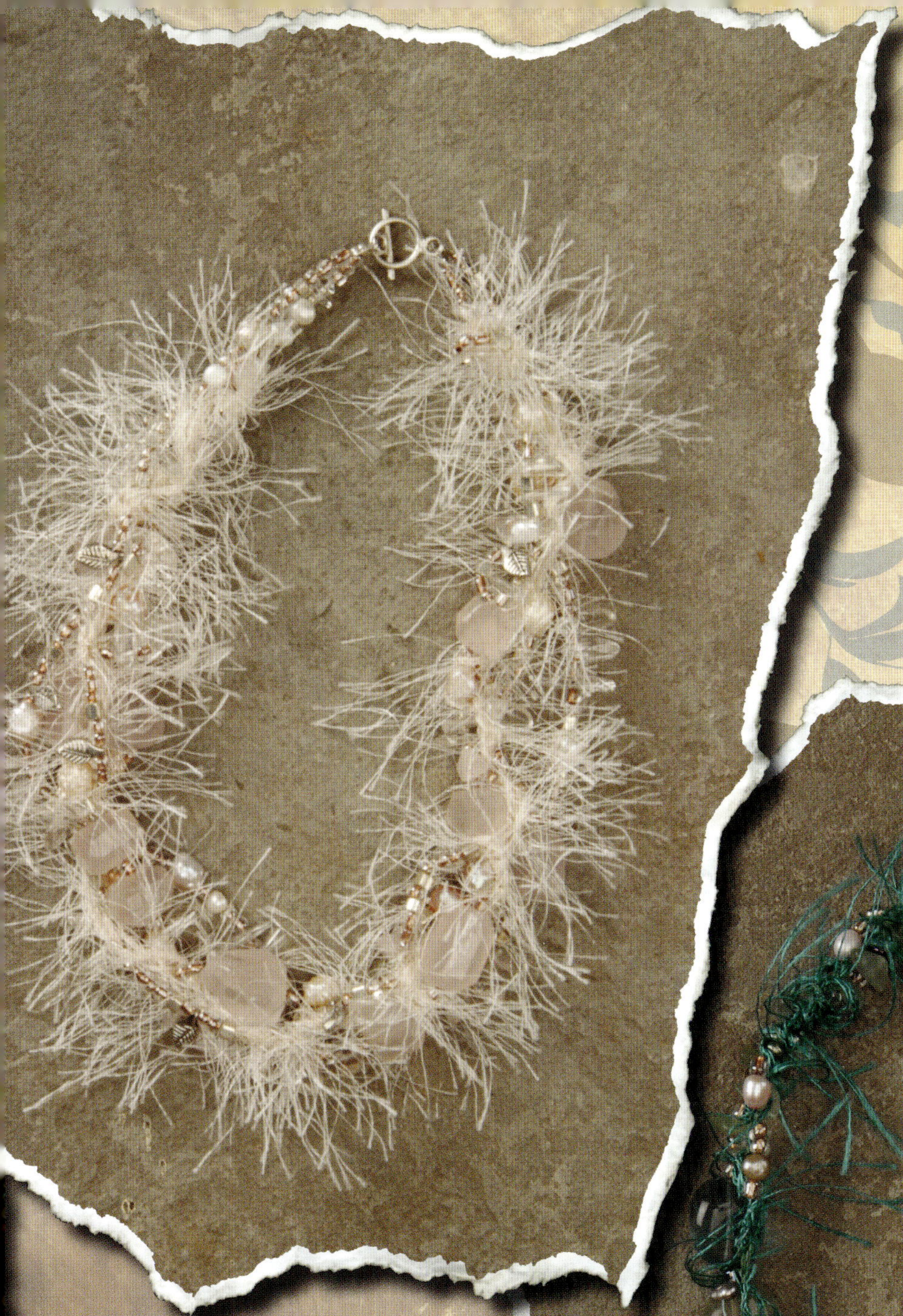

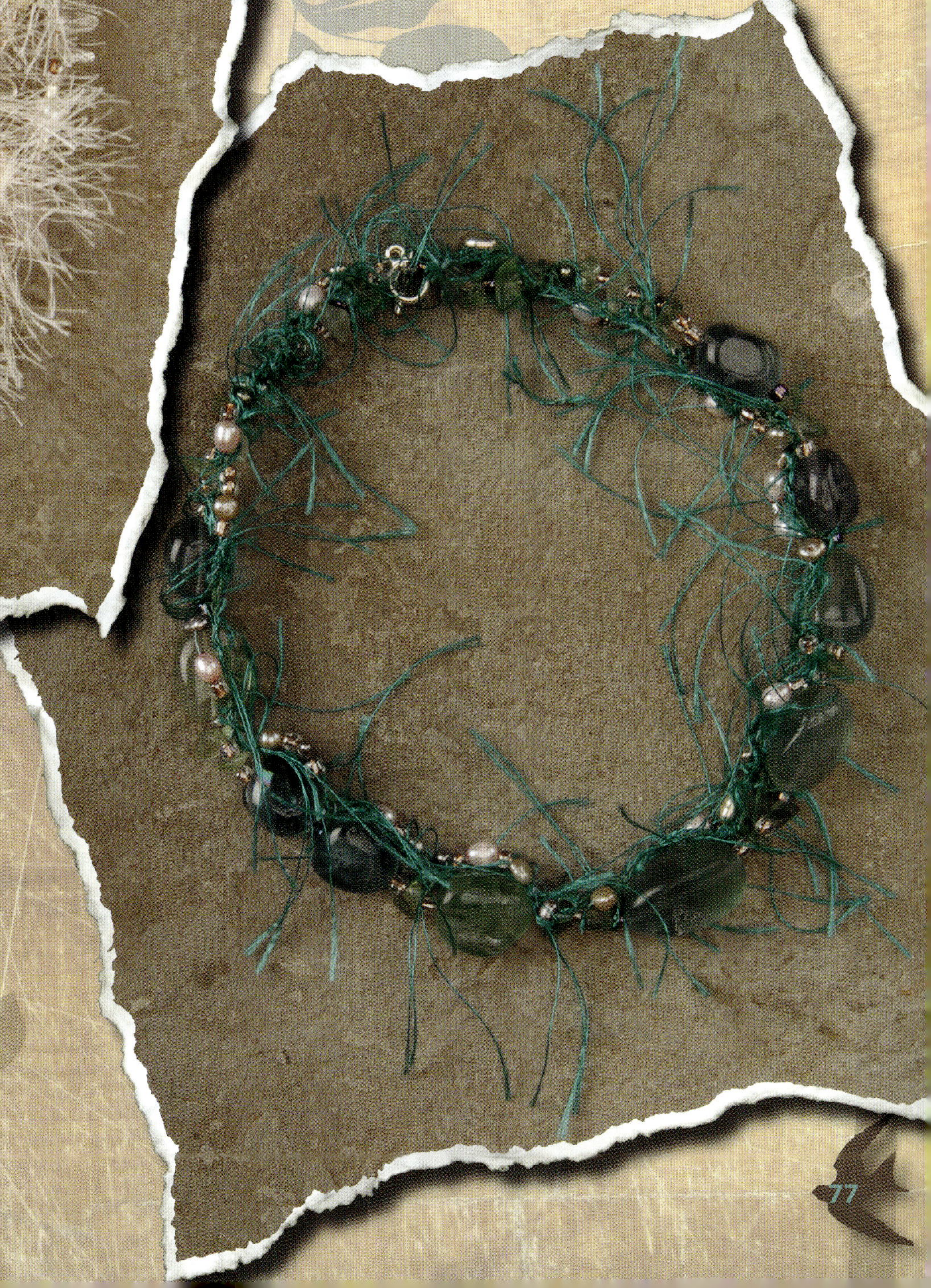

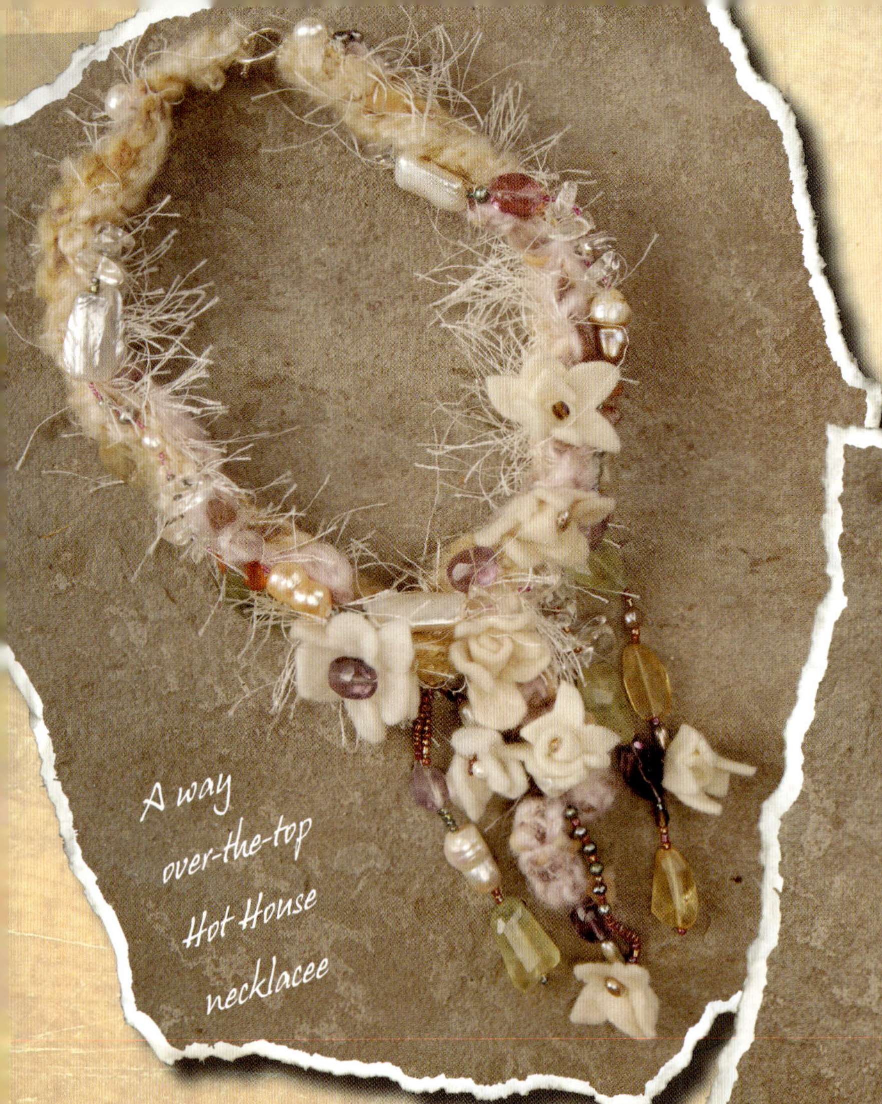

A way over-the-top Hot House necklacee

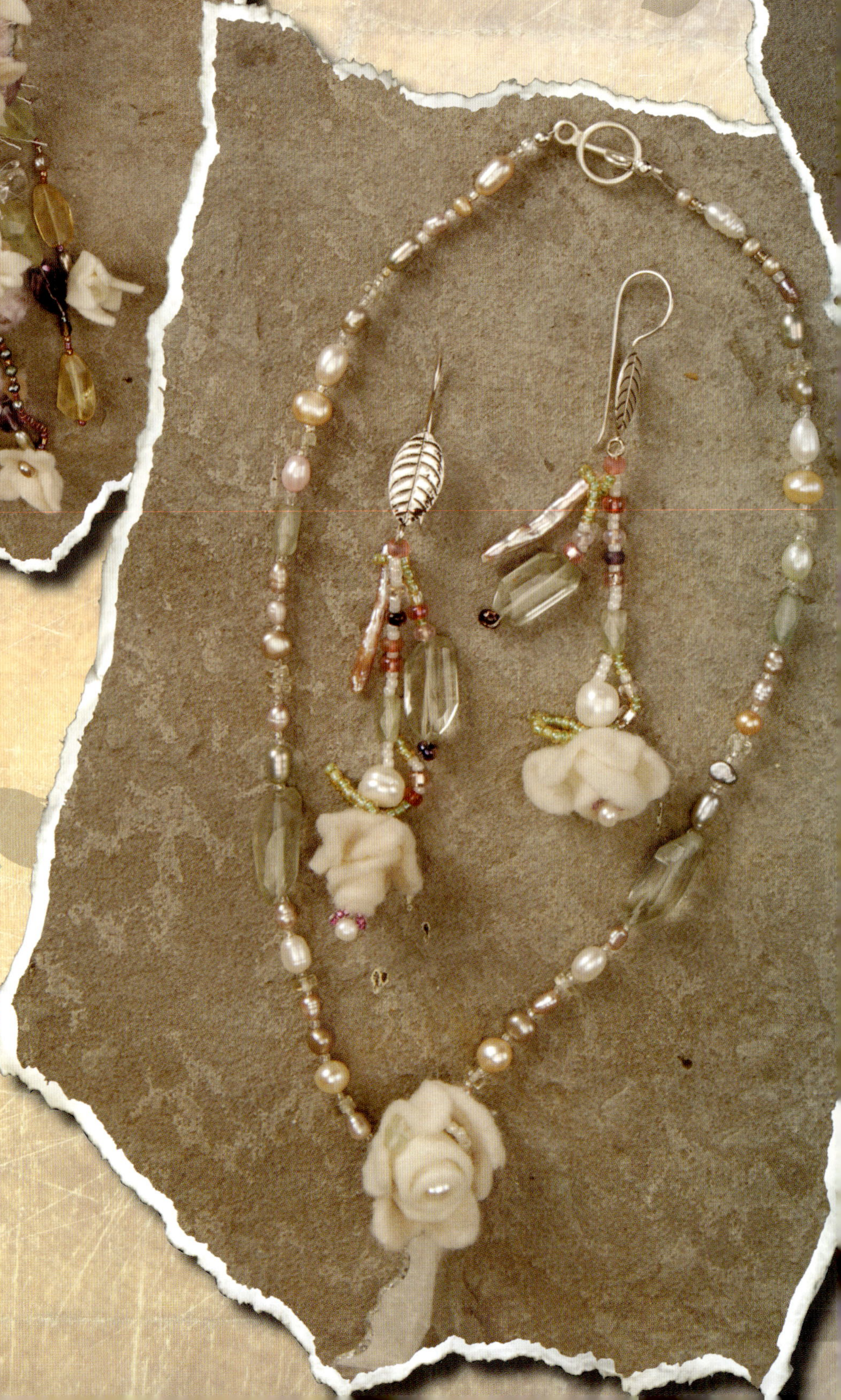

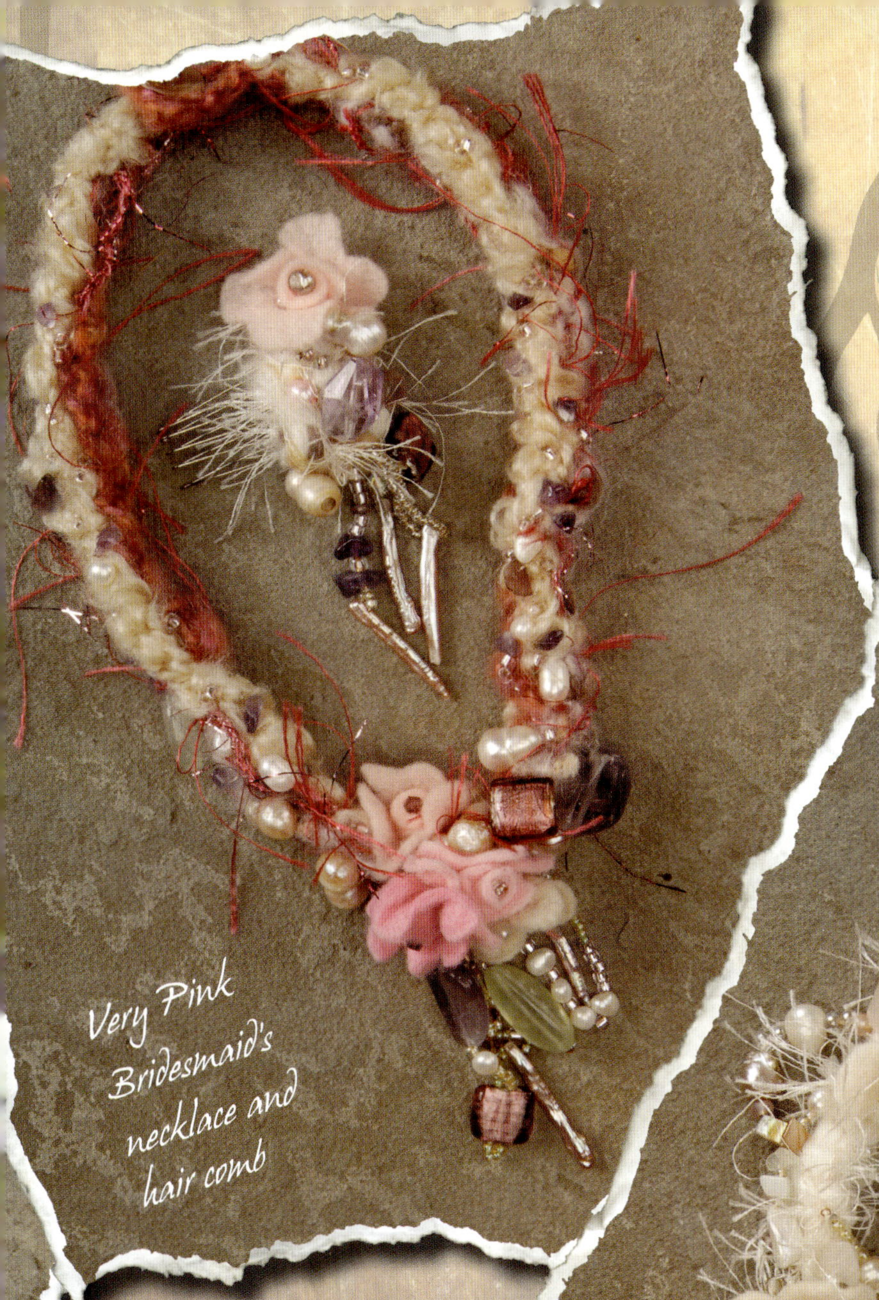

Very Pink Bridesmaid's necklace and hair comb

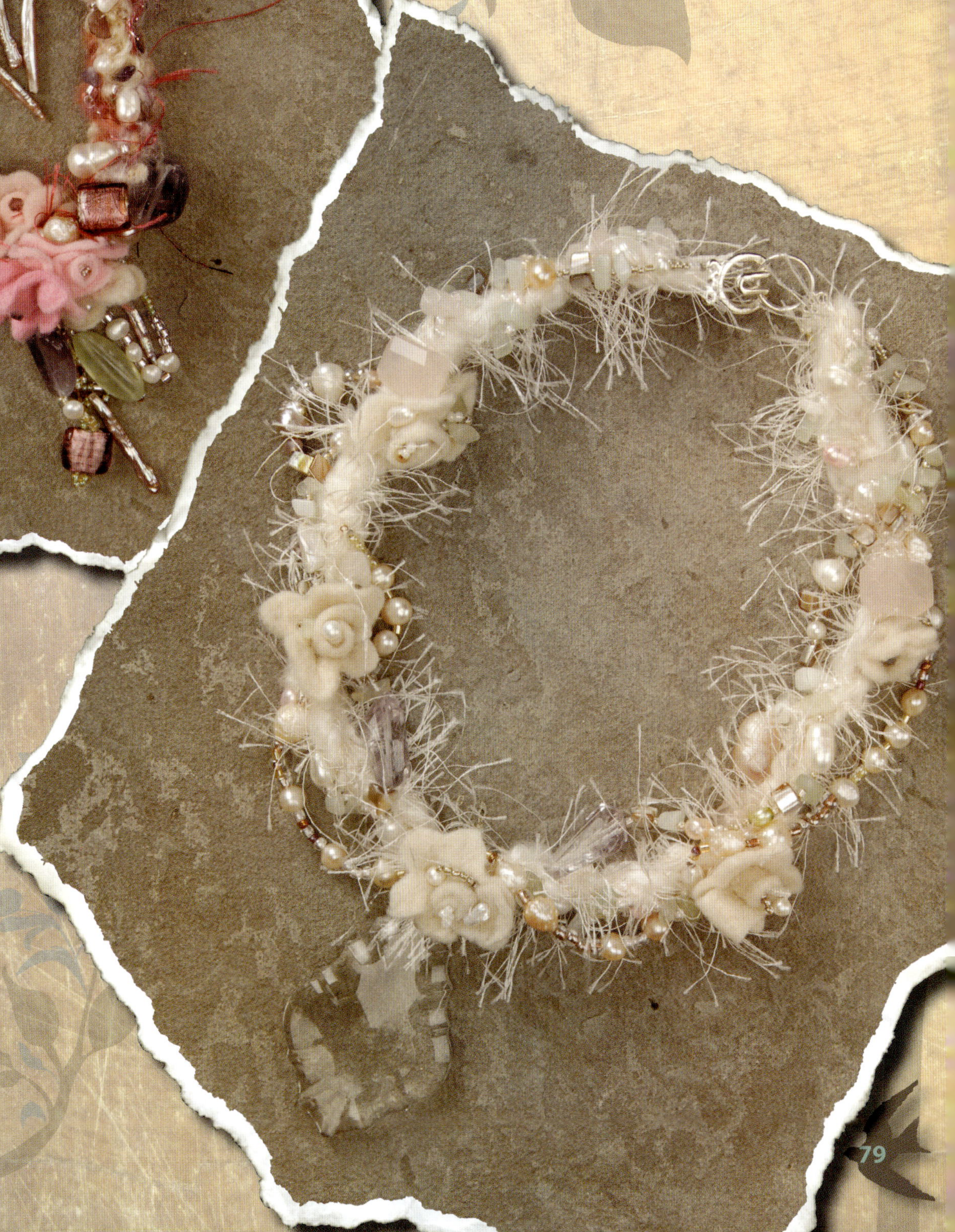

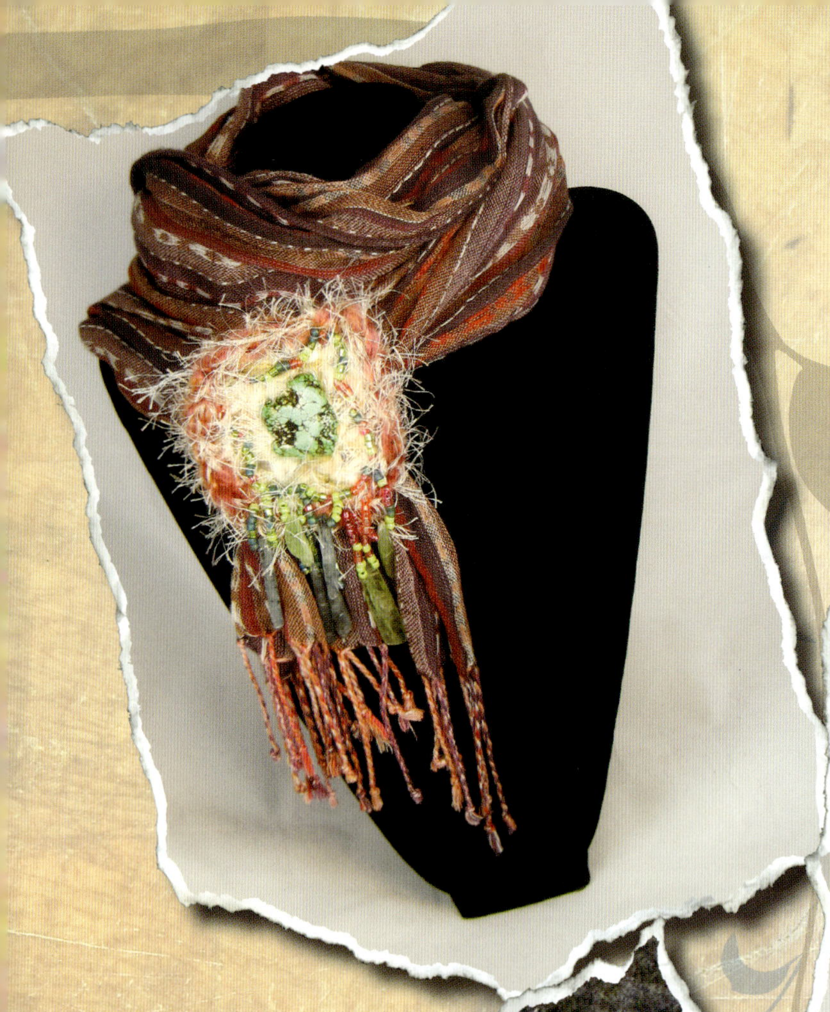

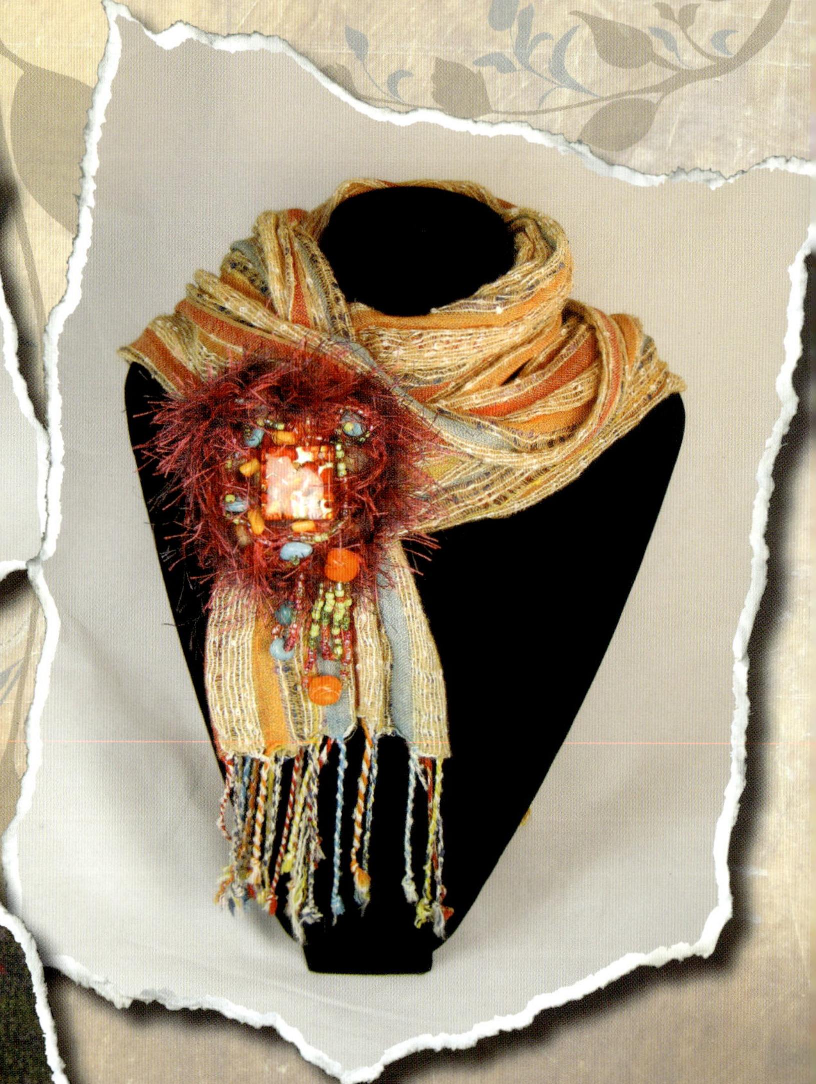

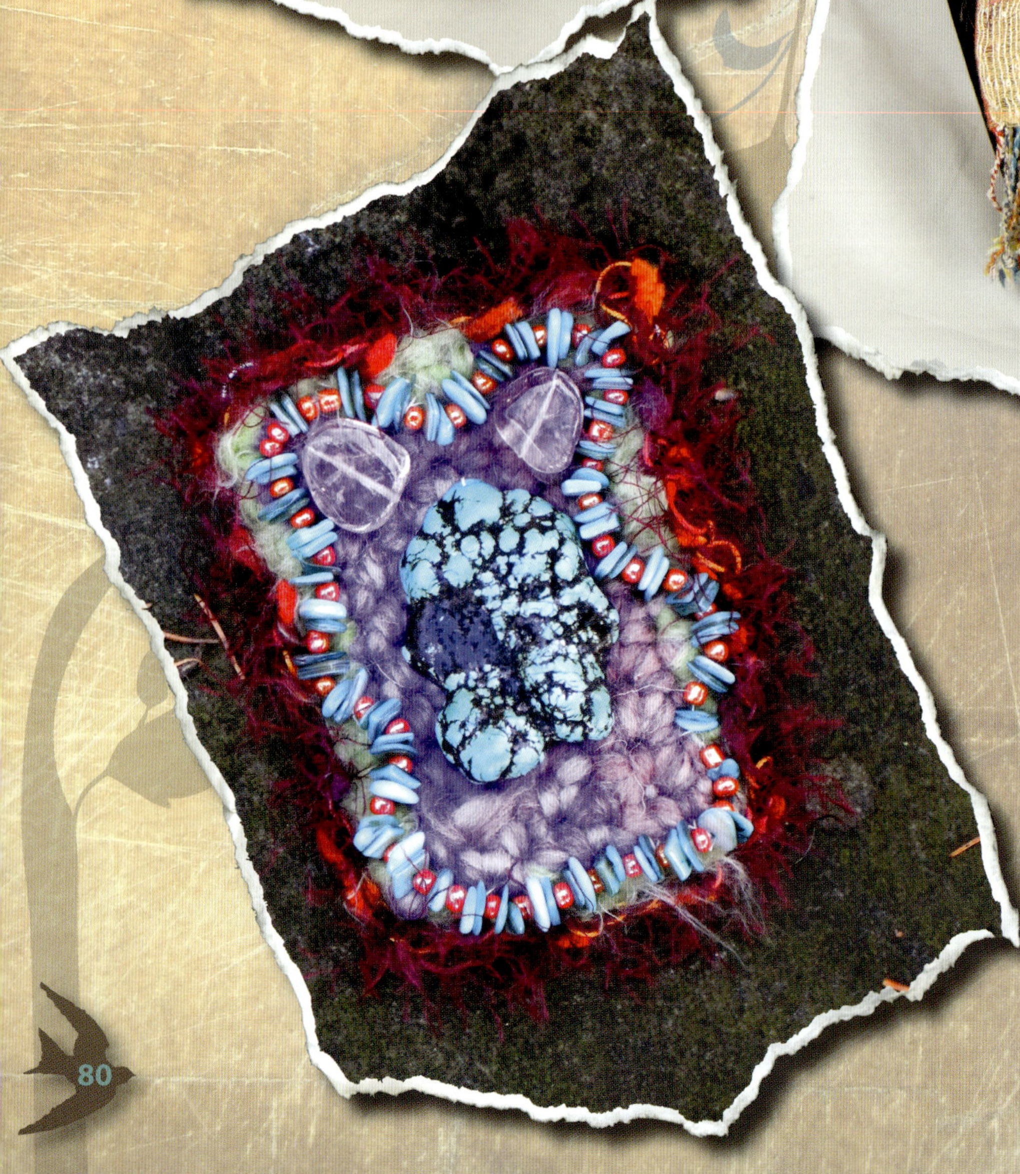

My End, Your Beginning

I've been asked by friends whether I'm nervous about writing this book because people might copy my unique designs and style. Absolutely not! I'm flattered that I have been given the opportunity to share my insights through the projects in this book. My hope is that this book will stir your creative juices! For me, the act and process of making a piece of jewelry is as important as the piece itself. Picking out your fibers, gem stones and beads should be fun and an expression of your own personal sense of style! Many how-to books tell you exactly what to do (and by all means, feel free to copy the samples in this book exactly). However, that is not necessary. Those of you who think that you could never dream up your own creative designs, think again. Believe me, you can. At least give it a try! My dear, dear friend Reagan is a perfect example. Reagan had no confidence in her own creativity. Her older brother was always the artist in the family (and is quite talented). When I tried to woo her to be my studio assistant for Plain Jane furniture, she always referred me to him. However, after a bit of coaxing (only 3 years!), I finally won her over. After she learned the basic techniques, and got a sense for my design style, she blossomed into an amazing furniture designer! The bottom line is that anyone who dresses or decorates their home with a sense of style by combining colors, textures and patterns in an interesting way, can express themselves by making their own jewelry. It is my heartfelt wish that you will find many hours of joy, as I have. Who knows, maybe one day I'll bump into you at the grocery store or the yarn shop and see you wearing a creation inspired by this book! I can only hope!

Suzanne

(www.ohsusannadesigns.com)

Resources

FIRE MOUNTAIN GEMS AND BEADS: This is an amazing resource! It is great for all your beading wants and needs. They have tools for every budget, an amazing group of findings in silver, gold and surgical steel, an assortment of beading wire and thread, and enough beads to make your head spin, from gemstones to Austrian crystals to clay. Also, their online support is terrific and I rely on them often for help. Be sure to ask them about any specials. I've gotten some fantabulous deals! They also have a retail store in Oregon. One day I'm going to go with a wad of cash and shop 'til I drop!

Here are some products I frequently purchase from Fire Mountain Gems: turquoise, large coral chunks, pearls, fine gemstones and glass seed beads. I also buy my sterling silver earring wires (including all of the ones shown in my earring projects) and fancy toggles.

www.firemountaingems.com
(800)423-2319

A.C. MOORE ARTS & CRAFTS and **MICHAELS:** These are both great "one stop" shops. You will be able to purchase all of your yarns, wires, beads and tools under one roof.

Here are some products I frequently purchase from A.C. Moore or Michaels: Large quantity discount packs of small, medium and large toggles in a silver finish, wire crimp beads and findings. Both are a great source for all your yarns—eyelash and novelty yarns in particular. I have found many a ball in the sale bin for a $1! I purchased the long, lamp glass beads that I used in Chapter Eight for Grandma Terri's Necklace at Michaels for a 1$ for a string of 6. Look how great that worked out!

www.acmoore.com
(800) acmoore
(choose option #2 for customer service)

www.michaels.com
(800) 642-4235

JO-ANN FABRIC AND CRAFT STORES: This is another basic craft store with an emphasis on sewing. They have a good selection of threads and needles, and they stock some really nice buttons that work beautifully as a interesting clasp. Be sure to check out their sale yarns. I have found a lot of eyelash and novelty yarns on sale!

www.joann.com
(888)739-4120

WEBS AMERICAN YARN STORE: This is a great online yarn source. The sales are great, the shipping is fast, and the customer service is knowledgeable and really helpful.

www.yarn.com
(800) for-webs

SHEEP AND WOOL FESTIVALS: Check your local listings! There are a ton of sheep and wool festivals around and they are a great and fun way to spend a day! (My whole family enjoys the events. Even my husband willingly joins in!) You will be able ogle and fondle almost every yarn imaginable, in every color, texture shade and hue. You can also see and pet (and even buy) angora bunnies, alpacas, lamas and every variety of sheep and goats. (I always go with a little kitty of money to spend that I have stashed away throughout the year.) This is a good time and place to splurge on something special for yourself or a loved one. (Cashmere, angora anyone?) In addition to the terrific yarns for sale, it will also be a day of dazzling inspiration. To see and chat with all of the wonderful artists and crafts people, and to see their handiwork in person, is a true treat. My local sheep and wool festival is:

Dutchess County Sheep and Wool Festival
Dutchess County Fairgrounds
6550 Spring Brook Ave
Rhinebeck, NY 12572
For more info:
www.festivalinfo@sheepandwool.com

YARN MARKET INC.: This is a good online yarn resource. It is easy to shop by category (i.e. eyelash yarns).

www.yarnmarket.com
(888)996-9276

NEW YORK CITY—BEAD, FINDINGS AND TRIM DISTRICT: When I have the time, the New York City bead, findings and trim district is where I go to stock up on gem stones, pearls, seed beads and findings. The district is located mostly on Sixth Avenue from about 35th Street to 40th Street, with some stores on the side streets toward Fifth Avenue. You can find just about anything in these stores. Give yourself time to rummage around and you'll discover some great deals. Picking that perfect strand can take some time, but is so, so much fun. Be on the lookout for limited time specials. If you love it, get it! It may not be there next time!

ETSY.com: I love to shop and sell my work on ETSY. You can find so many beautiful hand-made treasures. For example, you can find gorgeous, gorgeous rustic tree slice buttons. There are also shell buttons and hand-spun and dyed yarns to "dye" for (get it?). I love to support this creative shopping community.

THE STITCHERY: This is a small mom and pop shop that is bursting at the seams with the most gorgeous yarns imaginable. The owners Judy and Adam are very knowledgeable and will give you direction and advice (if needed). They offer an incredible selection of novelty yarns (like way more special than your typical eyelash stuff!) in cashmere silks and bamboos (to mention a few). They are fluffy, sparkly, and out-of-this-world unique. Splurge! Pick up a few skeins! Remember they will go a long way.

The Stitchery
49 East Central Ave
Pearl River, N.Y. 10965
(845) 736-4534

Mom and Pop yarn shops are a great resource for exotic and hand-crafted yarns. What I look forward to most when I go to my local yarn shop is fondling the fibers! There is nothing better than picking out your yarns in person and seeing all the subtle differences in color and texture. (Plus, I like to support small independent business.) So find out where your nearest fine yarn shop is and make the trip. You'll really enjoy yourself!

Central Shippee, The Felt People: These folks are an old-school felt company. They stock every type and color of felt imaginable. There is a fifty dollar retail minimum but if you really get into your projects or share with some friends you'll have no trouble making it. Their DURA FELT has every color that I use: old gold, mustard, white, eggshell, brown, currant, burgundy.

www.TheFeltPeople.com
(800)631-8968

More Schiffer Titles

www.schifferbooks.com

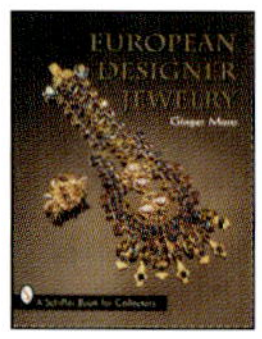

European Designer Jewelry. Ginger Moro. The dramatic evolution of 20th century European jewelry design, documenting the innovative trends, sources, and makers. Artists' limited-edition creations, as well as fashion and costume jewelry, are explored through the well-researched text, over 700 wonderful photos and vintage prints. Biographical sketches are provided for the artists and couturiers who worked closely with the fashion designers.

Size: 8 1/2" x 11"	707 photos	304pp.
ISBN: 0-88740-823-0	hard cover	$79.95

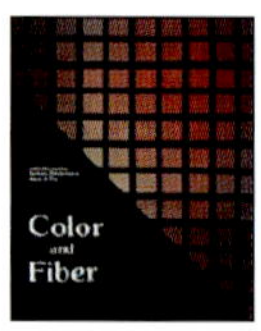

Color and Fiber. Patricia Lambert, Barbara Staepelaere, and Mary G. Fry. Fiber artists will welcome this opportunity to learn how to use and control color with this monumental and exquisitely beautiful book-whether they stitch, quilt, weave, work in macrame, hook rugs, knit, crochet, or experiment in mixed media.

Size: 8 1/2" x 11"	105 color photos, 18 charts, 49 b/w photos, & 71 line drawings	255pp.
ISBN: 0-88740-065-0	hard cover	$49.99

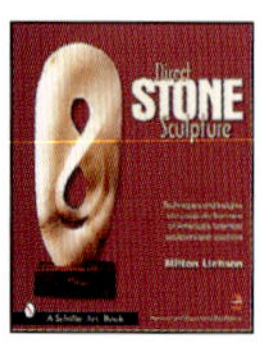

Direct Stone Sculpture, *Revised & Expanded 2nd Edition*. Milt Liebson. Here is your guide through the hands-on experience of sculpting in stone. Hundreds of photos of the progressive process and finished works by famous sculptors will inspire your own work. The types of stone and use of basic hand-sculpting tools are presented along with the use of power tools, methods of lamination, repair, and the business side of stone sculpture. Express your creativity in this ageless medium. This expanded edition includes 47 new pictures, updated stone-working techniques, and a gallery of students' work.

Size: 8 1/2" x 11"	300+ photos	160pp.
ISBN: 0-7643-1224-3	hard cover	$39.95

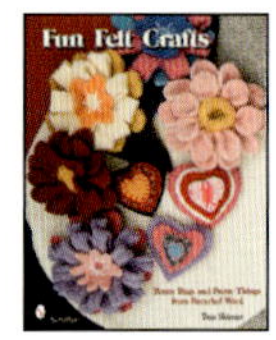

Fun Felt Crafts: Penny Rugs & Pretty Things from Recycled Wool. Tina Skinner. Christmas ornaments, decorative penny rugs, pretty pouches, and floral brooches are among the simple, featured projects. Recycle some wool clothing, buy a few pretty yarns and threads, sharp scissors, and a good needle and you're on your way. Clear, illustrated instructions and fun templates will help you create dozens of fun projects.

Size: 8 1/2" x 11"	150+ color photos	64pp.
ISBN: 978-0-7643-3299-9	soft cover	$12.99

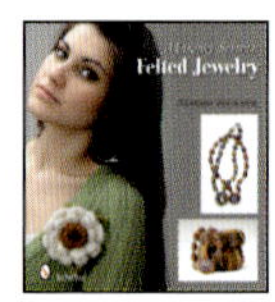

Making Simple Felted Jewelry. Marsha Fletcher. Make a brooch, necklace, wrap-around bracelet, and accessorize a purse and a hat. These fun, wool jewelry pieces are sure to freshen up all wardrobes. Step-by-step directions and basic techniques are demonstrated through 113 color images, along with 4 featured projects.

Size: 8 1/8" x 9 1/8"	113 color images & 1 b&w image	64pp.
ISBN: 978-0-7643-3570-9	soft cover	$9.99

Schiffer books may be ordered from your local bookstore, or they may be ordered directly from the publisher by writing to:

Schiffer Publishing, Ltd.
4880 Lower Valley Rd.
Atglen, PA 19310
(610) 593-1777; Fax (610) 593-2002
E-mail: Info@schifferbooks.com

Please visit our web site catalog at ***www.schifferbooks.com*** or write for a free catalog. Please include $5.00 for shipping and handling for the first two books and $2.00 for each additional book.
Full-price orders over $150 are shipped free in the U.S.

Printed in China